W9-BTP-303

"Thou Shalt Not Love"

"Thou Shalt Not Love"

What Evangelicals Really Say to Gays

Patrick M. Chapman, Ph.D.

Foreword by Daniel A. Helminiak, Ph.D

But now abide faith, hope, love, these three; but the greatest of these is love.

1 Corinthians 13:13

Haiduk Press
New York
2008

Haiduk Press, LLC
P O Box 1783
New Rochelle NY 10802-1783

www.haidukpress.com

haidukpress@gmail.com

Library of Congress Control Number: 2007943507

Printed in the United States
on acid-free paper with recycled content.

This book is dedicated to young homosexuals trying to find peace in the hope that it will help on your journey toward integrity in life, love, and faith.

❧

The Garden of Love
by William Blake

I laid me down upon a bank,
Where Love lay sleeping;
I heard among the rushes dank
Weeping, weeping.
Then I went to the heath and the wild,
To the thistles and thorns of the waste;
And they told me how they were beguiled,
Driven out, and compelled to the chaste.
I went to the Garden of Love,
And saw what I never had seen;
A Chapel was built in the midst,
Where I used to play on the green.
And the gates of this Chapel were shut
And "Thou shalt not," writ over the door;
So I turned to the Garden of Love
That so many sweet flowers bore.
And I saw it was filled with graves,
And tombstones where flowers should be;
And priests in black gowns were walking their rounds,
And binding with briars my joys and desires.

❧

CONTENTS

Tables

FOREWORD

When I speak on the Bible and homosexuality, people often ask how to respond to Biblical literalists who quote the Bible to prove that God condemns same-sex relationships. Considering the Bible's stark words — "abomination," "be put to death," "degrading passions," "shameless acts," "exchanged natural intercourse for unnatural," "not inherit the kingdom of God" — what can one say?

Of course, *there is* an answer. The main point is to insist that, as a baseline, the Scriptures mean what they meant to those who originally wrote them, not what they might happen to suggest to us who read them today. You allow that God inspired those sacred authors, and you also freely grant that this inspired word is inerrant (without error). Quibbling over these latter points just distracts from the real issue. Thus, you insist that what those ancient authors meant to say, as best we can determine, is what God intended to convey to us through their inspired and inerrant writings.

However, it turns out that what those biblical texts meant in their original languages and in their original situations has almost nothing to do with the questions we are asking about homosexuality today. The evidence to this effect is overwhelming. In text after text, with as much certainty as historical studies could ever achieve, the conclusion is the same. The Bible does not condemn homosexuality as we understand it, and the Bible was not even concerned about same-sex practices in its own day — except in one instance (male-male anal intercourse: "lying with a male the lyings of a women") for reasons of ritual purity that made sense in that ancient culture but have nothing to do with our current concerns.

This is the technical answer to Biblical literalism. This answer relies on historical evidence. It makes coherent sense of the evidence and compares this sense with our contemporary understanding of sexual orientation. It reasonably concludes that the Bible's genuine teaching implies no condemnation of homosexuality in our day. And it therefore responsibly chooses to take God's word *as it was written* — not as we read it — and stops condemning homosexual people on the basis of the Bible.

This is the answer, but it is of little use in this debate because Biblical Literalists would hardly ever accept such reasoning. Their worldview differs radically from what I just described. Their understanding of the Bible and their approach to determining its meaning are all their own. Their approach is novel, an early twentieth-century development. It is not coherent. It picks and chooses among texts. It switches emphasis as is convenient—interpreting Revelation symbolically, for example. It is filled with blind spots. And it rests solely on faith, a sheer choice—driven by fear of hell—to believe, simply because they insist that is what must be believed.

This approach to the Bible is so peculiar that I believe it actually constitutes a new religion in our day. A distinguishing feature of Judaism and Christianity is the insistence that God encounters us in human history and that the Bible is an instructive account of those encounters in exemplary cases. But Biblical Literalism is unwilling to attend to the historical particularities through which God's word comes to us. Literalists believe they can know God's word without investigating that history and its cultures, audiences, spokespersons, issues, languages, and semantic nuances. As I argue in *Sex and the Sacred*, on this essential point, this new kind of religion departs from the mainline tradition and is no longer Christian at all.

Holding this opinion, I have looked for other names for this new religion. *Biblical Fundamentalism* is the obvious one, but the adherents—for political reasons, not wanting to own this name, which, in fact, accurately describes their position—prefer the softer *Evangelicalism*. But the strains of "Evangelicals" are many, and not all are strictly literalist—except, almost universally, when homosexuality is the question. In my mind, the terms *Bible Religion* and *Biblicism* possibly name this new religion, which completely revolves around The Good Book. Still, ahistorical literalism is the pivotal issue, so I will continue to speak of this movement as Biblical Literalism, understanding its main tenet to be the need to believe the Bible as it reads, period.

Of course, all people of faith need to believe. No faith about God and the world-to-come is provable. But religion should at least be plausible; it should be reasonable. It should not be self-contradictory, and it should not contradict what is otherwise known to be so. One should not have to surrender one's God-given mind to be a faithful believer. But Biblical Literalism expects people to rest their beliefs on unthinking and unquestioning faith.

Accordingly, when asked about responding to the Biblical Literalists, I also propose a practical answer: Do not argue or try to convince them of anything; their position is impervious to argument. Certainly, never discuss a particular topic or particular text. At best, limit discussion to the general topic of how one determines the meaning of biblical texts. This general topic opens onto that question about history, and it needs to be addressed before any talk of particular texts can be fruitful.

The starkness of this practical answer tends to shock people, but the shock is part of the needed lesson. *Don't try to reason with irrational people.* Appeal to evidence through logical argument will get you nowhere.

Along with sensing people's shock, I also hear their protests. These come from kind and good-willed people, who want to be respectful of others, and also from Bible-believers, who take offense: "How could you be so insensitive toward people's religious beliefs?!"

The answer to this latter question lies in the book before you: it provides all the information you need. Blessed to have this book, you can understand for yourself why I speak as I do. Trusting that you now have this information at your disposal, I feel totally free to make my point directly and forcefully. Indeed, someone has to start naming the elephant in the room. Someone has to point out that the emperor has no clothes.

In no way do I intend to say that Dr. Patrick Chapman is doing this distasteful deed of calling Biblical Literalism irrational. In no way is he offensive or disrespectful in what he writes here. On the contrary, he is a former Evangelical Christian who speaks to and about his own people. His scientific restraint and Christian humility are exemplary. While his dispassionate presentation of the evidence serves to strengthen my point, in no way am I saying that this point is his.

Trained as an anthropologist, skilled in understanding and comparing cultures, armed with knowledge about widespread diversity among the peoples of the earth, comfortable with geology, biology, genetics, and evolutionary theory, schooled and re-schooled in the Bible, courageous in invoking his personal experience as a gay man, and dedicated to sharing his hard-won wisdom with sisters and brothers of the human family and the Christian churches, Dr. Chapman has presented a remarkable summary of current religious debate about homosexuality. Not only does he review the biblical evidence such as I presented in *What the Bible Really Says about Homosexuality*; he goes beyond the Bible to consider the available evidence from the sciences. Moreover, from the inside, he gives us a feel for the mindset of Biblical Literalism. He also summarizes the Literalists' responses to the scientific evidence, points out the flaws in their thinking, exposes the bias in their sources, coherently rebuts their counter-arguments, and calls them on their seemingly deliberate misinformation campaign against lesbian and gay people.

Thus, in addition to religion, Dr. Chapman presents a thorough discussion also of gender roles, comparative cultures, geological science, evolutionary theory, misleading ethnocentrism, and the documented biological and putative psychosocial bases of sexual orientation. *Thou Shalt Not Love* would make an excellent, balanced text for any course on current cultural debates. This book is an easily accessible compendium of contemporary information about homosexuality and fundamentalist religion. Perforce, this book also serves as an exposé of the problem with using a literal Bible to condemn lesbian and gay sex and relationships.

All this brings us back to my main point: Despite Dr. Chapman's restrained approach, his presentation, again and again, from a number of angles, on every consideration makes clear the inescapable truth that conservative Evangelical Christianity maintains its antagonistic teaching about homosexuality only by systematically ignoring all the counter-evidence. The Biblical Literalists' condemnation of same-sex love is not a reasonable or coherent position. It is a mistaken belief from a bygone age that refuses to die, a superstition that refuses to succumb to reason. It is an assertion of blind faith in the face of overwhelming contrary evidence.

If the Literalists would only admit some doubt—about the biblical teaching, about the causes of homosexuality, about the possibility of changing sexual orientation, about the happiness available to lesbian and gay people—their position might be reasonable. If they would only acknowledge that the exact meaning of the biblical texts has recently come under revealing scrutiny—if they would only acknowledge the facts, they would at least be crediting the evidence, at least be speaking honestly. I am not suggesting that they do a complete turnabout and teach that homosexuality is morally acceptable, but only that they acknowledge—as is the fact—that the wrongness or sinfulness of homosexuality is now in question. If, in light of this question, they were to admit that, as a particular religion and for whatever reason, they still choose to continue opposing homosexual relationships, at least they would be telling the truth. But no such admission is forthcoming: the Biblical Literalists stand their ground, insisting that God's own authority is behind their personal opinion and that the Bible unequivocally condemns homosexuality.

To justify their personal opinion "in the name of God," they rely solely on an ancient, complex, and ambiguous book, which they choose to read it in their peculiar way that differs from anything in the Christian tradition. They glory in the claim that they live by "faith," and they have little regard for reason, research, science, or scholarly findings. Out of hand, they disregard anything that disagrees with their chosen opinion. In his book on *Effective Biblical Counseling*, Lawrence J. Crabb, for example, approvingly quotes yet another Evangelical, J. R. McQuilkin, and proclaims the rejection of reason in the starkest of terms: "'When the teaching of Scripture conflicts with any other idea, the teaching of Scripture will be accepted as truth and the other idea will not be accepted as truth.'...The other idea, *regardless of its support from empirical research*, will not be accepted as truth" (p. 49, emphasis in original).

One can not reason with the irrational. By its very nature irrationality is immune to reason. The pages of this book make clear, again and again, from chapter to chapter, that the Biblical Literalist position is bankrupt of reason, and this bankruptcy does not concern this religious movement in the least.

Consider my point from another angle. Dr. Janet Buckingham presents herself as a Bible-believing Christian and is a leading opponent of gay marriage in Canada. I heard her speak at a public forum on this topic. Relying on her faith and on some literal biblical texts in translation taken at face value, she insisted that God opposes homosexuality and asked for respect for her religious belief. Appealing—rather disingenuously, I believe—to her well-educated audience, she expressed the firm expectation that no one would say she was wrong.

Her supposition seems to be that, because certain people believe something, everybody else is supposed to grant its validity. Does a belief become right just because someone believes it? Is everybody necessarily supposed to acknowledge as correct any religious opinion—or, at least, the Biblical Literalists' religious opinion? Irrationally, Dr. Buckingham does not expect anyone to say she is wrong although the bulk of research evidence discredits her opinion on every front.

The Literalists think that their opinion on homosexuality is the truth and no one should call it wrong. They rest their claim on the Bible's literal words, read apart from any historical awareness. They insist they accept the Bible, God's word, for exactly what it says. Yet, the Literalists are inconsistent in their acceptance of the biblical word. They do not generally believe in slavery although the Bible repeatedly endorses it (Ephesians 6:5-9; Colossians 3:22-4:1; 1 Timothy 6:1-2; 1 Peter 2:18). They do take interest on money and investments—"usury"—although the Bible repeatedly condemns it (Exodus 22:25; Deuteronomy 23:19-20, 24:10-13; Psalm 15:15; Proverbs 28:8; Ezekiel 18: 13, 17, 22:12). While insisting the world is only 6,000 years old because the Bible suggests as much, they do not believe the earth is flat, although the Bible presents it as such (Genesis 1:1-17; Psalm 24:1-2, 104:2-13). They often allow divorce although the literal words of Jesus strictly forbid it (Matthew 5:32; Mark 10:1-12; Luke 16:18).

Recalling such discrepancies in the claim to rely strictly on a literal Bible, from the audience at that public forum on gay marriage, I pointed out another discrepancy to Dr. Janet Buckingham. According to 1 Corinthians 11:8-10 and 14:34-35, women are not to speak in public and, above all, Dr. Buckingham should not be lecturing to me because, according to 1 Timothy 2:12, no woman is "to teach or to have authority over a man." In response, Dr. Buckingham only lamented that, on account of her minority religious beliefs, I was "marginalizing" her.

Dr. Buckingham should consider that it is not I, but the literal biblical word, that requires she not speak in public. After all, is this not the Biblical Literalists' standard defense of condemnation of lesbians and gay men? Don't blame them for the condemnation, they say; it is not they, but the Bible, that condemns.

As for my supposed offense in denouncing Dr. Buckingham's condemnation of homosexuality, she should consider that, in so doing, in no way do I mean to disrespect her person, but only to reject her opinion as wrong. After all, is this attitude not that of "hating the sin but respecting the sinner," which Bible-believers incessantly quote against gay and lesbian people?

This state of affairs raises troubling questions about the place of religion in a pluralistic society. How do we determine what is true? How do we decide what is good? If the Literalists' position were accepted, what would "truth" or "good" mean? Are their beliefs all true, just because they believe them, and everybody else's beliefs, therefore, false? Or are everybody's opinions correct just because people believe them religiously? And what if the opinions conflict—like the conscientious beliefs of the Biblical Literalists and the conscientious beliefs of lesbian and gay Christians? How do we decide?

Any solution must be open to all people regardless of religion, culture, or nation. We will never achieve peace on our shrinking planet unless our peace is respectful of everybody. The only solution I can imagine is to rely on the relevant evidence in open-mindedness, honesty, and reasonableness. To this solution any person of good-will should be able to agree. I have spelled out this solution in *Spirituality for a Global Community*. But Biblical Literalism and all forms of fundamentalism stand in direct opposition to this solution. The staunch Bible-believers seem to think that, because they hold something as true, it is true, period, and no one should dare call it wrong.

Am I mistaken, unfair, or unkind to say outright that such thinking is irrational? However you look at it, the Literalist claim to unquestionable truth in their selective use of the Bible is silly. It knows nothing of coherent reasoning or evidenced argument, and it wants to know nothing of it. How could one ever argue with such a position? The impossibility of any discussion evinces the irrationality of the Biblical Literalists' position.

I published my popular book on the Bible and homosexuality in 1994. I had hoped that the easy availability of solid scholarly information would have a softening effect on the Literalists' antigay agenda. The 2000 edition of the book reported even stronger, newly found evidence to the effect that the Bible has no concern whatsoever about homosexuality per se. Yet the voice of the Biblical Literalist minority is louder than ever. Its influence reaches from local neighborhoods and schools to the very halls of government, the boardrooms of business and industry, and the congresses of international affairs. In the extreme, apocalyptic belief— about the need for war in the Middle East to bring on the Second Coming of Christ—may even be undermining efforts to secure world peace and courts a nuclear holocaust. Such a belief is sheer insanity. Yet religious irrationality in biblical and other religions continues to spread while the fate of our world and of an egalitarian way of life teeters on the brink of catastrophe.

At this point in history, Dr. Patrick Chapman's book is most welcome. It should end the debate. It should cut through the darkness of Biblical Literalist irrationality. The scope of this book and the coherence of its presentation should finally stymie the Literalist juggernaut.

This book should effect all that, but, of course, like my book, it won't—precisely because the opposition is irrational while this book is a tour de force of evidence, reason, and cogent argument.

Nonetheless, all is not lost. This book will have a valuable effect if only it helps us to realize the extremes of the Biblical Literalist mindset. Then, no one would be shocked to hear my practical advice for responding to it. Despite respect for religion or the need for civil discourse, no one would hesitate to speak out against it.

In the private arena, on a person-to-person basis, there is also room for optimism. One person can have a healing effect on another by showing compassion, kindness, understanding, and good will. Among conservative Evangelicals there are many people of good will, some desperately searching for a way, in good conscience, to be more accepting of homosexual people, many totally unaware that their preachers and religious leaders have withheld and distorted information about the Bible and homosexuality. Honest and sincere one-on-one conversation with such genuine seekers can lead to a change of heart and mind. Authentic personal interchange affects people more than technical arguments ever could. Then the softened heart opens the mind to readmit reasonable thinking, to consider the technical arguments summarized in this book, and to choose responsible behavior.

I think especially of the Evangelical youth when I raise this hope. If they go to public schools and are allowed to watch TV or use the Internet at all, they are aware that their Biblical Literalist religion is out of step with much of the contemporary world. I would not suggest they should go with the world just to be in step. But confronted with this majority, they cannot help but wonder if their religion might not be mistaken. If the majority is, indeed, right, our youth ought to follow it. But is it right? This is the all-important question.

This book can help any thinking young person come to a reasonable conclusion. If reasonableness matters at all for humanity and before God, I am certain this book will help many youth — and their torn parents — to come to a rational, sane, healthy, and, perforce, holy resolution of their quandary. Please, God, let's not have still another generation waste their lives and suppress their loves because of misplaced religious guilt.

In the public arena, however, in the anonymity of the mass media and amidst religious competition for souls — and money — the prognosis is less optimistic. Where a society allows the free expression of ideas, no easy way to silence foolishness exists. Yet we cannot allow foolishness to control our communities, nations, and globe. In the face of irrationality, most important is to recognize it for what it is. One must not hesitate to name it and, then, as with any public threat, restrain it, and try to contain it. One must publicly challenge it, use every honest means to discredit it, and stop its creeping hegemony over public opinion. One must recognize the danger and do all in one's power to minimize its destructive effects.

Only reluctantly do Christians and other people of good will adopt such an aggressive strategy of self-defense. Yet even Jesus, when slapped by the temple police, protested the injustice: "If I have spoken wrongly, testify to the wrong. But if I have spoken rightly, why do you strike me?" (John 18:23). In some cases, to turn the other cheek is only to enable the forces of evil. In the present case, to refuse to take a stand—even for the noble motives of religious tolerance or holy charity—is to expose the structures of civilization to the onslaught of barbarian caprice.

The only thing that tolerance cannot tolerate is intolerance, for unleashed intolerance destroys any possibility of tolerance. If anything stands for intolerance, it is the Biblical Literalists' irrational claim of God-given authority. Like it or not, comfortable or not, genuine Christians and responsible citizens need to take defensive action.

Therefore, we all owe a debt of gratitude to Dr. Patrick Chapman. Through years of dedicated labor, he has crafted for us a book that lucidly defines the parameters of the current "culture wars." Later, when confronting demonic forces in daily life, if ever we are duped, if ever we begin to doubt our reality, we can again look up parts of this book—I certainly will—and recall the evidence to reconfirm our sane realization of Biblical Literalism's irrationality. In contrast to it, the "Word of God," Jesus' command to love, and responsible citizenship all coincide. Inevitably, they entail openness, honesty, humility, and good will.

Daniel A. Helminiak
September 29, 2006
Feast of St. Michael the Archangel
Quis ut Deus?

Acknowledgements

While I am responsible for the content of this book, I must acknowledge a great debt to many individuals who have inspired and helped me. The idea for this book developed through my friend David. As I watched him struggle with his faith and his sexuality, I thought there must be a book that would address his questions, but I was unable to find any that sufficed. Thus, the idea that I should write this book took root, but the real push for the work came when I was teaching in London, England in the fall of 2003. At that time the Massachusetts State Supreme Court declared that homosexuals should have the right to marry. Immediately after the court's decision the evangelical community began its move to change the Constitution to permanently prevent homosexuals from marrying. Some of my colleagues and associates in London, many of whom were homosexuals with Christian backgrounds, encouraged me to respond to the developing social conflict. They thought I had a unique view of the situation, given my anthropological training and standing as a Christian and homosexual.

Not all of the following agreed with what I say in this book, but I appreciate their feedback nonetheless. In particular, I thank my colleague and friend Erica Dixon for her tireless enthusiasm for reading drafts of each chapter and providing helpful comments and encouragement. Alexandra Gouirand helped with preliminary editing; George Darkenwald, Gerard Dolmans, April Kindrick, Kamau Kinuthia, and Ryan Clark provided helpful suggestions at various stages of the project. Philip Yancey, one of the evangelical authors I respect, graciously read a draft of this book and provided critical remarks. Susan Jones and Scott Stilson tracked down a number of books and articles for me. My sincere gratitude also to Bea Ferrigno, editor for Haiduk Press, for her help in expressing my thoughts. Finally, I thank my family for their encouragement and acceptance.

1 THE RAINBOW AND THE CROSS

Some parents have gay children. That probably isn't their first choice. . . . Even if they understand and accept the phenomenon of homosexuality, their first thought is likely to be: 'What sort of future awaits my child? How hard will his life be? What about the discrimination? What about the loneliness?'

— Jonathan Rauch[1]

In the 1950s and 1960s the New York City police frequently raided homosexual bars, jailed their patrons on charges of indecency, and published their names in the newspaper. On the night of June 27, 1969, however, homosexuals fought back. Judy Garland, a popular gay icon who died on June 22nd was buried on the 27th, an event that left the patrons of the Stonewall Inn gay bar in a less than submissive mood. When the police appeared, one drag queen, Sylvia Rivera, reportedly pitched a bottle at them. Others joined in and the police became targets of various projectiles, including bricks and rocks. Several nights of resistance followed. Homosexuals in New York City would no longer accept the routine of injustice and abuse. They began a collective move out of the closet in an effort to find happiness on this side of the rainbow. The "rebellion" at Stonewall is commemorated every year during the last weekend of June as part of the Gay Pride celebrations.

The events precipitated at Stonewall are analogous to the lives of individual homosexuals. Like many, I remained silent for years about my sexual orientation, passively accepting what was being said about homosexuals along with the unspoken rule that I should keep my preferences secret. Finally, I could no longer accept that my heterosexual friends could be completely open about their sexuality, while I effectively had to deny its very existence. My coming out process was long and difficult, a frequent experience among homosexuals, especially for those from Christian families.

This book collects what I learned as my worldview shifted from that of a typical evangelical Christian to the one I now hold as an anthropologist, a Christian, and a homosexual. It recounts how I realized that what my evangelical pastors taught about homosexuality was wrong (Chapters 2 through 5), and it summarizes scientific investigations of homosexuality (Chapters 6 and 7). It is my hope that young homosexual Christians will benefit from my experience so that their journey to wholeness may be a memorable and exciting adventure rather than a long, solitary passage through the "valley of the shadow of death."

This book also examines issues related to homosexuality and marriage, currently topics of intense public scrutiny (Chapters 8 through 10). It presents and critiques views of conservative evangelical Christians and the assumptions behind their arguments in the marriage debate. The counterarguments I offer are based on the research of biblical scholars, anthropologists, sociologists, psychologists, and other scientists and scholars. My intent is to encourage a more balanced, compassionate, and honest dialogue on homosexuality in American society.

The rainbow and the cross mentioned in this and other chapter titles reflect their association with homosexuality and Christianity, but more importantly, both are biblical symbols of hope. In Genesis 9:8-16 the rainbow appears in the sky to signify that God would never again destroy humanity in a flood. The cross represents Christ, through whom humans are reconciled to God. It is in hope of tolerance and reconciliation that I write. In particular, I hope this book will help homosexual Christians reconcile their sexual orientation with their Christian identity as I have done, and that it will also help evangelical Christians to welcome homosexuals into fellowship with a spirit of true love, compassion, and understanding. While I do not expect evangelicals to accept homosexuality, I do hope they will eventually extend the same grace and compassion to homosexuals as they do to gluttons, the proud, those who have divorced and remarried, and others whose behavior they consider sinful. The barriers to reconciliation are high, but some Christian denominations have already begun the process of dismantling them.

Who are evangelicals?

Scholars have difficulty defining exactly who is evangelical, primarily because there is a wide range of beliefs among adherents. Many evangelicals I know cannot define themselves; they simply assert that they are evangelical in their beliefs. One common definition is that evangelicals are "Bible-believing" Christians, with "Bible-believing" usually meaning someone whose interpretation of the Bible is similar to their own; neither too literal or fundamentalist, nor too liberal like mainstream Christians.

The Apostles' Creed

I believe in God, the Father almighty, creator of heaven and earth. I believe in Jesus Christ, his only Son, our Lord. He was conceived by the power of the Holy Spirit and born of the Virgin Mary. He suffered under Pontius Pilate, was crucified, died, and was buried. He descended into hell. On the third day he rose again. He ascended into heaven, and is seated at the right hand of the Father. He will come again to judge the living and the dead. I believe in the Holy Spirit, the holy catholic Church, the communion of saints, the forgiveness of sins, the resurrection of the body, and the life everlasting.

Sociologist and evangelical author Tony Campolo defines an evangelical as someone who accepts the doctrinal statements in the Apostles' Creed, the Bible as an "infallible guide" for beliefs and behavior, and who has a "personal spiritual relationship" with Christ.[2] The current form of the Apostles' Creed, which dates back to the early 8th century, represents one of the many statements Christians use to define their faith.

Didi Herman, author of *The Antigay Agenda*, explains that evangelical beliefs have two main components: that the four gospel accounts and, to a lesser extent, the Hebrew Bible are inerrant, true in all their detail; and that Jesus will rescue believers from the impending chaos to result from the rule of the Antichrist and the battle of Armageddon by rapturing them into heaven.[3] I have found that most evangelicals view the entire Bible, not only the four gospels and the Hebrew Old Testament, as the authoritative "word of God." They essentially have an all-or-nothing view of the Bible's authority: it is either completely inspired by God or it is not inspired at all. I would also add a third characteristic to Herman's pair: evangelicals place great emphasis on converting non-evangelicals, including other Christians, such as Roman Catholics and mainline Protestants, to their beliefs. In this book the term "evangelical" is used in a broad sense, encompassing all of the points mentioned above, while acknowledging that there is diversity of thought and activity within the evangelical community.

Over the rainbow

When I was growing up in the 1970s and early 1980s, I had no role model to help me learn how to deal with my homosexuality because I did not know any homosexual men, much less any homosexual Christians. There were no positive images of homosexuals in popular media, and certainly no homosexual characters in any of the books I read. I could not benefit from the experiences of other homosexual Christian men like Bruce Bawer, Andrew Sullivan, Mel White, former NFL defensive lineman Esera Tuaolo, and former New Jersey governor James McGreevey, because their books had not yet been written. There was no one I could talk to about my desires and longings. One afternoon I almost told one of my sisters about my attraction to other males, but the societal silence about homosexuality impressed upon me that I should not speak of "the love that dare not speak its name." Thus, I spent my childhood in silence with no inkling that there were many others who shared my feelings and experiences, nor anyone to advise me that only by admitting my homosexuality could I live a life of honesty and integrity.

During high school I never understood why other guys were so interested in girls, the fascination was just not there for me -- I was attracted to guys. While my friends were day-dreaming about cheerleaders, I worried about avoiding showers after gym class: I could not risk an unexpected arousal in the locker room where I was surrounded by attractive and completely naked men. During this time I learned to control my mind and body and to repress all sexual desire.

In college I became a "born-again" evangelical Christian and started attending a "Bible-believing" church where I was taught that homosexuality is a sin, that homosexuals stand in God's judgment and will go to hell. I learned that a Christian could not be homosexual; it was only the non-"Bible-believing" churches that said the two were compatible. "Bible-believing" churches reassured me that if I accepted my homosexual desires I would go to hell because that is what "God's word" teaches. As an evangelical I was taught to trust only evangelical leaders and especially not to trust scientists. The "biblical" worldview was truth; Satan has darkened the minds of non-believers, tricking them into accepting a scientific worldview that denies God and accepts homosexuality. But this same church held out hope that I could change my sexuality if I had enough faith in God.

At the age of 23, during counseling sessions with my pastor, I first admitted to having homoerotic attraction. My pastor explained that the attraction had developed because my father did not create an adequate bond with me during my formative years. He suggested that I needed to develop healthy non-sexual relationships with male role models who exhibited masculine behavior consistent with evangelical Christian beliefs. My pastor and other evangelical authorities encouraged me to date girls. They suggested that as I developed a sense of my masculine identity, I would develop erotic feelings for females. By dating girls I would prepare myself for the day when a heterosexual attraction would replace my homosexual one.

During counseling sessions my pastor encouraged me to believe that I could become like other guys, lead a normal life and, more importantly, not go to hell simply because of who attracted me. So I kept my sexual inclinations hidden, continued counseling, and developed friendships with masculine role models who were also devout evangelical Christians. Over the course of several years I realized that those relationships did not diminish my homosexual desires; rather, they strengthened my need for emotional fulfillment with other men. Dating girls simply filled me with guilt: I was not attracted to them and knowingly dated them primarily out of a desire to change my sexuality. That did not sit well with me because I always tried to treat others the way I wished to be treated: I would not want to be used in that way. As time went by, family, friends, and coworkers became more insistent about fixing me up with women. This simply increased the pressure I felt to be honest about my orientation.

In the closet

Encouraging homosexuals to keep their orientation secret implies they should be ashamed of who they are. Secrets often hide shame, some aspect of life or history that is considered unacceptable. Family secrets are a common problem; for homosexuals, keeping the secret can cause significant psychological and emotional difficulties. James McGreevey's experience is typical:

> Through most of these years I lived at arm's length from myself, unable to use my self-knowledge to live an honest life. I will say in my defense that it's an awful thing to expect a child of thirteen to pit himself against everything he holds dear – from his outsized ambitions to his beloved family and the church of his salvation – for the sake of something so small as private happiness. I could not do it at thirteen, and once I had started down the path of self-denial, I saw no alternative but to stay the course. . . . I never forgot for a minute that I was what my childhood friends mocked, what I thought my parents would reject – what my loving God supposedly condemned to limitless suffering.[4]

The internal conflict can be resolved by coming out of the closet, which is not a single event but rather a process of acknowledging first to oneself, and then to one's family, friends, and coworkers, that one is gay or lesbian. Homosexuals who come out of the closet also help to reduce discrimination against gay and lesbian people: it is difficult to discriminate against a group when someone familiar would be affected.

Many people do not understand the implications of denying one's sexuality. Former Roman Catholic priest and now psychology professor Daniel Helminiak explains:

> Sexuality means much more than physical arousal and orgasm. Attached to a person's sexuality is the capacity to feel affection, to delight in someone else, to get emotionally close to another person, to be passionately committed to him or her. Sexuality is at the core of that marvelous human experience, being in love – to be struck by the beauty of another and be drawn out of yourself, to become attached to another human being so powerfully that you easily begin measuring your life in terms of what's good for someone else as well as for yourself.[5]

When people deny their sexuality, they also deny themselves intimacy and emotional transparency along with their capacity to express love to another person. So when my pastor and other evangelical leaders instructed me to deny my homosexuality, they were really telling me to not love.

Andrew Sullivan asserts that this denial of love deprives homosexuals of their essential humanity, just as in Orwell's *1984*, the betrayal of Winston Smith's love signified the breaking of his spirit. For a homosexual, this betrayal often occurs in childhood, at the hands of those closest to him or her, the parents; this undermines the child's self-image and possibilities for future happiness in a committed relationship.[6] During childhood homosexuals are generally isolated from others who are similar to them; this exacerbates the problem, as John Boswell explains: "Gay people are for the most part not born into gay families. They suffer oppression individually and alone, without benefit of advice or frequently even emotional support from relatives or friends."[7]

A new hope and disappointment: reparative therapy

As my hope of change continued to fade while the pressure to marry increased, a new possibility arrived. During my graduate studies at the University of Wyoming, on his radio program James Dobson interviewed a man who had apparently overcome his homosexuality through what is known as reparative therapy. Dobson is the founder and chairman of Focus on the Family, an organization that is extremely influential among evangelical Christians. He suggested this man was "one of thousands" who had succeeded in changing their sexuality through reparative therapy. The "ex-gay" man had gone through a process of psychological counseling and support group therapy that supposedly enabled him to become heterosexual. Many evangelicals argue that such a change is possible because "the totality of Biblical canon reject[s] modern day theories and philosophies of being 'born gay.'"[8] Thus, shortly before my 29th birthday I began attending an "ex-gay" ministry.

Reparative therapy offered nothing new. I was encouraged to pray, to read the Bible, to seek God, and always to identify myself as heterosexual. The idea that my homosexuality developed from a weak paternal bond was reinforced, as was the belief that faith in God would help cure me. The facts were, however, that I had faith in God long before my sexual attraction developed; and I had followed biblical teachings even before becoming an evangelical Christian. So I came to think that perhaps God was not helping me change because he rejected me as a person. After all, evangelical leaders said thousands of homosexuals had changed their sexuality with God's help, yet God apparently was not helping me in those efforts. Perhaps I was to blame. This was a severe blow at the time, even though I now see the premise as ridiculous.

In *Stranger at the Gate* Mel White discusses the trauma, crisis of faith, and suicidal depression he suffered after his reparative therapy failed. White's Christian counselor had assured him that if he had sufficient faith in God he could completely change his homosexual orientation. But White never succeeded and believed it was because he lacked faith in God.[9] Mel White also recounts the story of a homosexual acquaintance who took the Bible literally and removed parts of his genitals with a razor.[10]

Eventually, like many others in my situation I realized, despite what evangelical leaders assert, that change was impossible and that I had been seriously misled. I re-examined the Bible and discovered that it is not as clear on the topic as many evangelical leaders claim. For example, many passages cited to condemn homosexuality are either irrelevant or are taken out of their cultural context. While modern English translations of the Bible contain a handful of verses that seem to condemn homosexuality, the historical, scriptural, and cultural contexts call that interpretation into question. I also undertook some research and learned that psychologists long ago discredited Freud's idea that homosexuality is a learned behavior caused by bad parenting or early sexual abuse. Also dismissed was the belief that a person's homosexuality can be changed. Finally, I discovered that many evangelical leaders in the "ex-gay" movement, who claim to have changed their sexuality, in fact have not. This includes Focus on the Family's John Paulk who, shortly after receiving national publicity for being "ex-gay" and claiming to be completely healed,[11] was found frequenting a gay bar: while Paulk's *behavior* may have changed, in that he married a woman and was no longer openly living as a homosexual, his *orientation* never budged.

As I read more about homosexuality in the church, I found my experiences were not unusual. Lutheran bishop Paul Egertson recounts his family's experience when his oldest son announced he was a celibate homosexual after accepting that his earnest prayers for change, over the course of many years, were in vain:

> But God did not change him. Did that mean he was so defective that even a gracious God did not love him? ... Since divine intervention did not occur, we pursued psychological therapy, only to discover that most psychiatrists and psychologists had long since come to the conclusion that homosexuality is not an illness and that no known system of treatment can change it. ... The best that therapy can do is help gay and lesbian persons accept the reality of their being before the socially imposed shame and the personal pain drive them to despair, drink, drugs, or death by suicide, all of which it does to numerous persons in our world.[12]

The story of Egertson's son closely parallels my own. The main difference is that I attempted reparative therapy on my own initiative. It was years before I finally accepted who I am; after that I could tell my family about my homosexuality. I had to learn from personal experience that the promises of change offered by James Dobson and other evangelical leaders are not consistent with scientific findings.

A culture of blame

When I finally stopped trying to change my homosexuality and accepted my orientation, my evangelical friends responded with a variety of accusations. Some told me I did not try hard enough, while others said I lacked faith in God. Many simply stopped associating with me. Missiles of blame were launched at me, fostering depression, anger, and a crisis of faith. Indeed, evangelical leaders have created a culture of blame: homosexuals are chastised for not being obedient to God, for not changing their desires, and for causing grief to their families and friends. For example, evangelical pastor Ronnie Floyd, author of *The Gay Agenda*, says "The son who returns home on a holiday and reveals to his father that he has a gay lover drives a wedge between himself and his parents,"[13] and "It saddens me to see fathers and sons separated because of homosexuality. A young man 'comes out' and the resulting years of silence destroy what once was a vital relationship."[14] Floyd blames the son's orientation and honesty about it for the breach between the son and parents, instead of recognizing that the silence was partly due to the parents' inability to love their son unconditionally.

A pamphlet designed for the families of homosexuals by Focus on the Family also instills a sense of guilt in homosexuals. It suggests that homosexuals are hurting their loved ones solely because of their sexual orientation: the closer the relationship, the more deep the hurt the homosexual causes, even though nothing can be done about it.[15] But here blame is also laid on the family: "Guilt is a huge issue, especially for parents. It's common for them to ask, 'Where did we go wrong?' They feel like total failures in one of their most important God-given roles."[16] It is no surprise that parents of a homosexual feel guilty: influential evangelical leaders tell them their son is gay *because* the father was too distant, or *because* the mother was too domineering; their daughter is lesbian *because* the mother was not nurturing, or *because* the father was too passive or unavailable. Many evangelical leaders blame the family instead of honestly stating that homosexuality is a natural condition, that scientific evidence indicates it cannot be changed in most individuals, and that homosexuality probably develops from a combination of factors, including genetics.

Many evangelical leaders blame homosexuals and their families because they simply do not understand homosexuality and may even fear it: homosexuality runs counter to their values and perception of natural order; it represents the unknown, the mysterious, and the foreign. And they have convinced themselves that God hates it (see Chapter 5). Evangelicals hold assumptions, beliefs, and values that may be surprising to people who are not familiar with that branch of Christianity. The evangelical worldview and perception of homosexuals are radically different from those of mainstream America. I was taught to view myself through those assumptions and beliefs. I could not reconcile my sexual and emotional life with the views of my trusted evangelical leaders, and so struggled for years with that internal conflict. It was not resolved until I accepted that I had been misled: I simply could not change my sexual orientation.

Of course, I still had doubts about going to hell for my sexual orientation. Not long after this a Christian student came to me for help with a similar conflict. I was compelled to articulate for the first time some of the choices he faced: he could live a repressed and unfulfilled life, isolated from love, happiness, and emotional fulfillment; he could reject God and become a full participant in the gay subculture; or he could consider that God might be more concerned with how he treated others than with the gender of his lover. With that, I finally accepted that my Christian faith and my homosexual orientation are compatible.

---

1 Jonathan Rauch (2004 , 80).
2 Tony Campolo (2004, 56).
3 Didi Herman (1997, 12).
4 James E. McGreevey (2006, 6-7).
5 Daniel A. Helminiak (2000, 25).
6 Andrew Sullivan (1995, 155-156).
7 John Boswell (1980, 16).

8 Darryl Foster (no date).

9 Mel White (1994, 107).

10 Ibid (70). "And if your right eye makes you stumble, tear it out, and throw it from you; for it is better for you that one of the parts of your body perish, than for your whole body to be thrown into hell." – Matthew 5:29.

11 John Paulk (July 2000).

12 Paul Wennes Egertson (1999, 25-26).

13 Ronnie W. Floyd (2004, 30).

14 Ibid (13).

15 Bob Davies (2002, 3)

16 Ibid (3).

2 EVANGELICAL REALITY

From a biblical standpoint, the rise of homosexuality is a
sign that a society is in the last stages of decay.

— Pat Robertson[1]

Evangelicals have gained considerable attention since the 2004 presidential election. The press has been curious about what evangelicals believe and how they emerged as an important political force. Evangelicals believe they are following God's call. Many, however, submit to the authority of their leaders without questioning several assumptions that underlie their teachings. This sometimes creates an unquestioned allegiance to views that are based in error. This can have serious consequences, especially when the civil rights of millions of Americans are affected.

Within evangelical Christianity there are a variety of opinions on many issues, including those presented here; not every evangelical agrees with the statements or beliefs of the prominent leaders discussed in this book. Also, evangelical Christianity is only one expression of the Christian faith. While it may seem to many Americans that James Dobson and Pat Robertson are spokesmen for all of Christianity, they are not. Although other major Christian traditions disagree with evangelical Christianity they are less often seen in the national spotlight; meanwhile certain evangelical leaders are frequent guests on news programs as representatives of the Christian perspective.

Evangelical leaders

The evangelicals' worldview explains their motivations and actions in opposing homosexuality. Many prominent evangelical leaders such as James Dobson, Pat Robertson, and the recently deceased Jerry Falwell, are represented in this book by quotations that express the predominant evangelical views. Although these individuals and their organizations rely heavily on the internet to communicate with their followers, there is no shortage of press releases and commentaries from them on issues surrounding homo-sexuality. Therefore, we will examine their backgrounds and statements, as well as those of other influential evangelicals.

James Dobson is the founder and chairman of Focus on the Family; he considers himself "America's foremost family counselor."[2] He is referred to as "Dr. Dobson," due to his Ph.D. in child development, which gives him a stamp of authority seldom questioned by his followers. He has written numerous books on the family and society. His influence can be gauged by a report that Abercrombie & Fitch received 300 phone calls an hour with complaints about their marketing practices after Dobson criticized the company on his radio program.[3]

While many evangelicals view Dobson as a kind and soft-spoken psychologist who is concerned with America's families and children, the homosexual community has a different view. As Episcopalian author Bruce Bawer notes, "When it comes to wicked propaganda about homosexuality, Dobson takes a backseat to few."[4] This may appear to be a very harsh appraisal, but Bawer has good reasons for his critique. Dobson misrepresents scientific findings, omits crucial qualifying statements in his proclamations, promotes malicious stereotypes about homosexuals, and misleads the public on many issues involving homosexuality, including whether it is possible to change one's sexual orientation.

Pat Robertson is the founder and president of Regent University in Virginia and of the Christian Broadcasting Network, with its popular television show, *The 700 Club*. Robertson, who trained to be a lawyer at Yale University but failed the bar examination, takes a special interest in law and politics. He is a former presidential candidate who lost the 1988 Republican nomination to George H. W. Bush. In 1989 Robertson founded the Christian Coalition to influence American politics toward his brand of evangelical Christianity.

We turn again to Bruce Bawer for a different view: "Robertson loves the parts of the Bible that depict God as avenging, punishing, destroying; he loves the scriptures' *Sturm and Drang*. Yet the gospel passages about love seem lost on him."[5] Bawer also suggests that Robertson, partly through the Christian Coalition, influenced the 1996 Republican Party platform.[6]

Recently deceased evangelical leader, Jerry Falwell, founded the Moral Majority in the 1970s. He was also the pastor of Thomas Road Baptist Church in Virginia, president of Liberty University, and host of the *Old Time Gospel Hour* radio and television show. He made regular appearances as a guest on cable news programs to put forth the "Christian" perspective on various issues. As did Robertson, Falwell gained considerable publicity and notoriety when he blamed homosexuals and others for the destruction of the World Trade Center.[7]

Mel White, who served as a ghostwriter for Falwell before White accepted his own homosexuality, wrote to him about his attitude toward homosexuals:

> You seemed compassionate and understanding that night. Then, today, I received a copy of the October 1991 fund-raising letter describing me and millions of men and women like me as "perverts" who "unashamedly flaunt their perversion." The letter declares "homosexuality a sin." It warns that "our nation has become a modern day Sodom and Gomorra" [sic] and that you have decided to speak out against this "perversion" for the purpose of "moral decency and traditional family values." . . .
>
> Jerry, I am also worried about the motives behind your letter. I remember clearly in one of our interviews that you described a noisy confrontation you once had with "radical activist gays" in San Francisco. "They played right into my hands," you said to me. "Those poor, dumb fairy demonstrators gave me the best media coverage I've ever had. If they weren't out there, I'd have to invent them."[8]

Two influential, but less visible evangelical leaders are Philip Yancey and Tony Campolo. Yancey is an editor-at-large for *Christianity Today*, a leading evangelical publication founded in part by Billy Graham. Yancey has written many award-winning and best-selling books that challenge and encourage evangelical Christians to live as Jesus did, with a spirit of grace and forgiveness. He also honestly and compassionately addresses controversial issues such as racism within the church and homosexuality. Although Yancey opposes homosexual behavior, he also opposes the judgmental and unloving response of many evangelicals to homosexuals, as demonstrated in his book *What's So Amazing about Grace?*[9]

Tony Campolo is professor emeritus of sociology at the evangelical Eastern University in Pennsylvania. He represents evangelical Christians who focus on the social gospel of Jesus; a major thrust of their mission is to help the poor, needy, societal outcasts, and those who are sick. Rather than being included with the "religious right," evangelicals such as Campolo oppose many Republican policies, including those that affect the environment and recent tax cuts for the rich at the expense of social programs. In *Speaking My Mind*[10] Campolo challenges evangelical Christians to recognize that God is a god of compassion who commands us to love people as they are; he asserts that evangelicals should be at the forefront of fighting for the rights of others, including homosexuals.

Evangelical assumptions about the Bible

Many people might dismiss some of the basic assumptions underlying the evangelical worldview as childlike and innocuous. However, when we recognize the strength of the evangelical social and political force, and understand that the goal of many evangelical leaders is to reshape America into a society based on these assumptions, the situation becomes serious. Evangelical assumptions have significant consequences when applied to other matters, such as the teaching of evolution in science classes and the debate over the "day after pill".

The mission statement of Jerry Falwell Ministries presents the evangelical worldview. Their beliefs include that

> the Holy Bible was written by men supernaturally inspired; that it is truth without any admixture of error for its matter; and therefore is, and shall remain to the end of the age, the only complete and final revelation of the will of God to man; the true center of Christian union and the supreme standard by which all human conduct, creeds, and opinions should be tried . . . By "The Holy Bible" we mean that collection of sixty-six books from Genesis to Revelation which, as originally written, does not only contain and convey the Word of God but IS the

very Word of God. By "inspiration," we mean that the books of the Bible were written by holy men of old, as they were moved by the Holy Spirit, in such a definite way that their writings were supernaturally and verbally inspired and free from error, as no other writings have ever been or ever will be inspired.[11] [Emphasis in original.]

The creed also insists that the creation accounts in Genesis are literally true: humans were created as-is in God's image, evolution did not occur, and God instituted the seven-day week, with the final day being a day of rest. These beliefs ignore the many errors, contradictions, and inconsistencies found within the Bible as well as its cultural and historical contexts, which are essential for critical understanding of any ancient writing.

When asked why evangelicals believe the Bible is *inerrant*, a term used to establish the literal Bible as the inspired and infallible "word of God," with no errors or contradictions, most evangelicals refer to 2 Timothy 3:16-17 (see below). Without any regard for the historical and cultural contexts of this passage, evangelical followers are assured that because the Bible says *all* scripture is inspired by God, it is therefore God who "wrote" the Bible.

Circular reasoning aside, there are solid reasons to doubt the evangelical conclusion. First, at the time the letter to Timothy was written there was no New Testament, nor was there even a "Bible" as we know it. Instead, both the Jewish tradition and the early Christian church viewed a variety of writings as authoritative; many, but not all of them were later incorporated within the Bible. Thus, the author of 2 Timothy, assumed to be the apostle Paul by evangelicals, although biblical scholars find that questionable,[12] could not have been referring to the Bible as we know it because it did not take its present form until the late 4th century.[13] Second, many of the New Testament books had not yet been written. Thus, if the author was referring to all the authoritative writings of his time, he could not have been including much of the New Testament. Third, in learned Jewish society there was a debate about whether only the Torah, the first five books of the Bible, was useful for teaching or a broader collection of works used in synagogues should also be considered authoritative. Therefore, the comment in 2 Timothy 3:16-17 may have been simply the author's opinion on this debate. Finally, inerrancy of a literal Bible is a recent doctrine, first officially stated in 1895, although there were leaders who assumed the inspiration of the Bible throughout the Christian era.[14] However, what the early leaders actually meant by inspiration is not necessarily what is meant by the concept today. For example, many early Christians treated the Old Testament as inspired allegory, not as literal truth.[15] A simple examination of all of the early Christian statements of faith and doctrine, such as the Apostles' Creed, reveals that the idea of biblical inerrancy was not an essential part of early Christian beliefs.

> All Scripture is inspired by God and profitable for teaching, for reproof, for correction, for training in righteousness; that the man of God may be adequate, equipped for every good work. – 2 Timothy 3:16-17

It seems untenable to insist that the Bible is the literal, inerrant "word of God," when there are obvious mistakes and contradictions in it. While evangelical leaders can creatively explain away most errors to their satisfaction, it is difficult to convince skeptics that Leviticus 11:6 is "inerrant truth" because rabbits do not chew cud, it only *looks* as if they do. Thus, the Bible is wrong about this biological fact. It is also beyond reason to accept the Bible's assertion in Joshua 10:13 that the sun and moon stood still for an entire day. Such an event could not occur within the basic laws of physics and astronomy, and would have caused havoc on earth because of the gravitational effects of the moon.

> The rabbit also, for though it chews cud, it does not divide the hoof, it is unclean to you.
> – Leviticus 11:6
> So the sun stood still, and the moon stopped, until the nation avenged themselves of their enemies. Is it not written in the book of Jashar? And the sun stopped in the middle of the sky, and did not hasten to go down for about a whole day. – Joshua 10:13

The belief that the Bible is the inspired "word of God" is essentially universal among evangelicals. However, the belief that it should be taken literally in all its detail is not, although that is assumed by most of the important leaders. Allowance is usually made for biblical teachings that contradict Western values, such as the acceptance of slavery, prohibitive dress codes, and instructions on hair length or head coverings. When biblical teachings contradict Western values, evangelicals maintain that the Bible simply reflects the cultural views of the ancient world,[16] but, as we shall see in Chapter 5, they ignore the same cultural context when it relates to homosexuality.

Evangelicals believe the Bible is accurate because they see it as God's word: God could not be mistaken about historical events. This view, however, ignores the possibility that God could convey important morals or lessons in fictional stories, as Jesus did in the parables. These considerations are relevant to the book of Genesis, which documents events that supposedly happened up to 3,000 years before Hebrew became a written language, around the 10th century BC.[17] According to the Genesis account, God created the universe about 6,000 years ago and destroyed virtually everything on earth with a worldwide flood about 4,500 years ago. In addition, it suggests that all of humanity spoke the same language about 4,300 years ago, when God dispersed the peoples and languages to prevent the Tower of Babel from being completed. Another biblical story tells us Jonah was swallowed by a big fish and remained inside it for three days before emerging at Ninevah. The fish would have had to circumnavigate the continent of Africa in three days: Jonah was thrown into the Mediterranean Sea and Ninevah is on the Tigris River, which empties into the Persian Gulf. If the literal Bible is considered completely accurate in its history and science, then many of the foundational discoveries of physics, chemistry, biology, medicine, and astronomy are in error.

Many evangelical leaders simply ignore scientific findings when the results do not agree with their interpretation of the Bible. They claim that science is inherently flawed and can only be trusted when the results are made to fit the biblical stories and assumptions. This belief is explicitly stated in *Creation* magazine:

The Bible records the true history of the universe. Thus, we should use the Bible as our starting point in science, especially sciences like geology that deal with Earth history. . . . So, what should we do if a geological interpretation doesn't fit with the Bible? Question the geological interpretation! Often we will need to re-examine the evidence directly. Frequently, even the 'facts' reported in geological books are not facts, but interpretations. When we carefully observe the evidence directly, and interpret it starting from the true history given in the Bible, we can confidently expect to find that the evidence fits the truth of the Bible, God's infallible revealed Word.[18]

Thus, if the facts do not fit the Bible, they must be reinterpreted until they do. The notion of reinterpreting facts to make them fit a predetermined outcome is considered unethical in science. However, evangelicals believe in a literal Bible and suggest that scientists should do exactly that in order to justify the evangelical's belief in "God's word."

Many evangelicals reject the scientific view that human biology is no different from that of other animals; this derives mainly from their interpretation of Genesis 1:27. They argue that because humans are the only creatures made in God's image, human biology is inherently different from that of the animals. However, this premise assumes that the biblical passage refers to our biological characteristics and not to some other aspect, such as the ability to be creative or to have emotional capacity. Many mainline Christians do not believe the passage refers to biological matters because it would imply that God has biological characteristics similar to humans, including DNA, two arms, two legs, a heart, and -- no disrespect intended -- a penis: God is always referred to in the masculine by evangelicals, even though "he" made humans in "his" image, male and female. The biology of humans is supposedly intrinsically different from that of animals, so arguments based on homosexuality in nature and research on the cause(s) of homosexuality in various animals and insects are considered irrelevant by evangelicals as clues to the cause(s) of homosexuality in humans.

Nonetheless, many evangelical leaders ignore the incompatibility between the belief that human biology is different from ani-

And God created man in His own image, in the image of God He created him; male and female He created them. – Genesis 1:27

mals because we are made in God's image and the view that being made in God's image has nothing to do with biology. In addition, they ignore the facts that the genetic code of humans is extremely similar to that of animals, that pig organs are used as transplants for humans, and that animals are frequently employed as substitutes for humans in the testing of products destined for human use. They also ignore that humans acquire communicable diseases, such as SARS, HIV, and bird flu, from animals. Science demonstrates that humans are indeed biological animals, very similar to the apes. The Christian belief that humans, unlike animals, also have a soul is not contradicted by the view of biological science that humans are animals. For example, Christian apologist C. S. Lewis suggests that a human is "an animal; but an animal called to be, or raised to be, or (if you like) doomed to be, something more than an animal."[19] From a Christian standpoint, we humans are biological animals with souls, which makes us in God's image.

The evangelical belief that humans were created in God's image highlights another important assumption by evangelicals: sex and gender are interchangeable concepts. Social scientists assert that gender is a social construct resulting from a culture's behavioral expectations for the different sexes, while sex is biological and based on a person's genitals. However, many evangelical leaders believe that biology automatically determines gender: God made males, who are always masculine, to be the providers, and females, who are always feminine, to be nurturers. For example, James Dobson argues that the two sexes are designed to physically and emotionally "fit together," with male stability and "productivity" only possible through union with a female.[20] Unfortunately, this view ignores anthropological and sociological data, which demonstrate that gender is culturally, not biologically, determined. See Chapter 7 for a full discussion of culture and gender.

If the Bible is the literal and inspired "word of God" in the sense that God communicated each word to the writers, then any biblical condemnation of homosexuality represents God's opinion and is not a reflection of societal values at the time of writing, or of the authors' personal biases. Significantly, the Genesis story suggests that humans and other animals die because of Eve's sin (although Christians frequently refer to it as Adam's sin, it was Eve who first committed the act of disobedience by eating the forbidden fruit). This original sin allowed evil to enter the world, leading to human suffering and illness. One of the consequences of the original sin, according to evangelical leaders, is that human sexual desires became perverted from what God intended. Therefore, homosexuality is viewed as an unnatural sexual act that resulted from human disobedience to God's original plan. Eve's original sin also corrupted nature, which helps evangelicals explain why there are homosexual animals.

Many evangelicals also believe in absolute truth and the existence of absolute good and evil. Absolute truth is defined as the Truth found in the Bible: "God's word is Truth" is a meaningful phrase to evangelicals. Thus, if the apostle Paul says that women should be submissive to men because God made woman for man and not vice versa, that is absolute Truth. God and Satan represent absolute good and evil, respectively. Most evangelicals consider Satan to be an actual being who is in control of our world, aided by his army of demons. Satan and the demons actively encourage people to disobey God's revealed Truth. Satan is also aided by liberals, homosexuals, feminists, abortionists, and Hollywood in his attempts to destroy "one nation under God." Thus, evangelical leaders view the culture war not just as a battle between true Christians (evangelicals) and their allies against liberals, but also as a war between God and Satan. Evangelical leaders believe that homosexuals are doing the work of Satan in trying to lead America further astray from the "biblical foundation" upon which it was supposedly established. Thus, many evangelical leaders believe they must oppose equal rights for homosexuals and other liberal causes; this makes homosexuals who are evangelical enemies of their fellow believers.

Evangelical leaders also assume that they understand biblical teachings exactly as the ancient authors intended them to be understood. In other words, the Bible is independent of culture -- the different assumptions held by ancient authors and modern

Americans do not affect how the passages are interpreted today. Thus, the Bible's commands are frequently universally applied, with very little attention to the context in which they were written. The assumption that the Bible is essentially independent of culture alters what the original biblical authors intended because no document can be immune to culture. Western culture, which is very different from that of the ancient Mediterranean, confounds our understanding of the ancient texts. Therefore, it is not wise to apply uncritically the moral, legal, and social codes of an ancient pre-industrial society to a modern one, which has a completely different understanding of the world. It raises the potential for considerable abuse of individual freedoms as well as the specter of discriminatory practices, such as slavery and Jim Crow segregation laws. In fact, the Southern Baptist church split from the American Baptists because the Southern Baptists asserted that slavery was indeed biblical and within God's will.[21]

The assumption that biblical truths are universally applicable ignores the variations and values of other cultures. An anthropologist studies many cultures and readily recognizes that the values evident in the Bible are characteristic of pastoral and agrarian societies. These values, such as a male-dominated society that views women as possessions, are not universal and would not be functional in other types of societies. The assumption that biblical values can and should be universally applied is a preconception that wreaked havoc in many societies that came under the influence of evangelical or other Christian missionaries. Culture allows people to adapt to their unique environment. The cultural practices and values derived from a culture in a semi-arid environment simply cannot work in other conditions such as a tropical island. The kosher food laws of Leviticus and Deuteronomy, for example, are meaningless in New Guinea or the Amazonian jungle, where many of the animals and foods mentioned do not exist. Many evangelical leaders are not trained in anthropology or cultural sensitivity and never question the universality of biblical values or consider whether they are appropriate to a particular culture.

One problem with the actions of many evangelical leaders is that they attempt to force their beliefs on the rest of American society. This is particularly evident in the teaching of evolution at various public schools around the country. Many evangelical leaders actively attempt to undermine the teaching of evolution, which is the bedrock of the biological sciences, because it does not agree with their belief in a literal Genesis.[22] If evangelical leaders succeed in establishing their worldview in mainstream America, much of what is taught in science classes will have to be altered to fit a literal Bible. This will significantly impact research grants to scientists, which will in turn have a negative impact on scientific and medical breakthroughs.[23]

Evangelical assumptions about Christianity

Another important assumption made by many evangelicals is that their beliefs represent true Christianity.[24] Some evangelical leaders consider the Catholic Church to be an apostate religion and hold that Catholics are not true Christians. Didi Herman notes that *Christianity Today* routinely denounced Catholics in the 1960s in a manner very similar to their treatment of homosexuals today.[25] Specifically, many evangelicals oppose the "worship" of Mary which they claim is an integral part of Catholicism; they also oppose the Catholic view that salvation can be achieved through the church's sacraments. Evangelicals believe salvation is only gained by faith that Jesus was the Messiah, the son of God, born of a virgin, lived a sinless life, and came to earth to die for our sins. Contrary to this evangelical belief, when a man asked Jesus how to acquire eternal life, Jesus simply responded that he should love God with all his heart, soul, strength, and mind and that he should love his neighbor as himself (see below). Evangelical beliefs are largely based on writings attributed to the apostle Paul and on Christian tradition. The belief in salvation by faith alone demonstrates that many evangelical leaders actually prefer the writings of Paul to the teachings of Jesus, although they believe Paul's teachings are consistent with those of Jesus.

Many evangelicals are suspicious of the Christianity practiced by the more liberal Protestants of mainline churches, including the Episcopal, Presbyterian, Methodist, and Lutheran denominations, because these generally do not take the Bible literally. Many evangelicals perceive this as a denial that the Bible is "God's word," and so determine that these are not "Bible-believing" denominations. Other groups, such as the Mormons, Seventh Day Adventists, and Jehovah's Witnesses are considered to be cults. Many evangelical leaders are resolutely opposed to ecumenical movements within Christianity because they believe they will compromise their true "Bible-based" beliefs by joining evangelical churches with denominations they regard as not truly Christian.

One method many evangelicals employ to discredit those who challenge their interpretation of the Bible is to suggest that they are simply "twisting scripture" to fit a personal bias, or not accepting the authority of the Bible. This allows evangelicals to ignore any criticism and avoid examining their basic assumptions. For example, Ronnie Floyd suggests that "Champions of the Gay Agenda can and do try to *twist the Scriptures* to their advantage, or at least to cause enough doubt in regard to issues of interpretation that they can effectively cloud what God has to say on the issue"[26] [emphasis added]. Therefore, any argument that indicates homosexuality is not condemned by the Bible is simply the result of "twisting scripture" to fit one's personal bias. This is further demonstrated by a discussion between two students that appeared on the *Youth on the Rock* internet chat forum after I presented a lecture on what the Bible does and does not say about homosexuality.[27] The first student explained she attended the lecture and that my "audacity" for giving such a lecture frightened her, that God would look at me "very sternly" and that Jesus was

> And behold, a certain lawyer stood up and put Him to the test, saying, "Teacher, what shall I do to inherit eternal life?" And He said to him, "What is written in the Law? How does it read to you?" And he answered and said, "You shall love the Lord your God with all your heart, and with all your soul, and with all your strength, and with all your mind; and your neighbor as yourself." And He said to him, "You have answered correctly; do this, and you will live." – Luke 10:25-28

crying. The second student quoted verses from 2 Timothy 3:5-7 in arguing that it's "false prophets" like me that devout Christians must avoid. She further stated that because of my views the blood of many would be on my hands. She advocated a simple childlike faith in the Bible and that "God means what He says in His word." These two students demonstrate a sincere compassion for those they consider unsaved. They also demonstrate the evangelical tendency to accept the modern English translation of the Bible as inspired by God and of unquestionable authority. Anyone who examines the English translation of the original Greek and Hebrew texts is seen as challenging God's authority. Such an uncritical appeal to authority creates a group of believers who simply follow the biblical interpretation of a few leaders. Any disagreement with them is regarded as "twisting scripture" or rejecting God's authority.

Evangelical assumptions about America

Many evangelicals also believe that American society was founded on the Judeo-Christian tradition and that societal acceptance of homosexuals will directly or indirectly destroy the United States. In their view, modern American society is straying from the Judeo-Christian tradition and morality is declining. Many evangelicals accept such premises and repeat them without question. The moral decline is a serious issue among evangelical leaders because they believe God gave America its prosperity and influence only because it had been true to the Bible.[28] Those who accept this view must either ignore history or accept that the brutal form of slavery practiced in America was biblically acceptable. They must assume that the United States was a more moral society when African Americans in the South could not drink from the same water fountains as whites, when blacks were the property of white slave owners, when children worked in factories, when women were not able to vote, when homosexuals were imprisoned or castrated solely because of their sexual orientation, when Japanese Americans were interned in prison camps and when treaties with Native Americans were regularly broken so that whites could usurp their land and resources.

Some evangelical leaders argue that homosexuality is a sign of a decaying civilization increasingly rejected by God. Others suggest that because God destroyed Sodom and Gomorrah, supposedly because of homosexuality, God will also destroy the United States. Thus, recognizing the humanity and dignity of homosexuals and treating them with equality will anger God so much that God will destroy the entire country. It is a strange god who turns a blind eye to one of the most brutal forms of slavery that has existed and then gets upset when an entire group of people is treated with dignity, respect, and equality. Yet this is the god of many evangelicals, and the fear of this god has prompted them to oppose the homosexual rights movement. Evangelical leaders rely on the linguistic connection between Sodom and "sodomy," while ignoring what the Bible actually says about the destruction of the cities (see Chapter 5 for a full discussion). Nowhere does the Bible attribute the destruction of Sodom and Gomorrah to homosexuality.

The belief that God will destroy the United States partly because of homosexuality seems farfetched to the average American who is not of the evangelical mindset. However, the responses of Pat Robertson and Jerry Falwell to the September 11th terrorist attacks demonstrate its force within the evangelical community. Robertson issued a press release that explains why, in his mind, the attacks occurred:

> Don't ask why did it happen. It happened because people are evil. It also happened because God is lifting His protection from this nation and we must pray and ask Him for revival so that once again we will be His people, the planting of His righteousness, so that He will come to our defense and protect us as a nation.[29]

Robertson lists a number of reasons why God is supposedly "lifting His protection from this nation," including secularism; the pursuit of health, wealth, material pleasures, and sexuality; allowing abortion and pornography; portraying the occult on television; and courts that are "removing God" from public schools.

On Robertson's *The 700 Club* television program of September 13, 2001, Jerry Falwell directly blamed, among others, homosexuals for being the primary reason that "God allowed" the terrorists to strike America:

> I really believe that the pagans and the abortionists, and the feminists, and the gays and the lesbians who are actively trying to make that an alternative lifestyle, the ACLU, People for the American Way, all of them who have tried to secularize America, I point the finger in their face and say "you helped this happen."[30]

Robertson's statement reveals the basic premise of the belief that homosexuality will directly or indirectly lead to the destruction of the United States:

> For those who love this country, we are facing judgment. There has been no society who [sic] has turned itself to widespread homosexuality that has survived. The Greeks were into it, but they didn't survive. Sooner or later God destroys them just like [sic] He did Sodom and Gomorrah.[31]

The argument is that God protects societies that adhere to "biblical morality" and allows the destruction of those that do not. Thus, as homosexuality becomes more acceptable, God will destroy the nation for straying from "biblical morality." However, historian John Boswell points out that the collapse of the Roman Empire was preceded by increasing intolerance of homosexuality, rather than increasing acceptance.[32] The argument that God will destroy the United States because of its increasing acceptance of homosexuality is not supported by the facts of history.

Historian Stephanie Coontz discusses changes in American families and culture, especially the considerable changes in sexual mores. For example, she writes that "as late as 1886, the 'age of consent' for girls was only 10 in more than half the states in the union."[33] She also notes that the perception of increasing violence in American society is not accurate, for in the 1950s considerable violence was directed at many different minority groups:

> There was tremendous hostility to people who could be defined as "others": Jews, African Americans, Puerto Ricans, the poor, gays or lesbians, and "the red menace." Yet on a day-to-day basis, the civility that prevailed in homogeneous neigh-

borhoods allowed people to ignore larger patterns of racial and political repression.[34]

However, because most white Americans lived in homogeneous neighborhoods, they were able to ignore the underlying problems of social tension, repression, and hostility. Coontz also observes that the portrayal of the family on 1950s television shows did not represent the true American family: "At the time, everyone knew that shows such as *Donna Reed, Ozzie and Harriet, Leave It to Beaver* and *Father Knows Best* were not the way families really were. People didn't watch those shows to see their own lives reflected back at them."[35] It would be more accurate to say that American morals, including sexual morals, have not declined, but have simply changed.

A result of the evangelical loyalty to tradition, which favors a conservative outlook, is that evangelicals generally associate the Republican Party with traditional Judeo-Christian values and Democrats with liberalism and a rejection of traditional values, in other words a rejection of God. The association of Republicans with "biblical" values becomes self-evident for the evangelical who examines the positions on social issues taken by the two political parties: Democrats tend to favor keeping abortion legal, while Republicans generally oppose it; Democrats are tolerant or accepting of homosexuality, while Republicans tend to oppose it. Republican opposition to homosexuality is evidenced by their support of a federal marriage amendment to the Constitution that would deny equal rights to homosexuals. The 2004 platform of the South Carolina Republican Party advocated further discrimination against homosexuals, stating: "Although we support tolerance, we don't agree that unnatural or unhealthy sexual practices ought to be legitimized or promoted in the classroom, nor do we believe that known practicing homosexuals should serve as teachers in public schools."[36] Republicans generally share evangelical views on issues such as this; many evangelicals are staunch conservatives who believe Jesus had similar values. In fact, the 2000 and 2004 presidential election exit polls indicated that some 80 percent of those who considered themselves to be conservative or evangelical Christians voted for George W. Bush, the Republican candidate.[37]

The predominant association of evangelicals and Republicans indicates both groups hold a biased view of Jesus and the Bible. It is evident from the gospels that Jesus focused much more on social concerns, including justice for the oppressed and the welfare of widows, orphans, and other outcasts: these are issues typically of concern to Democrats.[38] Jesus fiercely condemned the conservative social forces in his society, specifically the religious leaders and the rich, groups frequently associated with Republicans.[39]

Jesus did not necessarily support or promote the traditional values of his time. Indeed, the gospels mention how Jesus criticized the Jewish religious leaders who were strong supporters of tradition. Rarely did Jesus correct the behavior of anyone except religious leaders. Instead, he focused substantial attention on teaching people to love their neighbors as themselves and to show compassion and mercy to others.[40] This is quite different from the message of many evangelical leaders who promote a "pro-family" agenda at the expense of single parents and homosexuals.

Tony Campolo speaks for the minority of evangelicals who strongly disagree with the conservative majority. While liberal evangelicals are pro-life, they are also critical of President Bush's environmental policies and tax cuts that benefit the rich. Furthermore, they support universal health care and legal protection for homosexuals.[41] Although a vast majority of evangelicals are conservative, Campolo demonstrates the diversity of thought within the evangelical community and reminds us to be cautious with generalizations.

Coinciding with the conservative politics of most evangelicals is the association of the family with evangelical Christianity. Many evangelical leaders consider themselves to be the voice of the traditional family that is supposedly being eroded by the liberal social movement and, in particular, the homosexual rights movement. Evangelical leaders believe that the preservation of the "traditional family," to the exclusion of other types of families, is crucial for the preservation of American society.[42] Thus, we see the strong focus on the family by evangelicals who frequent the Family Christian Bookstore, listen to "family friendly" radio or watch the Family Network on TV, originally owned by Pat Robertson. "Family" has actually become one of the main code terms used by many evangelicals to identify something as their own. It seems that any organization with "family" in its title is evangelical in its worldview. These groups include Focus on the Family, Family Research Council, Family Research Institute, Culture and Family Institute, and American Family Association. These evangelical organizations consider themselves "pro-family," implying that those who disagree with them are anti-family.

Perhaps the most influential evangelical organization is James Dobson's Focus on the Family ministry, which includes long-running radio programs that are "heard on over 3,000 radio facilities in North America," translated into 27 languages, and heard by over 220 million people worldwide.[43] Dobson created Focus on the Family in 1977 because of his "increasing concern for the American family." The organization's mission is "to cooperate with the Holy Spirit in disseminating the Gospel of Jesus Christ to as many people as possible, and, specifically, to accomplish that objective by helping to preserve traditional values and the institution of the family."[44] "Family" in this context means only two-parent heterosexual families. While Focus on the Family attempts to help two-parent heterosexual families, they actually hinder other families. Didi Herman argues that Focus on the Family has taken over the now defunct Moral Majority's role in "vociferous antigay campaigning;" it has produced "volumes of antigay material."[45]

> Do not think that I came to bring peace on the earth; I did not come to bring peace, but a sword. For I came to set a man against his father, and a daughter against her mother, and a daughter-in-law against her mother-in-law; and a man's enemies will be the members of his household. He who loves father or mother more than Me is not worthy of Me; and he who loves son or daughter more than Me is not worthy of Me. – Matthew 10:34-37

Contrary to the Focus on the Family mission statement, Jesus did not connect spreading the gospel with the institution of the family. An examination of Jesus' comments on the family reveals that Dobson and Jesus have very different ideas, both on its importance related to the gospel, and on what actually constitutes a family.[46] For example, in Matthew 10:34-37 (see above) Jesus states that he came to set the members of a household against each other (the specific relations mentioned in the passage all lived under one roof in ancient Israelite society; the son-in-law is not mentioned because the bride moved in with the groom's family). Thus, Jesus' idea of spreading the gospel is *not* based on preserving the traditional family.

In addition to "family," a second important code term for evangelicals is "Bible-believing." A "Bible-believing" church is one that is evangelical in doctrine. Mainline Protestant churches focus on the social gospel of Jesus, interpreting "love your neighbor as yourself" as actively meeting a person's social and physical needs. However, as we have already seen, many evangelicals do not consider these churches as true "Bible-believing" churches because they generally interpret the Bible in terms of its cultural and historical contexts.

Janice Crouse of the evangelical Concerned Women for America recognizes the existence and the importance of evangelical code words by highlighting their use in President Bush's 2004 State of the Union speech:

> The second base that the President touched was with language. He clearly stated that our nation must defend the "sanctity" of marriage and that marriage is defined by "moral tradition." Though he shied away from addressing the question of homosexual civil unions, he linked the marriage issue to America's moral tradition and the sanctity of marriage. . . .

> For years, the Far Left has had its own rhetorical language where certain words carry special meanings to those "in the know." Now, conservatives have their own way of conveying messages that have unique significance for them. In the State of the Union Address, *Christians heard special messages that were conveyed with skillfully placed words.* For believers, the "sanctity" of marriage is rooted in those biblical principles that sustain marriage; just so, defining marriage through its "moral tradition" carries specific ramifications in terms of Judeo-Christian values and beliefs.[47] [Emphasis added.]

Of note, Crouse's use of "Christian" refers only to those who share her evangelical outlook, because "believers" oppose same-sex marriage. Therefore, anyone who does not oppose same-sex marriage, which supposedly violates the "sanctity of marriage," is not a believer regardless of religious affiliation.

Evangelicals define "homosexual" based on behavior, not biology

One of the most important components of how evangelicals view homosexuality, and by extension same-sex marriage, is that homosexuality is defined by sexual behavior. Scientists, however, define it according to sexual orientation. The evangelical definition implies that person can change his or her sexual behavior and become "ex-gay, " as mentioned on The Parsonage, a web site of Focus on the Family: "Thousands of men and women have overcome homosexuality and are able to lead celibate lives."[48] In the evangelical context, "ex-gay" means someone who abstains from homosexual sex; it does not imply any change in sexual orientation, desires, or emotional longings. A person who has homosexual desires but remains celibate has "overcome homosexuality" and is now "ex-gay."

To illustrate the confusion between the differing definitions for homosexuality, consider the following statement by Scott Ross of the Christian Broadcasting Network: "While some say that one can be born a homosexual, the Bible indicates that an individual has a free choice and chooses to be a practicing homosexual."[49] Ross' statement has two parts, each of which is essentially true, despite his presentation of them as conflicting. First, based on the weight of scientific evidence it appears true that some people are born homosexual. Second, it is also true that one chooses to be a "practicing homosexual," as opposed to a celibate homosexual. The concept of a celibate homosexual, however, is not one that most evangelical leaders accept because their definition of homosexuality is based on behavior rather than orientation: a person, celibate or not, who does not engage in same-sex behavior is heterosexual because that is the way God supposedly made all people.

Peter Sprigg, author of *Outrage: How Gay Activists and Liberal Judges Are Trashing Democracy to Redefine Marriage*, further illustrates the problems arising from different definitions for homosexuality. Discussing why he opposes same-sex marriage, Sprigg comments on

"gay citizens" being denied their "constitutional right to marry." This is nonsense. . . . many "gay citizens" have already been married. On the other hand, many people who once identified themselves as "gay" have now abandoned homosexual behavior and are happily married to people of the opposite sex.[50]

Sprigg ignores two important points. First, he assumes that bisexuals do not exist: people are either homosexual or heterosexual, according to their behavior. However, scientists recognize that sexuality exists on a continuum.[51] I know several bisexuals who switch between heterosexual and homosexual relationships. While their relationships change, their sexuality does not -- they remain bisexual. A good analogy is handedness. Ambidextrous people can use either hand effectively: if they choose one day to use their right hand for a particular task, and the next day use the left hand, that does not imply that their handedness changed. The only change is in behavior. This is a significant difference that is overlooked by many evangelical leaders. It also directly relates to the second oversight by Sprigg: anyone can choose to engage in sexual behavior that is not in accord with his or her orientation. A homosexual can choose to engage in heterosexual sex: many have had to for centuries. Likewise, a heterosexual can also choose to engage in homosexual sex: it certainly occurs in prison.[52] This does not mean that the person's sexuality changes. When I was 13 years old I decided to teach myself how to write with my left hand. While I was never as proficient as I was with my right hand, I was able to do it effectively enough. I had altered my *behavior* even though my natural right-handed *orientation* never changed. Thus, Sprigg's comment demonstrates the evangelical definition of homosexuality as behavior rather than orientation, which overlooks some fundamental considerations.

Therefore God gave them over in the lusts of their hearts to impurity, that their bodies might be dishonored among them. For they exchanged the truth of God for a lie, and worshiped and served the creature rather than the Creator, who is blessed forever.

Amen.

For this reason God gave them over to degrading passions; for their women exchanged the natural function for that which is unnatural, and in the same way also the men abandoned the natural function of the woman and burned in their desire towards one another, men with men committing indecent acts and receiving in their own persons the due penalty of their error. – Romans 1:24-27

Evangelicals believe that homosexuality is inherently immoral

Evangelicals believe the Bible clearly condemns homosexuality as immoral and cite "many biblical passages." In the original texts, however, only one passage, Romans 1:24-27, possibly mentions both male and female homosexuality. Any claim that a multitude of passages deals with the subject is false.

In *Solid Answers* James Dobson includes answers to various hypothetical or theoretical questions on topics of interest to his readers,[53] including one about the morality of homosexuality:

Homosexual activists claim their lifestyle, which in some cases includes thousands of sexual partners, should be sanctioned, protected, and granted special rights by society. Their rationale is that since their sexual nature is inherited, it is involuntary and therefore should be considered morally neutral. Would you critique this stance?[54]

The question is couched in terms consistent with evangelical stereotypes of homosexuals. Dobson's lengthy response is largely based on evangelical assumptions.

He first compares homosexuality to promiscuous heterosexuality, declaring that because heterosexual lust and promiscuity are not morally defensible, even though they are supposedly inherited conditions, homosexuality is also not morally defensible.[55] The original question is whether or not homosexuality is morally *neutral* because it is biologically determined and therefore involuntary. In other words, if homosexuality is morally neutral then homosexual behavior can be either moral or immoral depending on the context. However, Dobson immediately changes the question to whether or not *all* aspects of homosexuality are morally *defensible*. What Dobson has done is compare homosexuality to what he considers to be immoral heterosexuality, instead of comparing the moral neutrality of homosexuality to the moral neutrality of heterosexuality. He is arguing that because *aspects* of heterosexuality are not morally defensible, then homosexuality *in general* is not morally defensible. The issue of moral *neutrality* is never discussed. Dobson is assuming, and rightly so, that heterosexuality is morally neutral and that how it is expressed determines whether it is moral or not. If that is the case for heterosexuality, then why is it different for homosexuality? A logical conclusion is that if some aspects of heterosexuality are moral and some are immoral, in other words that heterosexuality itself is morally neutral, then the same argument can be made for homosexuality. However, Dobson completely ignores the question of whether or not homosexuality is morally neutral. As do most evangelical leaders, Dobson defines homosexuality according to behavior. He believes all sex outside of marriage is immoral; so because homosexuals cannot marry, all homosexual behavior is immoral.

C. S. Lewis, the highly respected Christian author, correctly states that

> Sex in itself cannot be moral or immoral any more than gravitation or nutrition. The sexual behaviour of human beings can. And like their economic, or political, or agricultural, or parental, or filial behaviour, it is sometimes good and sometimes bad.[56]

Lewis recognizes that sex is simply a natural, biological act and that it cannot implicitly be moral or immoral. It is what a person does with it that makes it one or the other. Lewis argues that if a person engages in sex with an attitude of love and good faith, it is moral. If the person is selfishly using the sexual act, or if it brings harm to one of the individuals, or possibly to a third party, as in the case of adultery, then it is immoral. Therefore, one can argue that sex is morally neutral, whether it is homosexual or heterosexual.[57]

Dobson continues his critique on the moral neutrality of homosexuality by comparing it to pedophilia.[58] Pedophilia involves the sexual obsession of an adult with a prepubescent child, which is an illness and, if acted upon, is illegal. Specifically, the adult is abusing the child for selfish sexual pleasure. If we were to use Jesus' teaching on the Golden Rule to explain why it is immoral, we would conclude that the pedophile is not doing to another person as he would like to have done to himself. He is harming the child for his own personal pleasure, therefore the action is wrong. However, legitimate homosexual relationships involve two individuals who have come of age and engage in mutually consenting acts considered normal by medical science. Thus, the comparison of homosexuality and pedophilia fails. Nonetheless, Timothy Dailey, author of *The Bible, the Church & Homosexuality: Exposing the 'Gay' Theology*, directly identifies men who burn with "insane love for boys" as homosexuals, when in reality they are pedophiles. [59] Homosexuals do not crave little children.

Psychologists recognize that homosexuality and pedophilia are completely different behaviors with different causes.[60] Homosexuality, like heterosexuality, is an orientation wherein one post-pubescent individual is sexually and emotionally attracted to another post-pubescent individual, whereas pedophilia is a pathology, wherein an adult attempts to gain or assert power over a child. Psychologists note that pedophiles, many of whom are former victims of pedophilia, frequently have difficulty being sexually aroused by another adult: homosexuals are no more or less likely to be attracted to those below the age of consent than heterosexuals. Thus, it is inappropriate to connect homosexuals with pedophiles. Nonetheless, many evangelicals fear that homosexuals will prey on their children, evidenced partly by the Boy Scout ban. The Concerned Women for America argued against the United Way's threat to stop funding the Boy Scouts of South Florida by suggesting that the Boy Scouts were simply refusing "to allow homosexuals access to children through its programs."[61] Such fears are unfounded because homosexuals are not normally attracted to young children.

In the Focus on the Family booklet *Teaching Captivity*, the authors suggest homosexual activists recruit children while they are vulnerable,[62] even though the notion that homosexual men are more likely to sexually abuse children than heterosexual men has already been thoroughly disproved.[63] Sociologists have documented that the typical scenario for pedophilia involves an adult man with a young girl.[64] In addition, research indicates that it is most likely the girl's father, the mother's male partner, or another close relative who commits the sexual abuse. In spite of the evidence, evangelical leaders continue to equate homosexuals with pedophiles and argue that homosexual men should not be given access to children.[65] Based on the evidence, if evangelical leaders were consistent in their actions they would instead attempt to restrict heterosexual males from being around young girls, for that is the most common context for the sexual abuse of children. The association of homosexuals with pedophiles is simply an attempt by evangelical leaders to portray homosexuals in a negative light.

Tony Campolo rebukes his fellow evangelicals for associating homosexuality with pedophilia: "Sexually molesting children is a horrendous evil, but to declare from the pulpit that homosexuals are more likely to commit such a hideous crime than are heterosexuals is just an out-and-out lie."[66] Dobson's comparison of homosexuality to pedophilia to determine if the former is morally neutral is irrelevant, inappropriate, misleading and once again avoids the actual question.

Dobson's next analogy compares homosexuality to alcoholism, that is, to both a behavior and a disease.[67] Exactly how this applies to whether homosexuality is morally neutral is unclear. Dobson explains that a genetic predisposition for immoral behavior does not make that behavior morally acceptable.[68] Fair enough, but this still does not address the issue of moral neutrality. Here Dobson begs the question by *assuming* homosexuality to be immoral. Furthermore, drinking alcohol is considered morally neutral by most people, even though some Christian denominations condemn it. It is abusing alcohol in a way that is destructive to oneself and others that is considered immoral. The best comparison in this otherwise faulty analogy would be to compare alcoholism to promiscuity (homosexual or heterosexual). Both drinking alcohol and sex are morally neutral: abusing alcohol and engaging in a sexual relationship that is destructive to the participants or others are immoral. Regardless, Dobson has again ducked the question of morality.

Finally, Dobson argues that "promiscuity for unmarried heterosexuals is the moral equivalent of promiscuity for homosexuals."[69] The main difference between unmarried homosexuals and unmarried heterosexuals is that heterosexuals *can* marry someone they love and desire, while at present in most of the United States, homosexuals cannot. Here Dobson solely focuses on the sexual act and completely ignores the motivation of love in a relationship. Furthermore, promiscuity among homosexuals is actually the moral equivalent of promiscuity among heterosexuals, not just among unmarried heterosexuals.

Dobson's statement invites a further question: if promiscuity for homosexuals is the moral equivalent of promiscuity for unmarried heterosexuals, then is faithfulness in a homosexual relationship the moral equivalent of faithfulness in a heterosexual marriage? Or would faithfulness in the homosexual relationship be even nobler than faithfulness in a heterosexual marriage, because homosexuals are faithful despite not being allowed to make a formal, socially recognized, vow of fidelity to each other?

Dobson repeatedly fails to respond to the question of whether homosexuality is morally neutral. He also fails to provide a reasonable explanation of why he believes homosexuality should be considered immoral. Instead, he approaches the question from an assumption that homosexuality is immoral, the very point under debate. His comparisons to heterosexual promiscuity, alcoholism, lust, pedophilia, and unmarried heterosexuals in no way address the question of the moral neutrality of homosexuality, nor do they demonstrate that homosexuality is immoral. What they do demonstrate most effectively is some of the many stereotypes evangelical leaders have of homosexuals.

Evangelicals assume that homosexuals are inherently promiscuous

Peter Sprigg summarizes the predominant evangelical view: "Among homosexual men in particular, casual sex, rather than committed relationships, *is the rule and not the exception*"[70] [emphasis added]. Focus on the Family bases the "fact" of homosexual promiscuity primarily on four studies of homosexual men conducted in the 1980s and 1990s.[71] Three of the four studies focus on the first men who acquired HIV or AIDS,[72] while the fourth study focuses on homosexual men infected with Hepatitis A.[73] Logically, the more partners a man had, the greater his chance of acquiring AIDS and other sexually transmitted diseases, especially before HIV/AIDS had received much publicity. Thus, rather than representing the average homosexual man, these data represent the most promiscuous of homosexual males. Certainly those who were not promiscuous would be much less likely to have acquired the disease and would not have been included in the study.

In an online discussion regarding the Massachusetts Supreme Court ruling permitting same-sex marriage, Peter Sprigg provides insight into how evangelical leaders view homosexual relationships: "Furthermore, the short duration of most homosexual partnerships and lack of sexual fidelity among such partners (demonstrated by abundant research) are dramatically different from the average heterosexual marriage."[74] When an online guest asked Sprigg to cite the "abundant research," he could only reference one study from the Netherlands.

The Dutch study examines rates of HIV infection in homosexual males and suggests that a significant proportion of the infections occur in males with steady partners. This finding was explained by suggesting that the partnered homosexual males had on average eight sexual partners outside of the relationship each year.[75] Sprigg uses the Dutch findings to compare the behavior of the Dutch homosexual males to that of married American heterosexual males, suggesting: "This is an astonishing contrast to the typical behavior of married heterosexuals, among whom 75 percent of the men ... report never having had extramarital sex."[76] However, Sprigg's comparison of homosexual partnerships and heterosexual marriages are not equal. Homosexual partnerships can refer to a civil union or simply to two individuals who live together as an unmarried heterosexual couple might, many of which are also of short duration and are not necessarily exclusive. These types of heterosexual partnerships are not included in studies using data solely from heterosexual marriages. Also, Sprigg draws his conclusion from two different types of data: he does not compare the percent of Dutch homosexual males who have had sex outside of the relationship to the percent of American heterosexual males who have, or the average number of extra-marital relationships both have had. From a statistical perspective it is impossible to compare the two different types of data and derive meaningful results. Furthermore, Sprigg's comparison of Dutch homosexuals to American heterosexuals ignores the impact of cultural views toward relationships and marriage. It is possible that Dutch society does not have as puritanical a view of relationships as American society. Therefore, in order for the comparison to have some merit, Sprigg would have to compare Dutch homosexuals to Dutch heterosexuals.

An additional consideration regarding Sprigg's analysis is that homosexuality has a tradition of being stigmatized by Western societies, including in the Netherlands and Belgium, both of which now permit same-sex marriage. Although same-sex marriage is legal in those countries, it does not imply that a majority of members in the societies accept it. John Boswell argues that promiscuity "must be viewed in conjunction with the variable of social hostility. It is obviously very much to a gay person's advantage in hostile environments not to be part of a permanent relationship."[77] One cannot ignore that cultural attitudes and expectations do influence the behavior of individuals in a society. Evangelical leaders routinely label homosexuals as promiscuous and sometimes treat them with general condemnation or hostility. It is therefore not surprising to find some homosexuals who act in ways that are consistent with the labels attached to them; an idea that is consistent with sociological theory.[78] However, to imply that all homosexual relationships are promiscuous and short-lived is to deny reality.

Peter Sprigg argues that homosexual women are also highly promiscuous. "Startlingly, lesbians have higher rates of promiscuity as well – with men."[79] Arguably, the women to whom Sprigg refers are bisexual, not homosexual: lesbians prefer to have sex with women.

In trying to argue that lesbian relationships are inherently unhealthy, Focus on the Family suggests that:

most women who have sex with women do not do so exclusively. Approximately two-thirds of women surveyed have also had sex with men within the last five years. Sexually transmitted disease rates for bisexually active women are as much as twice that of those who engage in exclusively lesbian activity.[80]

In other words, lesbians in committed relationships have significantly *lower* rates of sexually transmitted disease than bisexual women. So the issue does not appear to be women in lesbian relationships but women who switch between heterosexual and homosexual behavior. Focus on the Family's leaders appear unable to distinguish between homosexuals and bisexuals because in both cases a person is having sex with someone of the same gender.[81] Once again this demonstrates the evangelical tendency to define sexuality based solely on behavior. To argue that lesbian relationships are unhealthy because bisexual women have higher rates of STDs is a *non sequitur*. However, it does highlight that the women are probably acquiring the diseases from heterosexual men, although leaders at Focus on the Family do not then condemn all heterosexuals as they do homosexuals when discussing STDs. Furthermore, Focus on the Family leaders fail to establish whether or not the mental and physical health of lesbians are better in a homosexual relationship or in heterosexual marriage, where they are denying their basic romantic and emotional affections, and their sexual orientation. To solely equate health with physical health is to ignore other vital aspects of the human condition, including emotional and psychological health.

It is difficult to obtain accurate data about homosexuals in America because they are still stigmatized and consequently many do not publicly acknowledge their sexuality.[82] The societal stigmatizing of homosexuals may actually create an environment that encourages promiscuity. Ancient Greece and Rome showed little hostility towards lawful homosexual relationships. Most of the Roman emperors had homosexual relationships, and some had what constituted legal same-sex marriages, even though the citizens disapproved. Contrary to the evangelical stereotype of homosexual relationships, many of the homosexual relationships were exclusive, permanent, and considered the most stable in society.[83]

The assumption of the inherent promiscuity of homosexuals is based on biological determinism: men are naturally aggressive and sexually promiscuous, requiring women to tame them.[84] James Dobson explains that

> without positive feminine influence, [a man's] tendency is to release the power of testosterone in a way that is destructive to himself and to society at large. . . .
>
> Stated positively, a man is dependent for stability and direction on what he derives from a woman, which is why the bonding that occurs between the sexes is so important to society at large. Successful marriages serve to "civilize" and domesticate masculinity, which is not only in the best interests of women, but is vital for the protection and welfare of the next generation.[85]

Dobson argues that homosexual men have no such tempering influence and therefore allow their natural impulses to go unrestrained. This, of course, is not only unproven but ignores that homosexual men are just as capable of controlling their sexual behavior as devout, but unmarried, Christian men.

Homosexuality as a disease

Many evangelical leaders consider homosexuality the equivalent of a behavioral disease, with alcoholism most frequently used as an analogy. The idea is that homosexuality is not a natural, normal variant of human sexuality, but the result of abnormal tendencies stemming from a genetic predisposition or a detrimental postnatal environment. One reason the association with alcoholism is popular among evangelical leaders is that it helps them reconcile how homosexuality could be inborn, as many scientists suggest, but not approved of by God. For example, "ex-gay" author Mike Haley says a genetic link to some behaviors does not prove the idea of normalcy or rightness. Look at alcoholism or propensities toward anger. While these have been promoted as having a genetic linkage, there are few, if any, in our society who would promote these behaviors as OK just because they are linked genetically.[86]

Most evangelical leaders believe homosexuality is a learned behavior, so the analogy with alcoholism provides them a basis for condemning homosexuality, even if scientists have shown it has at least a partially genetic cause. What Haley overlooks is that homosexual behavior, unlike alcoholism, is found throughout the animal kingdom.[87] While that has little bearing on morality, it does indicate that there is nothing unnatural about it.

Jeffrey Siker, a Presbyterian minister and New Testament theology professor, suggests that the analogy with alcoholism is flawed in additional ways. First, while the harmful effects of alcoholism are obvious, the same cannot be said for homosexuality. Second, while recovering alcoholics understand the need to abstain from alcohol, most homosexuals do not believe homosexuality is inherently problematic. Finally, to become an alcoholic one must first drink alcoholic beverages. [88] Siker's last point deserves elaboration. Homosexuals have same-sex desires whether or not they have ever had sexual relations. Alcoholics may not know they have a predisposition to alcoholism until they begin drinking. For the homosexual the desires are not only sexual; they also involve emotional affection for another person. Presumably, heterosexuals do not view their partners only as sexual outlets; their partners provide emotional comfort that cannot be achieved with members of the same sex. Just as heterosexuality involves all aspects of a person, not only his or her sexual partnership, homosexuality also involves a person's total being. In other words, homosexuality is not simply about sex. A heterosexual orientation exists whether or not a person has ever engaged in sex; the same is true for those with a homosexual orientation.

In *Virtually Normal* Andrew Sullivan offers a further critique of the alcoholism analogy:

For one thing, the act of having a drink is immoral only for alcoholics. Moderate drinking is perfectly acceptable, according to the [Catholic] Church, for nonalcoholics. Analogizing to homosexuality, this would mean that sex between people of the same gender would be – in moderation – fine for heterosexuals, but always out of bounds for homosexuals: an argument that even the most nitpicking of theologians might regard as a little perverse.[89]

Thus, the comparison of homosexuality with alcoholism fails in many ways, yet this remains the best analogy that many evangelical leaders can produce for why homosexual behavior should be considered immoral.

Because many evangelicals believe homosexuality is equivalent to a disease, they think it can be prevented. Focus on the Family's Bob Davies provides readers with steps they can take to help ensure their children will not be homosexual.[90] These include promoting an atmosphere in the home that will allow the family to talk openly about sex, providing "accurate" information on homosexuality, reinforcing "appropriate" gender roles in children, discouraging behavior that would be contrary to social expectations, demonstrating physical affection for the child, and encouraging identification with role models of the same sex, particularly biblical heroes, Boy Scout leaders, or Sunday school teachers. If the parents follow these guidelines the belief is that their children will not struggle with gender confusion and will "remain" heterosexual. This view, based on Freud's psychoanalytical perspective and on traditional sociological theories, is now known to be incorrect. This will be discussed more fully in Chapters 6 and 7.

Evangelicals believe they must fight homosexuals to win the culture war

Many evangelical leaders view homosexuality not as a biological condition in which some humans are simply different because they do not have the predominant heterosexual orientation, but as an evil that threatens American society and must be eradicated. Many evangelicals believe homosexuals should not be given societal acceptance or equal rights with heterosexuals, whether it be in marriage or non-discrimination in work or housing, for that would only hasten America's destruction by God. Therefore, evangelical leaders have established a clear agenda that is promoted by such influential leaders as Dobson, Falwell, and Robertson. It is designed to combat society's growing acceptance of homosexuals and the societal recognition that homosexuality is simply a natural variation of human sexuality, similar to some people being left-handed instead of right-handed. Pastor Ronnie Floyd acknowledged the seriousness of the situation: "Make no mistake, two irreconcilable agendas are at war."[91]

A point overlooked by the evangelical leaders engaged in this culture war is that there is very little in Jesus' teachings to support it. Jesus did not instruct his disciples to force their version of morality on others. Jesus' command to go out and make disciples of all the nations is not a command to force others to live by evangelical morality but to spread the gospel of direct access to and forgiveness by God, and to treat others the way we want to be treated.[92] He never suggested that individuals who practice an immoral act -- I am not suggesting homosexuality should be regarded as such -- should be discriminated against and opposed. Instead, Jesus taught that if we do not want to be discriminated against for any reason we should not discriminate against others. Significantly, the *only* instance of Jesus telling an individual to "repent and sin no more" is not in the earliest manuscripts of John's gospel, and is therefore considered unreliable.[93] Jesus' focus is primarily on the individual's behavior toward other people: we are to be critical of our own unloving attitudes toward others; we are to deal with our own sins before we focus on other people's actions.[94] Jesus was very critical of those who attempted to judge others while holding themselves in high regard. He condemned the religious leaders of his time, the Pharisees, for claiming the moral high ground yet holding hatred and prejudice in their hearts. Jesus made it quite clear that loving God and loving our neighbor as ourselves are the bases of Christian morality and fulfill all of the Old Testament laws. He also specified that following those two commands would result in eternal life.[95] The evangelical leaders' focus on legislating morality to avoid God's wrath, based as it is on fear rather than love, does not fit very well with the teachings of Jesus.

The use of negative stereotypes and inappropriate comparisons for homosexuality that are widespread among evangelical leaders have been condemned by some in the evangelical "ex-gay" movement. For example, Joe Dallas criticizes fellow evangelicals for resorting to sensational exaggerations and stereotypes to "gross people out" about homosexuality.[96] Unfortunately, the evangelical community has yet to change this destructive and deceptive practice. An example of the misleading information presented by some evangelical leaders comes from Paul Cameron of the Family Research Institute. Cameron has consistently promoted the belief that homosexual parenting has a negative impact on children and that homosexuals are prone to acquiring serious diseases. Even though there is a long bibliography of research upholding the idea that lesbians and gays can make fine parents,[97] many prominent evangelical leaders continue to cite Cameron's writings.[98] They do this despite the fact that Cameron's work has been discredited by national scientific organizations: it was fabricated to make homosexuals appear unfit as parents.[99]

Awareness of the major assumptions evangelicals have about homosexuality is crucial to understanding the current societal debate on the subject. From the points presented above we see that evangelical leaders teach young homosexuals to regard their sexuality as a curse, something that is abhorrent and must be overcome. Young homosexual Christians are taught that they must either change or deny their sexuality, or face going to hell. Unfortunately, this leads to a variety of different responses: some repress their sexual and emotional desires and seek to live a life in accord with evangelical views by entering into dishonest marriages, keeping an important part of themselves secret; some reject their religious upbringing and live in a manner that also rejects many of the moral foundations they learned as children; others embrace the stereotypes attributed to them and live lives of promiscuity, repeatedly exposing themselves to life-threatening infections; unfortunately, too many others lose hope and see suicide as the only option, evidenced by significantly higher suicide rates among homosexual youth as compared to heterosexual youth.[100]

Building bridges

The current debate on homosexuality all too often creates animosity between homosexuals and evangelicals. According to many evangelical leaders, homosexuals are trying to undermine Christianity and the foundations upon which America was built. Homosexuals frequently view evangelical leaders as judgmental bigots who fan the flames of hostility, violence, and discrimination against them. Many of the leaders and activists in both groups do little to encourage dialogue. There are notable exceptions, however, that will allow us to conclude this chapter on a more positive note.

Tony Campolo believes his fellow evangelicals must actively fight *for* homosexual rights, even though he agrees with them that homosexual behavior is wrong. Because he believes all Christians are called to love people, even (or perhaps especially) societal outcasts,[101] he encourages evangelicals to make churches welcoming to homosexuals, free from harmful generalizations and rhetoric, and to fight for gay civil rights: "Unless heterosexual Christians are willing to champion calls for justice for gays and lesbians, it will be just about impossible to declare that the church loves them."[102] The most impressive aspect of Campolo's statement is that he does not find the phrase "heterosexual Christians" redundant. Too many evangelicals incorrectly believe that being a Christian means one is also heterosexual. Campolo's statement demonstrates his affirmations of the value and humanity of homosexuals and that people with a homosexual orientation can also be Christians.

Popular evangelical author Philip Yancey is also to be commended for compassionately addressing the issue of homosexuality in his book *What's So Amazing about Grace?*[103] Yancey discusses how his long-time friendship with a homosexual man changed his views on homosexuality and recounts hate mail that he received just for being mentioned in his friend's book.[104] He also describes the unfortunate treatment of his friend by some Christians: "Once I asked to see a batch of the hate-mail he gets from Christians, and I could barely make it through the letters. The pages were septic with hatred. In the name of God, writers rained down curses and profanity and threats."[105] Yancey honestly discusses the prejudice homosexuals face, especially from some Christians. When Jesus commanded people to love their neighbors as themselves he did not put any qualifiers on it: there is no "unless you don't like who they are or how they act." Although Yancey does not approve of homosexual behavior, he writes in the spirit of treating others the way he wants to be treated. Yancey demonstrates what compassion is and provides an example of why it is important for homosexuals to come out of the closet: it can change how others treat homosexuals.

Finally, Yancey also highlights the Christian belief that reconciliation was an important part of Jesus' ministry:

> The apostle Paul – initially one of the most resistant to change, a 'Pharisee of the Pharisees' who had daily thanked God he was not a Gentile, slave, or woman – ended up writing these revolutionary words: 'There is neither Jew nor Greek, slave nor free, male nor female, for you are all one in Christ Jesus.' Jesus' death, he said, broke down the temple barriers, dismantling the dividing walls of hostility that had separated categories of people. Grace found a way.[106]

These words resonate with truth. The apostle Paul mentioned the three major categories that separated people in ancient Israel; what remains is for the spirit of the words to be internalized and applied by Jesus' modern followers so they can lower the walls that separate gay and straight people.

The views of Tony Campolo and Philip Yancey are welcome signals that evangelical churches might develop tolerance, if not acceptance, of homosexuals. Two of the greatest obstacles to this are the evangelical interpretations of science and the Bible.

Many evangelical leaders argue that the Genesis creation accounts affirm that God intended humans to be heterosexual. They agree with the apostle Paul's apparent declaration in Romans 1 that homosexual desires are not natural. Claims of what is or is not natural can be examined scientifically, but any appeal to nature by either evangelicals or scientists will inevitably result in a discussion of creation and evolution. For example, Cardinal Ratzinger, now Pope Benedict XVI, arguing that homosexual behavior is not natural, appeals to the Genesis story of creation as the foundation for the debate on homosexuality.[107] Louis Sheldon of the Traditional Values Coalition also directly appeals to the creation story in his opposition to same-sex marriage: "When you advocate homosexual marriage, you are violating the mandate of the Creation narrative."[108] In order to better understand the foundation of the basic arguments that many evangelical leaders have about homosexuality and how their reality is different from that of non-evangelicals, we must turn to the great debate of the 20th century, evolution and creation.

---

[1] Pat Robertson (2001).
[2] This is part of the subtitle for *Solid Answers* (James Dobson, 1997).
[3] Family Research Council (December 12, 2003).
[4] Bruce Bawer (1997, 254).
[5] Ibid (175).
[6] Ibid (182).
[7] Falwell's comment occurred in CBN's *The 700 Club* on September 13, 2001.
[8] Mel White (1995, 292, 295).
[9] Philip Yancey (1997).
[10] Tony Campolo (2004).
[11] Jerry Falwell Ministries (no date).
[12] Calvin J. Roetzel (1998).
[13] David F. Wright (1990, 108-109).
[14] See Bruce Bawer (1997) for more information on the historical development of this doctrine. Calvinism is one Christian tradition that was founded in a belief in the inerrancy of the Scripture.
[15] For example, see John Boswell (1980, 137-143) and David F. Wright (1990, 103-106).
[16] For example, see Stanton L. Jones and Mark A. Yarhouse (2000, 167-170).
[17] The Hebrew alphabet derives from the Phoenician script, which developed about 1100 BC. See Philip J. King and Lawrence E. Stager (2001, 300-304) and Glenn E. Markoe (2000, 108-113).
[18] Tas Walker (December 2001-February 2002).
[19] C. S. Lewis (1958, 115).
[20] James Dobson (2004, 10).
[21] See Bruce Bawer (1997, 82).

[22] For example, see Focus on the Family (no date (a)).

[23] The Associated Press (May 6, 2004) reports that the U.S. is falling behind other nations in science education. Including creation science or intelligent design into the curriculum will only exacerbate the problem.

[24] For example, see Didi Herman (1997, 10-11).

[25] Ibid (42-44).

[26] Ronnie W. Floyd (2004, 102).

[27] Youth on the Rock (March 4, 2004). The comments were posted at 5:53 pm and 8:05 pm, respectively.

[28] For example, see Pat Robertson (2004, ix-xiv).

[29] Pat Robertson (September 2001a).

[30] A transcript of the entire conversation, which occurred on September 13, 2001, is available from the People for the American Way's web site www.pfaw.org. Afterward Falwell claimed to have been taken out of context, while Robertson claimed to not have understood Falwell's remarks. But consider the following quote from Robertson's book *The Ten Offenses* (2004, 204):
"A great nation can slowly be destroyed by pervasive moral decay. We sow the seeds of our own destruction, or God Himself can strike sudden devastating blows – violent earthquakes, hurricanes, tornadoes, massive flooding, extended drought, widespread disease, even the impact of an asteroid. Or God can raise up fierce enemies who delight only in destruction and death.
Knowingly or unknowingly, the ACLU, the National Abortion Rights Action League, Planned Parenthood, the National Organization of Women, the Gay-Lesbian Alliance, the American Atheists, Marxists, People for the American Way, Americans United for Separation of Church and State, advocates of political correctness in education, and all of their allies across the land in Congress, the state legislatures, and the media are hastening the destruction of the United States of America and the freedoms and lifestyle we all enjoy. "
Robertson includes the very same groups mentioned by Falwell and suggests that they are "hastening the destruction" of the country, partly through fierce enemies that God has raised up against the United States. It appears that Robertson's disclaimer that he did not fully understand Falwell's comments is misleading.

[31] Pat Robertson (August 11, 2003).

[32] John Boswell (1980, 73).

[33] Stephanie Coontz (1997, 15).

[34] Ibid (39).

[35] Ibid (38).

[36] South Carolina Republican Party (2004).

[37] ABC News's 2000 exit poll indicates that 14 percent of voters identified themselves as conservative Christian, while CNN's 2004 exit poll indicates that 23 percent of voters identified themselves as white evangelical or born again Christian.

[38] The gospels regularly show Jesus helping those who were in need. For example see Luke 14.

[39] For examples, see Matthew 6, 23, Mark 7, 10:17-31, Luke 6, 11, 12:13-21 and 16:19-31.

[40] See Matthew 19:19, 22:39; Mark 12:31; and Luke 10:27-28 for four examples.

[41] Tony Campolo (2004, 26).

[42] For example, see James Dobson (2004, 26-27).

[43] Focus on the Family (no date (b)).

[44] Focus on the Family (no date (c)).

[45] Didi Herman (1997, 66).

[46] See L. William Countryman (1988, 168-189) for a more thorough discussion on Jesus' frequent negative statements and actions regarding the family.

[47] Janice Shaw Crouse (January 21, 2004).

[48] *The Parsonage* (1999).

[49] Scott Ross (2003).

[50] Peter Sprigg (October 28, 2003).

[51] Kinsey *et al.* (1948) and Kinsey *et al.* (1953).

[52] John M. Coggeshall (1993).

[53] James Dobson (1997).

[54] Ibid (510).

[55] Ibid (510-511).

[56] C. S. Lewis (1964, 14-15).

[57] Lewis himself did not approve of homosexuality, although he did not consider sexual sin to be as serious a sin as others (see Lewis, 1943, 183 and Lewis, 1955, 104). For example, Lewis (1955, 104) suggests that "cruelty is surely more evil than lust." However, at the time of his writings the prevailing scientific view was that homosexuality was a disease, was changeable and that it was not a natural variation of human sexuality. Elsewhere (Lewis, 1958) he interpreted scripture in the light of scientific evidence.

[58] James Dobson (1997, 511).

[59] Timothy J. Dailey (2004, 30).

[60] See Kenneth V. Lanning (1992, 265-273, 279-285).

[61] Concerned Women for America (no date).

[62] Focus on the Family (2002a, 8).

[63] Steven E. Barkan (2001, 293).

[64] Ibid (2001, 293).
[65] See Peter Sprigg and Timothy Dailey (2004, 121-142) for a thorough treatment by evangelicals, including the various errors and assumptions.
[66] Tony Campolo (2004, 73).
[67] James Dobson (1997, 511).
[68] Ibid (511).
[69] Ibid (512).
[70] Peter Sprigg (November 19, 2003).
[71] The *Straight Answers* booklet cites no sources for the "many studies" it draws upon to make this assertion. During an interview on *Larry King Live* (September 5, 2003, on CNN) James Dobson stated that the average homosexual man has between 300 and 1000 lifetime partners. I requested clarification from Focus on the Family and their response included the studies discussed here (Timothy Masters, personal communication, September 24, 2003).
[72] Focus on the Family provided me with the following citations for their comments: A. P. Bell *et al.* (1981), H. Meyer-Balburg *et al.* (1991) and G. Rotello (1997).
[73] L. Corey and K. K. Holmes (1980).
[74] Peter Sprigg (November 18, 2003).
[75] Maria Xiridou *et al.* (2003).
[76] Peter Sprigg (2004, 96).
[77] John Boswell (1980, 26).
[78] John J. Macionis (2001, 198-205).
[79] Peter Sprigg (2004, 46).
[80] Mike Haley (2001, 19).
[81] Also see the Family Research Council's Peter Sprigg and Timothy Dailey (2004, 84) for similar statements.
[82] Stanton L. Jones and Mark A. Yarhouse (2000, 28).
[83] See John Boswell (1980) and Louis Crompton (2003).
[84] For example, see Glenn T. Stanton and Bill Maier (2004, 22).
[85] James Dobson (2004, 10-11, 11-12).
[86] Mike Haley (2001, 10).
[87] For example, see Bruce Bagemihl (1999).
[88] Jeffrey Siker (1994, 183).
[89] Andrew Sullivan (1995, 43).
[90] Bob Davies (2002).
[91] Ronnie W. Floyd (2004, 15).
[92] The Great Commission is found in Matthew 28:19.
[93] The command is from John 8:11. Jesus rescues the woman caught in adultery and tells her accusers that whoever is without sin should cast the first stone.
[94] Matthew 7:1-6.
[95] Luke 10:25-28.
[96] Joe Dallas (1999, 6).
[97] Gary Sanders (1999, 199).
[98] For example, see John Ankerberg and John Weldon (1994) and Robert A. J. Gagnon (2001).

[99] Gary Sanders (1999, 199).
[100] Shelly Reese (1999, 140).
[101] Tony Campolo (2004, 57).
[102] Ibid (56, 73-74).
[103] Philip Yancey (1997).
[104] Ibid (163). The book Yancey references is Mel White (1994) *Stranger at the Gate.*
[105] Philip Yancey (172).
[106] Ibid (155).
[107] Joseph Cardinal Ratzinger (1994, 41).
[108] Louis Sheldon, in David Crary (March 7, 2004).

3 FAITH VERSUS SCIENCE

> *Evolution can only be accepted on blind faith . . . because it cannot be proven. On the other hand, you* can *prove God's existence.* [Emphasis in original.]
>
> — Ray Comfort[1]

Many evangelical leaders assume that science is wrong on many issues because they believe the Bible is God's ultimate truth and that it cannot be wrong in any of its details. This belief shapes the evangelical worldview and responses to homosexuals and issues about homosexuality. It also directly impacts various areas of culture that evangelical leaders want to influence, including education and marriage. For example, evangelical leaders are actively attempting to alter sex education curricula and the teaching of evolution in public schools. In January 2004 a school superintendent in Georgia decided to remove the word "evolution" from its curriculum, along with language suggesting that the earth has a long history, in order to make it acceptable to those who believe the biblical chronologies.[2] The curriculum was being altered not because evidence had been found to disprove the scientific theories, but solely because it did not agree with the evangelical worldview. After considerable public pressure was mounted against this change, evolution was reinstated in the curriculum. Evangelical groups succeeded in removing evolution from the curriculum in Kansas and Texas, while in Alabama they placed a disclaimer on biology textbooks to remind students that evolution is "only" a theory.[3] The disclaimer labels have since been removed by court order.

Many evangelical leaders advocate that creation science and intelligent design are legitimate scientific theories about the origins of humans and that they should have equal time with Darwin's theory of evolution. However, neither creation science nor intelligent design is scientific because they resort to the supernatural. We also know that the two creation stories in the Bible are contradictory and cannot represent the actual truth.

The American Anthropological Association reports that "legislation intended to undermine evolution education was introduced in no fewer than 15 states" in the last few years.[4] This highlights a potentially serious situation in which the teaching of science may be held hostage to one group's religious beliefs. If evangelical leaders are successful at eliminating evolution from the science curriculum, there will be significant repercussions in American society, for evolution is the foundation of the biological sciences. For example, geneticist Steve Jones argues that the rejection of Darwinian evolution by the leaders of the former Soviet Union had a significant and detrimental impact on agricultural production.[5] Furthermore, it is by means of evolution that viruses, such as HIV or the H5N1 bird flu, mutate into new strains that can infect humans, and bacterial diseases, such as TB and gonorrhea, become resistant to antibiotics. Only by understanding evolutionary theory can we hope to deal with these mutating organisms. While evangelical leaders have the right not to accept scientific methods or evidence, they have no right to prevent their being taught in public schools.

Evangelicals and science

Many evangelicals maintain that the Bible is "God's literal word" to humanity, even though the Bible itself says Jesus is the "word of God."[6] Because the Bible is "God's literal word" it must be true in all its detail: it is inerrant. Even the passages that we know are not true must somehow be correct. This creates a difficulty that is only resolved through denial, cognitive dissonance, or through creative explanations, such as that the original texts were true but have since been compromised. This evangelical belief in the inerrancy of a literal Bible creates a dilemma between their beliefs and scientific findings. One solution is simply to remain uninformed of basic scientific principles. For example, James Dobson implies that if a trait is not fully genetic in its causation, it is not biological,[7] a comment frequently seen in evangelical literature. However, we know that many of our biological traits actually develop from both genetic and environmental factors.

The evangelical approach to science is fairly simple: if scientists disagree with the Bible, the scientists are wrong. They are wrong when they say that humans evolved from an ape-like ancestor over millions of years because the Bible says God made us on the sixth day of creation.[8] The Southeast Christian Church demonstrates a second important aspect of evangelical thinking: "Many Christians have bought into the so-called 'science of evolution' *because they don't fully understand the implications* of believing in Darwinism"[9] [emphasis added]. What matters, in their view, is that Christians should not believe in evolution because of the *implications* it has on the Bible and their faith. In other words, it does not matter if evolution is *actually true* or not: it should be rejected because it disagrees with the evangelical interpretation of the Bible. Many evangelical leaders believe that because scientists are supposedly wrong on human origins, they must also be wrong on other things, such as whether or not homosexuality is an inborn characteristic.

Mike Haley of Focus on the Family demonstrates another notion promoted by evangelical leaders: "Hey, let's face it: science is fact ... *not* theory. So, when the media grabs hold of a theory of genetic links to homosexuality and promotes it as science, people are led astray" (emphasis in original).[10] In context Haley is stating that facts are scientific, while theories are not. However, theories are the foundation of science and are, by definition, supported by the scientific evidence. Therefore, Haley's dismissal of the argument that homosexuality is biological as unscientific demonstrates a misunderstanding of the scientific method.

How science works

The scientific method proceeds from observation of a phenomenon to an explanation of, or *hypothesis* about it. The hypothesis is then tested by collecting and analyzing data. If the result does not support the hypothesis, it is discarded and a new one is suggested. For example, we observe that some people are homosexual. Evangelical leaders posit the hypothesis that homosexuality is caused by a distant father and domineering mother. The hypothesis can be tested by observing homosexuality in other cultures, such as the Sambia of New Guinea. Sambian families are unlike those found in Western society: males and females essentially live in two separate worlds with minimal interaction; children associate primarily with the women's world.[11] For the first seven years of a boy's life, he has minimal interaction with his father. Among adult Sambia males, however, there is no unusual incidence of homosexual orientation. Thus, the hypothesis fails and is set aside.

A new hypothesis, including other factors that might explain the phenomenon, is then set up. For example, many scientists believe that homosexuality is the result of biological processes. To test this alternative hypothesis, we look for biological differences between heterosexual and homosexual males. We learn that the nucleus of a specific group of cells within the anterior hypothalamus region of the brain, which is important in regulating sexual behavior, is smaller in homosexual men than in heterosexual men.[12] Significantly, the average cell nucleus in homosexual men is similar in size to those found in females. This suggests a possible biological link to male homosexuality. The study is flawed, however, because assumptions were made about the actual sexuality of some of the subjects. So we retain the hypothesis and look for other ways to test it, such as studies in animals. From a study of sheep we learn that some rams exhibit only homosexual behavior and also have a smaller nucleus in the cells than heterosexual rams. Once again, the average size of the cells' nucleus in the homosexual rams is similar to those found in ewes.[13] Thus, initial scientific evidence supports the new hypothesis.

There are considerable data, both direct and indirect, that indicate a significant biological component for homosexuality.[14] For example, in addition to studies of human and sheep brains, studies of male and female twins show strong evidence for both a genetic component and a non-genetic biological component for sexual orientation.[15] Additionally, correlations between homosexuality and other biological traits, such as handedness, have also been reported.[16] Therefore, the weight of evidence that homosexuality is at least partly the result of biological factors continues to mount. The hypothesis, when tested repeatedly and in varied ways, yields the same result: this is sufficient to establish the theory that homosexuality is at least in part determined by biology. The theory, however, has not been *proven* because we have not identified beyond any doubt the *specific* biological mechanisms that cause homosexuality, nor have we established that they are causative in *all* homosexuals. Thus, this theory is not yet a scientific law, such as the second law of thermodynamics; it is, however, scientific and not to be dismissed simply because it does not fit an idiosyncratic definition of what science should be.

A theory is essential to science and represents a general explanation that encompasses hypotheses that are well supported by observations and experiments: no evidence has ever refuted the theory and all the predictions based on it have been accurate. Evolution is an established theory: while there may be arguments about *how* it occurred, there is no scientific debate about *whether* it occurred because all the available evidence indicates that it did. Thus, it is a theory grounded in solid scientific evidence and verified by the scientific method. That it is "only" a theory does not diminish its validity. Other theories that are completely accepted include aerodynamics and gravity, even though scientists still do not understand exactly what gravity is or how it works. These two concepts are scientific, even though they are "just theories."

Scientists believe that humans are not biologically different from animals in any significant way. For instance, homosexuality is observed in a wide range of animal species, including apes, and is considered a natural variant of sexual expression and behavior.[17] The implication from science is that if homosexuality is found throughout nature, and that humans do not differ in any significant biological way from the apes, then homosexuality is a natural variant of human sexuality as well.

For many evangelical leaders, however, the literal acceptance of the Genesis accounts for human origins and the corresponding rejection of evolution are primary assumptions underlying their arguments in the debate on homosexuality. God created Adam and Eve as models for humanity; it is assumed they were heterosexual. Therefore, God did not create homosexuality. Evangelical leaders believe that God made humans inherently different from animals because the Bible explicitly states that humans were made in God's image. Therefore, evangelicals consider the existence of homosexuality throughout the animal world irrelevant in the debate about whether it is natural for humans.

Darwin's theory of evolution

Charles Darwin's book *On the Origin of Species by Means of Natural Selection*[18] presents what is now the accepted scientific view of human origins. Darwin observed that life forms change over time through the process of natural selection: beneficial traits are preserved and harmful traits are eliminated. The slow changes that accumulate over many generations result in significant differences between members of the same species that have become isolated from one another. These separated populations continue to diverge in appearance and behavior and eventually become separate species, no longer capable of successful breeding with each other. Through this process humans evolved from ape-like ancestors that existed some five to seven million years ago: today the chimpanzees and bonobo apes are our closest cousins. These apes acquire the same diseases as humans, have similar anatomy and physiology, and even exhibit behavioral characteristics similar to those seen in humans.[19] Thanks to human instruction, they communicate with each other and with us through sign language. They have been observed intentionally deceiving others; chimpanzees have committed genocide against other members of their species.

Chimpanzees and humans share about 98 percent of their genes.[20] While there seem to be great differences between chimpanzees and humans, a simple analysis shows that we could easily have had a common ape-like ancestor. According to the best current estimates, humans have about 25,000 genes that determine our physical traits.[21] A 98 percent similarity means that modern humans and chimpanzees differ in 1,250 genes. In the course of six million years, 1,250 genes in an ancestral chimpanzee or human would have to change to arrive at our current level of difference. This could be accomplished if only one gene changed in either ancestral line every 4,800 years. Evolution is a lengthy process that happens one step at a time. A problem arises when people view the beginning and the end and imagine it happening in one step. Many evangelicals have difficulty accepting the evolution of humans from an ape-like ancestor because they, consciously or otherwise, imagine it happening in one generation. Though it is impossible to go from one species to another in one generation, such a change is completed by an incremental process.[22]

Science and the origin of humans

When Darwin first presented his idea of evolution by natural selection there was not much of a fossil record, as he admitted. His idea was theoretical, based on observations of living species. However, he suggested that as fossils were discovered they would support his view. In other words, his hypothesis could be tested. We now have millions of fossils with which to test Darwin's theory. While some of his specific ideas, such as the rate of change from one species to another, are still under debate, the fossil record overwhelmingly supports the belief that life has evolved: the further back in time we look, the less complex the organisms are (Table 1).

Table 1: The Evolution of Life[23]

Period	Findings	Comments
3.6 billion years ago (bya)	Primitive life	Only single-celled organisms are present.
1.7 bya	Multicellular life	Sponge-like organisms exist.
540 million years ago (mya)	Chordates	The first organisms with a spinal cord appear in the fossil record at the time of the Cambrian radiation, when 33 of the 34 existing phyla developed from the pre-existing sponge-like organisms in a period spanning about 5 million years.

The Evolution of Life

530 mya	Vertebrates	The first organisms with a vertebral column surrounding the spinal cord appear.
425 mya	Fish	Fish, a type of vertebrate, appear.
360 mya	Amphibians	Amphibians, vertebrates that can survive on land or in water, appear.
256 mya	Mammal-like reptiles	Reptiles with some features common to mammals appear.
220 mya	Mammals	The first true mammals appear.
65 mya	Mammals diversify	After the dinosaurs become extinct, mammals diversify to fill the available ecological niches.
55 mya	Primates	The first true primates, mammals that include humans, apes, and monkeys, appear.
40 mya	Monkeys	Monkeys quickly spread throughout Africa and reach South America. The South American monkeys diverge in appearance from their African cousins.
23 mya	Apes	The first apes develop in Africa, and eventually diversify into many different types, spreading into Europe and Asia.
6 mya	Bipedal apes	Bipedal ape-like primates begin appearing in Africa.
2.5 mya	Tool use begins	The body proportions of the bipedal primates begin to change. In particular, the arms become shorter in relation to the legs. At about this time the bipedal primates begin making stone tools and their brain sizes increase slightly compared to other apes.

The Evolution of Life

1.5 mya	Brain size increases	Dramatic increases in the size of the brain in bipedal primates to more than double the size of a chimpanzee's and about two-thirds the size of a modern human brain. Body proportions are now the same as a modern humans'. However, the growth and development rates of transitional species are still intermediate to apes and humans.
500,000 ya	Growth rates change	Growth and development rates become human-like by 500,000 years ago. Brain sizes are within the lower end of the range found in modern humans, although facial features are still much more robust than those of modern humans.
300,000 ya	Final altertions	Individuals whose facial features are intermediate between modern humans and our most recent predecessors appear.
200,000 ya	*Homo sapiens*	Fully modern humans first appear in the fossil record.

One famous fossil from three to four million years ago, known as "Lucy," has a human-like pelvis and knee joint but an ape-like chest and skull.[24] In addition, the features of Lucy's teeth are intermediate to those of apes and humans. One creation science publication discredits the significance of Lucy by suggesting that "Nearly all experts agree 'Lucy' was just a 3 foot tall chimpanze [sic]."[25] However, to my knowledge no paleoanthropologist, the experts on ancient fossils such as these, says that Lucy was *just* a chimpanzee, mainly because no chimpanzee has a human-like pelvis or knee, or is bipedal. Furthermore, Lucy's characteristics are consistent with other bipedal apes from the same period. Given that Lucy's physical characteristics are exactly what would be expected if humans had evolved, Lucy probably represents one of the many intermediate species in the evolution of humans from an ape-like ancestor.[26]

While the fossil record clearly supports the evolution of life and of humans from an ape-like ancestor, it is evident that there is no single "missing link" directly between apes and humans. What we do find are fossils that show the different stages of a slow transition, including related species that eventually became extinct. Alterations in the skeleton resulting from bipedalism began the transition from an ape-like ancestor to humans, followed by changes in body proportions. As the body proportions became more like modern humans, the growth and development rates also changed from being ape-like to human-like. Brain size at first changed slowly and then rapidly as technology developed. As the brain became more like that of modern humans, the technology became even more sophisticated, ultimately resulting in creative expression and religion, which makes its first unquestioned appearance after the arrival of modern humans, around 200,000 years ago.[27]

The fossil evidence does not support the premise held by biblical literalists that humans and all other life forms were created in their present forms about 6,000 years ago. To accept the literalist premise we must believe that all of the extinct species evident in the fossil record were created only 6,000 years ago, that every species that was created by God intermediate to humans and apes is now extinct, and that they were layered sequentially in the fossil record so as to give the appearance that humans evolved from an ape-like ancestor. Accepting this premise would beg questioning the nature of these supposed coincidences, perhaps leading one to ask if God was purposefully causing people not to believe in the biblical account.

Evangelicals and the origin of humans

Many evangelical leaders who support the idea of a 6,000-year-old earth suggest that scientists are completely wrong in the techniques they use to date fossils. In other words, our knowledge of chemistry and geology, on which the dating techniques are based,[28] is unreliable even though that very same knowledge got us to the moon, enables us to heat and cool our houses, provides us with antibiotics and aspirin, and allows us to create jet planes and x-ray machines. Yet once again this is what the biblical literalists imply. Thus, it is important to understand the evangelicals' view of human origins and why biblical literalism is so important to them.

The six days of Creation

"Satan put fossils in the ground to deceive people into not following God."

"God put the fossils there to test our faith and determine who the true believers are."

"Dinosaurs are the result of humans and animals having sex before Noah's flood."

My students who are trying to maintain their faith in a literal Bible regularly offer such explanations for the fossil record. Many of them have been taught that doubting what the Bible says on the subject is un-Christian because it shows a lack of faith in God and in the Bible; that lack of faith might condemn them to hell for eternity. Thus, the only possible explanation for human origins is the biblical one: God created the universe in six days, about 6,000 years ago. This view derives from the first chapter in Genesis:

1. On the first day God created light and separated it from darkness.
2. On day two the heavens and the waters were separated, apparently with the earth as a result.
3. Day three saw dry land appear on the earth, followed by the creation of plants.
4. On the fourth day God created the sun, moon, and stars.
5. The next day animal life appeared, specifically fish and birds.
6. The sixth day brought the creation of land animals, including humans.

7. Then, on the seventh day God rested, indicating that the seven-day week is a divine construct and is not simply a cultural arrangement of time.

However, scientists, using the fossil record, find that life did not develop in that order. But evangelicals, rather than trying to understand the science they depend on every day, remain suspicious of science because scientists disagree with the Bible. I have even heard some evangelical leaders suggest there is a conspiracy among certain scientists to lead people away from God. Witness the impact on evangelical Christianity of a non-literal Adam. Theologian David Shackelford explains:

Adam is a 'watershed' topic concerning the biblical teachings of individual human beings, the sinful state of mankind as a whole, the incarnation of Christ, Christ's death atoning for sin, and even the relative age of the earth (i.e., billions of years vs six-ordinary-day creation about 6,000 years ago). If taken as a literal human being who was given a real wife and fathered real offspring, all of Scripture concerning the areas mentioned above, including the age of the earth, is consistent with the rest of the Bible. On the other hand, if Adam is considered not to be a real person, or if the earth is considered to be millions of years old as evolutionists and progressive creationists claim, contradictions with clear statements of Scripture are impossible to resolve.[29] [Emphasis in original.]

Thus, any scientific finding that renders Adam figurative means that many key evangelical beliefs are rendered implausible and the story of Adam and Eve is "nothing more" than a myth. If Adam and Eve are nothing more than myth, then their vital role in the evangelical understanding of homosexuality and marriage is undermined.

Two biblical accounts

A point many evangelicals overlook is that there are actually two different accounts of human origins in the initial chapters of Genesis. The first creation story (Genesis 1:1-2:3) recounts the events of the first week, while the second story (Genesis 2:4-25) tells how God first made Adam and then made plants to give Adam something to do (take care of God's garden). Afterwards, God made animals to help Adam. After deciding that none of the animals were a suitable helper for Adam, God took one of Adam's ribs and made Eve, thus establishing a male-dominated society as a God-ordained system: women were made to help men. Evangelicals believe that this first "marriage" somehow demonstrates God's desire that *all* marriages be heterosexual and monogamous.

Shackelford's explanation ignores the contradictions between the two stories because they are generally regarded as harmonious by evangelical leaders who argue that the second creation story is an elaboration on the sixth day of the first story. They argue the translation of the original Hebrew should not be that God created Adam *and then* plants and animals, but rather that God created Adam, having *already* created plants and animals. By translating the Hebrew in this fashion, all apparent contradiction is removed and the two Genesis accounts become harmonious. Scholars, however, do not accept this interpretation because it perverts the Hebrew text and because there is evidence that the two accounts were written at separate times by different authors: an idea that is part of the documentary hypothesis.[30]

Documentary hypothesis

I understand the skepticism of many evangelicals when they first encounter the documentary hypothesis, which indicates that the Torah was written by four different authors or groups at four different times in Israel's history. The first time I heard this view, I was skeptical as well. After all, I had been taught that Moses himself had written the Torah through God's inspiration. The documentary hypothesis is completely at odds with that teaching, so I needed proof.

The creation stories provide some evidence for separate sources. The first creation story refers to God as Elohim, normally translated in the Bible as "God."[31] In it Elohim creates plants, then animals, and finally humans. The second creation story refers to God as Yahweh Elohim, normally translated as "Lord God," and has the first human existing before plants and animals. So far the four-source hypothesis works, but the evidence was not yet convincing enough to me, especially because the stories are in two distinct sections and show no obvious signs of editing. However, the stories detailing Noah's flood proved to be different.

> And of every living thing of all flesh, you shall bring two of every kind into the ark, to keep them alive with you: they shall be male and female. Of the birds after their kind, and of the animals after their kind, of every creeping thing of the ground after its kind, two of every kind shall come to you to keep them alive. – Genesis 6:19-20

I quickly recognized that the story of Noah's flood uses both names for God, Elohim and Yahweh. I also recognized that many items in the story are repeated, just as scholars indicate. Some of the repeated information is very curious. For example, in Genesis 6:19-20 and Genesis 7:2-3 there is a contradiction in the number of animals of each kind that Noah was to take on board the ark. This made me curious, so I did a rudimentary textual analysis by sorting through the relevant passages, separating out the verses that referred to God as Elohim from those that used Yahweh. Verses that did not reference God were separated by vocabulary and writing style, as is typical in textual analysis. The results surprised and convinced me. Two stories emerged, each identifying a problem, a solution, and a conclusion, and the two give extremely different accounts of the flood (see below). In one version only two of every animal are taken on board the ark. In the other, seven pairs of clean animals and one pair of unclean animals are taken. This is an important point because the Bible does not explain what animals are considered clean or unclean until the book of Leviticus, whose events occur more than 1,000 years later in the biblical chronology. In one version, the flood's duration is 40 days and nights while in the other it is 150 days. Furthermore, one version is remarkably similar to the Babylonian account found in the Gil-

> You shall take with you of every clean animal by sevens, a male and his female; and of the animals that are not clean two, a male and his female; also the birds of the sky, by sevens, male and female, to keep offspring alive on the face of all the earth. – Genesis 7:2-3

gamesh Epic: Noah releases various birds to see if the land is fit for habitation, just as the hero does in the Babylonian account. Thus, the Genesis account of the flood gives every impression of originally being two separate stories that were edited together at some point in time, most likely during or after the Babylonian captivity of Israel.

Version 1: God as Yahweh[32]

The LORD saw that the wickedness of man was great on the earth, and that every intent of the thoughts of his heart was only evil continually. The LORD was sorry that he had made man on the earth, and he was grieved in his heart. And the LORD said, "I will blot out man whom I have created from the face of the land, from man to animals to creeping things and to birds of the sky; for I am sorry that I have made them." But Noah found favor in the eyes of the LORD. [Genesis 6:5-8]

Then the LORD said to Noah, "Enter the ark, you and all your household; for you alone I have seen to be righteous before Me in this time. You shall take with you of every clean animal by sevens, a male and his female; and of the animals that are not clean two, a male and his female; also of the birds of the sky, by sevens, male and female, to keep offspring alive on the face of all the earth. For after seven more days, I will send rain on the earth forty days and forty nights; and I will blot out from the face of the land every living thing that I have made." And Noah did according to all that the LORD had commanded him. [Genesis 7:1-5]

Then Noah and his sons and his wife and his sons' wives with him entered the ark because of the water of the flood. Of clean animals and animals that are not clean and birds and every-thing that creeps on the ground, there went into the ark to Noah by twos, male and female, and the LORD closed it behind him. [Genesis 7:7-9, 16b]

It came about after the seven days, that the water of the flood came upon the earth. And the rain fell upon the earth for forty days and forty nights. Then the flood came upon the earth for forty days, and the water increased and lifted up the ark, so that it rose above the earth. And the water prevailed and in-

creased greatly upon the earth, and the ark floated on the surface of the water. And the water prevailed more and more
upon the earth, so that all the high mountains everywhere under the heavens were covered. The water prevailed fifteen cubits higher, and the mountains were covered. [Genesis 7:10, 12,
17-20]

Thus He blotted out every living thing that was upon the face
of the land, from man to animals to creeping things and to
birds of the sky, and they were blotted out from the earth; and
only Noah was left, together with those that were with him in
the ark. Then it came about at the end of forty days, that Noah
opened the window of the ark which he had made; and he sent
out a raven, and it flew here and there until the water was
dried up from the earth. Then he sent out a dove from him, to
see if the water was abated from the face of the land; but the
dove found no resting place for the sole of her foot, so she returned to him into the ark, for the water was on the surface of
all the earth. Then he put out his hand and took her, and
brought her into the ark to himself. So he waited yet another
seven days; and again he sent out the dove from the ark. And
the dove came to him toward evening, and behold, in her beak
was a freshly picked olive leaf. So Noah knew that the water
was abated from the earth. Then he waited yet another seven
days, and sent out the dove; but she did not return to him
again. [Genesis 7:23, 8:6-12]

So Noah went out, and his sons and his wife and his sons'
wives with him. Every beast, every creeping thing, and every
bird, everything that moves on the earth, went out by their
families from the ark. Then Noah built an altar to the LORD,
and took of every clean animal and of every clean bird and offered burnt offerings on the altar. And the LORD smelled the
soothing aroma; and the LORD said to Himself, "I will never
again curse the ground on account of man, for the intent of
man's heart is evil from his youth; and I will never again destroy every living thing, as I have done. While the earth remains, seedtime and harvest, and cold and heat, and summer
and winter, and day and night shall not cease." Then the LORD

said, "My Spirit shall not strive with man forever, because he also is flesh; nevertheless his days shall be one hundred and twenty years." [Genesis 8:18-22, 6:3]

Version 2: God as Elohim

These are the records of the generations of Noah. Noah was a righteous man, blameless in his time; Noah walked with God. And Noah became the father of three sons: Shem, Ham, and Japheth. [Genesis 6:9-10]

Now the earth was corrupt in the sight of God, and the earth was filled with violence. And God looked on the earth, and behold, it was corrupt; for all flesh had corrupted their way upon the earth. Then God said to Noah, "The end of all flesh has come before Me; for the earth is filled with violence because of them; and behold, I am about to destroy them with the earth. Make for yourself an ark of gopher wood; you shall make the ark with rooms, and shall cover it inside and out with pitch. And this is how you shall make it: the length of the ark three hundred cubits, its breadth fifty cubits, and its height thirty cubits. You shall make a window for the ark, and finish it to a cubit from the top; and set the door of the ark in the side of it; you shall make it with lower, second, and third decks. And behold, I, even I am bringing the flood of water upon the earth, to destroy all flesh in which is the breath of life, from under heaven; everything that is on the earth shall perish. But I will establish My covenant with you; and you shall enter the ark--you and your sons and your wife, and your sons' wives with you. And of every living thing of all flesh, you shall bring two of every kind into the ark, to keep them alive with you; they shall be male and female. Of the birds after their kind, and of the animals after their kind, of every creeping thing of the ground after its kind, two of every kind will come to you to keep them alive. And as for you, take for yourself some of all food which is edible, and gather it to yourself; and it shall be for food for you and for them." Thus Noah did; according to all that God had commanded him, so he did. [Genesis 6:11-22]

Now Noah was six hundred years old when the flood of water came upon the earth. On the very same day Noah and Shem and Ham and Japheth, the sons of Noah, and Noah's wife and the three wives of his sons with them, entered the ark, they and every beast after its kind, and all the cattle after their kind, and every creeping thing that creeps on the earth after its kind, and every bird after its kind, all sorts of birds. So they went into the ark to Noah, by twos of all flesh in which was the breath of life. And those that entered, male and female of all flesh, entered as God had commanded him. [Genesis 7:6, 13-16a]

In the six hundredth year of Noah's life, in the second month, on the seventeenth day of the month, on the same day all the fountains of the great deep burst open, and the floodgates of the sky were opened. And all flesh that moved on the earth perished, birds and cattle and beasts and every swarming thing that swarms upon the earth, and all mankind; of all that was on the dry land, all in whose nostrils was the breath of the spirit of life, died. And the water prevailed upon the earth one hundred and fifty days. [Genesis 7:11, 21-22, 24]

But God remembered Noah and all the beasts and all the cattle that were with him in the ark; and God caused a wind to pass over the earth, and the water subsided. Also the fountains of the deep and the floodgates of the sky were closed, and the rain from the sky was restrained; and the water receded steadily from the earth, and at the end of one hundred and fifty days the water decreased. [Genesis 8:1-3]

And in the seventh month, on the seventeenth day of the month, the ark rested upon the mountains of Ararat. And the water decreased steadily until the tenth month; in the tenth month, on the first day of the month, the tops of the mountains became visible. Now it came about in the six hundred and first year, in the first month, on the first of the month, the water was dried up from the earth. Then Noah removed the covering of the ark, and looked, and behold, the surface of the ground was dried up. And in the second month, on the twenty-seventh day of the month, the earth was dry. [Genesis 8:4-5, 13-14]

Then God spoke to Noah, saying, "Go out of the ark, you and your wife and your sons and your sons' wives with you. Bring out with you every living thing of all flesh that is with you, birds and animals and every creeping thing that creeps on the earth, that they may breed abundantly on the earth, and be fruitful and multiply on the earth." And God blessed Noah and his sons and said to them, "Be fruitful and multiply, and fill the earth. And the fear of you and the terror of you shall be on every beast of the earth and on every bird of the sky; with everything that creeps on the ground, and all the fish of the sea, into your hand they are given. Every moving thing that is alive shall be food for you; I give all to you, as I gave the green plant. Only you shall not eat flesh with its life, that is, its blood. And surely I will require your lifeblood; from every beast I will require it. And from every man, from every man's brother I will require the life of man. Whoever sheds man's blood, by man his blood shall be shed, for in the image of God He made man. And as for you, be fruitful and multiply; populate the earth abundantly and multiply in it." [Genesis 8:15-17, 9:1-7]

Then God spoke to Noah and to his sons with him, saying, "Now behold, I Myself do establish My covenant with you, and with your descendants after you; and with every living creature that is with you, the birds, the cattle, and every beast of the earth with you; of all that comes out of the ark, even every beast of the earth. And I establish My covenant with you; and all flesh shall never again be cut off by the water of the flood, neither shall there again be a flood to destroy the earth." And God said, "This is the sign of the covenant which I am making between Me and you and every living creature that is with you, for all successive generations; I set My bow in the cloud, and it shall be for a sign of a covenant between Me and the earth. It shall come about, when I bring a cloud over the earth, that the bow will be seen in the cloud, and I will remember My covenant, which is between Me and you and every living creature of all flesh; and never again shall the water become a flood to destroy all flesh. When the bow is in the cloud, then I will look upon it, to remember the everlasting covenant between God and every living creature of all flesh that is on the earth." And God said to Noah, "This is the sign of the covenant which I have established between Me and all flesh that is on the earth." [Genesis 9:8-17]

Now the sons of Noah who came out of the ark were Shem and Ham and Japheth; and Ham was the father of Canaan. These three were the sons of Noah, and from these the whole earth was populated. Then Noah began farming and planted a vine-yard. And he drank of the wine and became drunk, and uncovered himself inside his tent. And Ham, the father of Canaan, saw the nakedness of his father, and told his two brothers outside. But Shem and Japheth took a garment and laid it upon both their shoulders and walked backward and covered the nakedness of their father; and their faces were turned away, so that they did not see their father's nakedness. When Noah awoke from his wine, he knew what his youngest son had done to him. So he said, "Cursed be Canaan; a servant of servants he shall be to his brothers. May God enlarge Japheth, and let him dwell in the tents of Shem; and let Canaan be his servant." And Noah lived three hundred and fifty years after the flood. So all the days of Noah were nine hundred and fifty years, and he died. [Genesis 9:18-25, 27-29]

While the story of Noah's flood readily lends itself to textual analysis, other parts of the Torah are much more complicated, and scholars still debate the origins of some passages. Nonetheless, many scholars do agree upon the basic four-source framework, given that it makes the most sense of all the data. It explains inherent inconsistencies in the stories of the flood and creation, and helps explain many passages that appear to be duplicates, such as Genesis 19 and Judges 19-20 (Chapter 5). The stories in those passages have similar outlines as well as wording.

Another textual duplicate is the story of how Abraham offers his wife to a king to avoid being killed. In Genesis 12, Abraham gives his wife to the Egyptian pharaoh; in Genesis 20, she is given to the king of the Philistines. The latter account is highly problematic because, according to biblical chronologies, Abraham lived around the 20th century BC, but the Philistines did not arrive in Palestine from the Aegean region near Greece until around the 14th century BC.[33] To take the Bible as literal fact on this matter requires assuming that the archaeological record, Egyptian written records, and the written records of other civilizations in the region are all wrong. The best explanation for the inconsistency is the documentary hypothesis, which indicates that the account with the pharaoh derives from one source while the account with the Philistine king is from another source.[34] When the latter was written, sometime around 850 BC, the author would have had no idea that the Philistines had not always lived in the region, but had actually arrived about 450 years previously. Thus, the account of Abraham and the Philistine king would not have been questioned when it was originally written.

The importance of being literal: Genesis

I believe there are three main reasons why many evangelical leaders cling to the literal account of Genesis. First is the idea that every word in the Bible was inspired directly by God and therefore must be literally true. Thus, because God created the universe and inspired the Bible, the two creation accounts must both be correct. Second, Jesus treats Adam and Eve as historical individuals; because evangelicals believe Jesus was fully God, he cannot be wrong.

The third point concerns the origin of sin, an important issue for evangelicals because of their reliance on a literal Bible and their view of the purpose of Jesus' life and death. According to Genesis, God created the world and declared it to be good. There was no sin and no death. Unfortunately, Adam and Eve disobeyed God by eating the forbidden fruit, with their subsequent punishment being eventual death. They brought sin into the world and we are all doomed to repeat their error: therefore we all die. The Bible states that anyone who is sinful cannot approach God's temple and that anyone who has sinned cannot go to heaven. So God had to find a way to redeem us and bring us back into our proper position in the universe.

The Old Testament presents a temporary means of restoring harmony: sin must be removed and, because it is punished with death, atoned for. Atonement requires that blood be shed, either that of the sinner or of a substitute. The Bible declares that a person's sins can symbolically be transferred to a goat, which is released into the wild to take the sins away.[35] In addition, a spotless lamb is sacrificed as a substitute for the person who sinned.[36] However, this temporary solution has the disadvantage that a great number of animals have to be slaughtered on a daily and yearly basis to make up for our wrongdoings. Evangelicals believe that God had a permanent solution that required a lot less bloodshed. They believe that Jesus, who they say was God in human form, came to earth to be sacrificed on our behalf. Being sinless, Jesus is considered to be both the spotless sacrificial lamb and the scapegoat that takes our sins away. Thus, the evangelical understanding of Jesus and the purpose of his existence are based on the sin of a literal Adam and Eve.

The evangelical dilemma

This brings us to the problem of human origins as perceived by many evangelicals: the Bible says God created Adam directly from dirt. Scientists, however, say that humans evolved from an apelike ancestor. If scientists are correct, then the origin of the first modern humans was about 200,000 years ago, not 6,000 years ago as suggested in the Bible (and the Bible is very specific about the time frame thanks to its genealogies and chronologies). Therefore, evolution eliminates the possibility of a literal Adam and Eve. In addition, because scientists say organisms died before humans ever came into the world, the Bible must be wrong when it says that death was the result of humanity's sin. Likewise, if Adam and Eve did not exist as actual humans, then the entire notion of sin entering a perfect world is wrong. If Adam and Eve are not historical, then Jesus was wrong when he referenced God's creation of them. If Jesus was wrong, he cannot be God. This creates a crisis of faith among evangelicals, but not necessarily for other Christians given that the literal view of Adam and Eve is not required in other Christian traditions.

> I also am mortal, like everyone else, a descendant of the first-formed child of earth; and in the womb of a mother I was molded into flesh, within the period of ten months, compacted with blood, from the seed of a man and the pleasure of marriage.
> – Wisdom of Solomon 7:1-2

The problem is amplified further in Luke 3:23-38, which traces Jesus' unbroken genealogy back to Adam. David Shackelford argues that the doctrines of the incarnation of Jesus and the atonement for sin based on his death all directly rely on a literal Adam.[37] Shackelford goes so far as to say that Jesus' genealogies in Luke and Matthew are consistent with one another. However, not only is the number of generations from Abraham to Jesus vastly different in the two accounts, there is also no agreement between them about Jesus' ancestors from David's son through Jesus' grandfather. Evangelical leaders explain this contradiction by suggesting that Matthew is following Jesus' ancestry through his father Joseph, while Luke's gospel follows it through Jesus' mother Mary. However, the only way this can be true is if we ignore eastern Mediterranean culture: a patriarchal and patrilineal society, such as ancient Israel, would *never* trace ancestry through the female line.[38] The cultural practice of tracing lineage is based on beliefs about procreation.

In ancient Israel, as in many agricultural societies, it was believed that the essence of reproduction was in the male semen.[39] Just as seeds were planted in the ground to receive nourishment and grow, children were thought to result from a seed planted by the male in the female whose blood nourished the seed and caused it to grow in her womb. The apocryphal Wisdom of Solomon 7:1-2[40] (see above) demonstrates that this concept was accepted by the ancient Israelites. The female was simply an incubator for the man's seed: the child grew from the seed, not the incubator. Therefore, in a patrilineal society similar to ancient Israel a person *never* belongs to his or her mother's lineage and an individual's genealogy *never* follows the mother's line. If the father of the child is unknown, the child has no social or legal standing because it cannot trace its ancestry, and therefore is illegitimate. Evangelical attempts to reconcile this biblical contradiction do not make sense when examined in the context of ancient Israel's culture.

Creation science to the rescue[41]

Evangelicals resolve the conflict between the biblical and scientific views of origins by means of explanations such as creation science and intelligent design. Creation science, which is not scientific because it is based on the supernatural, has five important assumptions:

1. The Bible is literally true, including what it says about human origins.
2. Adam and Eve were real people created about 6,000 years ago.
3. No macroevolution, evolution from one type of species to another, has occurred; therefore, humans did not evolve from an ape-like ancestor.
4. Dinosaurs and humans coexisted.
5. The fossil record is a result of Noah's flood.

Let us examine each of these assumptions.

The Bible is literally true. As we have already seen, creation science adherents believe God created the universe and all it contains. While the Bible may not give specific details on how God created, evangelicals are sure that the process happened exactly as recorded, given that the Bible is "God's word" and cannot be wrong in any detail. Therefore, God spoke everything into being and declared each thing to be good. The creation of everything in the universe occurred in the first week, with humans created on the sixth day.

Adam and Eve were created about 6,000 years ago. Many evangelicals believe that God made Adam from dirt and Eve from one of Adam's ribs. In addition, unlike animals, humans were made in the image of God about 6,000 years ago. However, some 1,500 years after Adam and Eve were created, God decided to destroy nearly all of creation in the famous flood, saving only Noah and those with him on the ark. Consequently, more than 6 billion humans today can trace their ancestry to Noah, who supposedly lived about 4,500 years ago. Estimates that the earth is 6,000 years old derive from biblical chronologies and genealogies that provide an unbroken timeline from Adam to the Babylonian captivity of Israel, which has an archaeologically established date. Some evangelicals allow for an older earth by noting that each day of creation lasted an unspecified length of time, while others suggest each day was 1,000 years. The latter view is based on 2 Peter 3:8, which states that a day is like a thousand years to God. If the six days of creation were really 6,000 years and the earth was created on the second "day," the earth would be about 10,000 years old, as opposed to the scientific estimate of about 4.5 billion years.[42] Because the Bible says that Adam and Eve were created on the sixth day, the first humans would still have been created only 6,000 years ago.

No macroevolution occurred. Although the evangelical view that God created nature as it currently exists eliminates the possibility that one animal evolved into another over time, some evangelicals do allow for evolution within animal types. For example, they are open to the idea that zebras, horses, and donkeys all had a common ancestor, but that ancestor was created by God separately from other animal types. Also, because God created the first human from dirt, it is impossible for humans to have evolved from an ape-like ancestor as scientists argue. This creates a substantial problem because the scientific evidence includes many fossils with traits that are intermediate between apes and humans. In fact, as shown above, the fossil record has a definite progression from an ape-like ancestor to humans. Of course, this evidence is unacceptable to many evangelicals who take the Bible literally. One of their most frequent explanations is that the fossils of human ancestors are extinct apes or abnormal humans.

Dinosaurs and humans coexisted. If the earth is only 6,000 to 10,000 years old, evangelicals who accept creation science have to believe in the coexistence of humans and dinosaurs. If God created all land animals and humans on the sixth day of creation, dinosaurs would have existed at the same time as humans. Some believers suggest that dinosaurs became extinct before Noah's flood, while others argue they survived the flood and became extinct later. According to the latter view, Noah would have had dinosaurs on the ark, given that he took at least two of every animal with him. Biblical "evidence"

Behold now, Behemoth, which I made as well as you; he eats grass like an ox. Behold now, his strength in his loins, and his power in the muscles of his belly. He bends his tail like a cedar; the sinews of his thighs are knit together. His bones are tubes of bronze; his limbs are like bars of iron. – Job 40:15-18

Can you draw out Leviathan with a fishhook? Or press down his tongue with a cord? Can you put a rope in his nose? Or pierce his jaw with a hook? – Job 41:1-2 for dinosaurs is usually found in the book of Job which mentions the behemoth and leviathan, two large animals thought to be dinosaurs by some evangelical leaders who need to find evidence that they coexisted with humans. If, in fact, dinosaurs coexisted with humans, why are they not mentioned in Egyptian hieroglyphics or Sumerian cuneiform tablets, writing systems that were in use 5,000 years ago in the area around the Middle East?[43]

The fossil record. Creation science adherents believe that the fossil record is the result of Noah's flood. Fossil discoveries in the 18th and 19th centuries led scientists to believe the world had to be much older than the Bible suggests. Many of the fossils of extinct animals (but never dinosaurs), such as those from the sewers of Paris, were found with ancient stone tools, some of which we now know were used by Neandertals. This was a surprise, for Paris traced its origins to Roman times, only 2,500 years or so after Noah's flood. Some people, such as the anatomist Georges Cuvier, argued that the fossils were remnants of animals destroyed in a great flood, an idea that still prevails among supporters of creation science. They believe that the fossil record simply proves there was a great catastrophe that eliminated a large proportion of life on earth: because the Bible mentions such a catastrophe, the flood must have created the fossil record.

To counteract the scientific argument that the farther down in the fossil record one goes the simpler the life forms are, creation scientists argue that the soil and rocks in the earth were disrupted during Noah's flood: they acted as filters so that the smaller life forms fell farther down into the earth's strata, while the larger animals remained higher up. Thus the smaller life forms appear to be older than the larger ones. This ignores the fact, however, that although some dinosaurs were among the largest animals that ever lived, they are not found at the top of the earth's strata, but underneath all except the earliest mammals, which vary tremendously in their sizes.

I encourage the reader who is unfamiliar with creation science arguments to remember that there is really no other alternative for evangelicals who hold a literal view of the Bible, which requires it to be correct in every detail. They must accept the Bible as literally true in every point, or admit that their faith is in vain and believe they might go to hell. Thus, it is no surprise to find believers trying to reconcile scientific findings with the Bible by denying the scientific conclusions. They are effectively forced to come up with something, *anything* to bring sense to the world.

Another way evangelicals resolve the "fossil problem" is blame the forces of good and evil supposedly at work in the world. Many evangelicals believe Satan is constantly trying to undermine people's faith in God; the fossil record is one means he uses to accomplish this. His devious scheme is to attack people's faith in a double-pronged fashion: he creates fossils and places them in the ground to give every appearance of the Bible being wrong and then creates a false system of belief -- evolution -- to lead people astray from the Bible, and therefore from God. Only the true believer is able to see through this clever deception.

Some problems arising from a literal Bible

Not only do some evangelicals dismiss the scientific findings, they also ignore the many contradictions and mistakes in the Bible. Their literal interpretation of the Bible cannot resolve the logical and scientific problems it presents. In addition to the contradictory creation stories mentioned above, here are a few of the difficulties that arise when the Bible is regarded as literally true.

Cain. Genesis 4:1-18 tells the story of Cain and Abel, the first two children of Adam and Eve. In the well-known story, Cain murders his brother and is exiled. Cain is fearful that people will kill him, so God gives him a mysterious mark to protect him. Cain eventually marries and founds a city called Enoch, located east of Eden.

There are three problems with this story. First, who did Cain marry? The usual assumption is that Adam and Eve had daughters who are not mentioned in the Bible. Thus, Cain married one of his sisters. Second, who did Cain fear would kill him? The Bible mentions only Adam and Eve as alive at the time; if creation stopped after Eve was made, there could be no other humans alive who were not part of that first "dysfunctional" family. The resolution is that either Cain's unmentioned brothers and sisters or

Abel's unmentioned children would avenge Abel's death by killing Cain. Finally, do three people a city make? It is rather farfetched to suggest that Cain founded a city when there are only three people (Cain, his wife, and their son) mentioned as potential residents. Even if Adam and Eve and their children multiplied at the rate of rabbits, there still would not be enough people to establish a city, particularly when the founder is an exile who fears for his life. Also, we should not ignore the limited genetic variation and problems with inbreeding that the high levels of incest would cause.

Noah's flood. There are many problems that arise from a literal belief in a worldwide flood. There is, however, archaeological evidence for a *regional* flood not too far from the Middle East. About 7,500 years ago the Black Sea was a freshwater lake, separated from the Mediterranean by a land bridge that joined the European and Asian parts of Turkey. Rising seas flowed over the land bridge and salt water poured into what became the Black Sea.[44] Fossils of freshwater fish and other marine animals have been found there, as well as remains of villages that now lie about 200 feet below the surface. Many regional tales and legends recount this flood, which may also have inspired the biblical story.

The documentary hypothesis demonstrates that there are actually two separate, significantly different accounts of the flood that have been edited together into what is now viewed as the biblical account. Aside from this major problem for biblical literalists, there are a large number of other issues that arise if we accept that a global flood occurred. According to the biblical account, water covered the earth for nearly an entire year. The Bible explains that animals were preserved on the ark, but says nothing about plants. Most plants could not have survived the 150 days it took for the waters to begin receding from the mountain tops. One could assume that Noah took seeds and clippings of all the plants that exist today, but that would not explain how an olive tree survived outside the ark so that a bird brought its leaf (or branch, depending on the translation) to show Noah that the earth was once again habitable.[45]

In addition to the botanical problems, there are numerous zoo-logical issues. For example, what did the carnivores eat while on the ark? How did Noah have enough food to feed all the animals, especially those adapted to particular environments -- from the arctic to the tropics -- which required specialized foods? After the continents split apart -- according to creation scientists, at the earliest stages of the flood -- how did the various animals reach the Americas and Australia? Why did virtually all the marsupials end up in Australia? If marsupials crossed the water to Australia, why did no placental mammals make it there, except the bat, which would have flown? While scientists can easily answer these questions, creation science adherents cannot, except by saying that God can do anything. But even this brings us back to the problem of the dinosaurs. *If* they coexisted with humans, and *if* they made it through the first 1,500 years of biblical history, what happened to them? I have a difficult time imagining a *Tyrannosaurus rex* on the ark with rabbits, goats, and sheep. Could the ark possibly have been big enough to hold at least two of every kind of dinosaur on it, even if they were not full-grown adults? Why did all the dinosaurs become extinct so soon after the flood? Why do we not find dinosaur skeletons associated with human remains? Why are there no cave drawings of dinosaurs, nor any written records of them from any part of the world, even though both cuneiform and hieroglyphic writing were in use *before* the flood? Creation science does not adequately address these problems.

Human longevity. The Bible records the ages at death of many individuals both before and after Noah's flood.[46] Many of their ages seem fantastic to us today: Adam died at the age of 930 years, while Methuselah made it to his 969th birthday, dying in the same year as Noah's flood. Adam's third son, Seth, lived to be 912 years old. Adam's grandson Enosh died after his 905th birthday. Kenan, Enosh's son, was 910 years old when he died. His son, Mahalelel, died at the ripe old age of 895 years and Mahalelel's son Jared died at the age of 962 years. The list continues through to Noah, who died at the age of 950 years, a full 350 years after the famous flood. Those who are not familiar with evangelical beliefs may be surprised to learn that many evangelicals believe these ages at death to be literally true. Given that most evangelicals who believe in a literal Bible recognize these "years" as being the same as our years, we must assume that either human biology was very different back then or the earth's cycle around the sun was much shorter.

Genesis says that before God destroyed virtually all life forms in the great flood, God stated that human life would be limited to 120 years,[47] but that did not happen immediately. Among Noah's descendants, Arpachshad died at 438 and Peleg at 239 years; Nahor, Abraham's grandfather, died at 148 years of age.[48] Although longevity decreases after the flood, 500 years later Abraham lived to 175.[49] Not until more than 1,000 years after the flood, according to biblical chronologies, does anyone die at the age of 120 years, Moses' exact age at death.[50]

As an anthropologist who specializes in skeletal traits, I have a further problem with these ages. Forensic anthropologists are able to examine a skeleton and estimate the age of the person at death. Quite a few ancient skeletons have been found in the region around Israel, yet none of them show any indication of unusual age at death. (There is also no evidence of the biblical giants that supposedly lived in the region; the stories of giants possibly resulted from early attempts to explain the fossils of ancient mammals.)[51] Thus, it takes a leap of faith to believe the biblical account. However, if scholars are correct that the flood story was written by two different authors and then edited together, the contradiction involving God's declaration to limit human longevity completely disappears, given that the declaration to limit ages and the exaggerated ages are from separate sources.[52]

Egypt. Archaeological evidence and Egyptian hieroglyphics indicate that the Egyptian kingdom dates back to about 5,000 years ago, roughly 1,000 years after biblical creation (Adam would have died less than 100 years before the Pharaoh Aha rose to power), and about 500 years *before* Noah's flood.[53] Here is the problem: if the Bible is literally true, which means that Noah's flood happened around 2500 BC, why is there a continuous reign of pharaohs from 3000 BC to the time of Christ? If only Noah and his immediate family survived a worldwide flood, how could there still be civilizations in Egypt and Mesopotamia at that same time? A further issue is brought up by the story of the Tower of Babel. Genesis 11:1-9 tells how humanity shared a common language after the flood. However, about 200 to 300 years after the flood, God became concerned that humans were achieving great things, evidenced by the Tower of Babel,[54] so God confused the people by giving them different languages. Thus, according to the Bible it was only about 4,200 years ago that different languages first developed. However, writing in different languages existed in Mesopotamia and Egypt 5,000 years ago.[55] The historical evidence contradicts the biblical story, which is based solely on oral tradition. Nonetheless, it is the oral traditions of Genesis that many evangelicals accept as the literal truth. I once posed many of these problems to an evangelical friend who had an interesting but predictable response: scientists are wrong. He argued that we should adjust science to make it fit the biblical chronologies. Thus, contrary to archaeological findings, he argued that the Egyptian dynasties did not begin until after Noah's flood. Therefore, Egypt could not have developed as a powerful state society until sometime between 2200 and 2000 BC, not around 3000 BC as archaeology indicates. Unfortunately, this altered timeframe creates significant problems.

If we assume a literal Bible, then the Philistine people, also known as "the Sea Peoples," were in Palestine at the time of Abraham, about 1900 BC. However, Egyptian hieroglyphics and a wealth of other archaeological data indicate that the Philistines did not arrive in the region until about 1300 BC.[56] Thus, if we assume that the Bible is correct and all other sources are incorrect, we must accept that the Egyptian hieroglyphics and archaeological data are off by about 600 years on this matter. Therefore, to fit the Egyptian kingdom into the biblical timeframe, we would have to compress 1,700 years of Egyptian history (from 3000 BC, when the pharaohs began their rule, to about 1300 BC, when Egyptian hieroglyphics mention the Philistines invading the eastern Mediterranean) into about 300 years (from after the flood to when Abraham interacted with the Philistine king). It is known, how-

ever, that nearly 100 pharaohs ruled during this period, many of
whom were sons of the preceding pharaoh.[57] If we are asked to
accept the Bible as literally true and historically accurate, then we
must also accept that although the descendants of Adam and Eve
were living many hundreds of years, the Egyptian dynasties had
sons replacing their fathers as pharaoh about every three years. In
other words, the Egyptian pharaohs lived only very short lives,
while the individuals mentioned in Genesis had incredibly long
lives. Thus we are left with the question of which tradition is more
reliable: the Egyptian written tradition, supported by archaeology
and the written records of other Middle Eastern civilizations; or
the Hebrew tradition as documented in the Old Testament, which
has no scientific evidence to support the stories in Genesis?

The Egyptian written tradition dates back 5,000 years, while
the Hebrew alphabet is derived from Phoenician, the first known
alphabet, which appeared about 1100 BC.[58] The best estimate for
the appearance of Hebrew as a written language is between 960 –
920 BC, during the reign of Solomon.[59] This creates another problem for those who believe in a literal Bible: if Moses was a historical person and he wrote the Torah, in what language did he write
it, given that Hebrew was not yet a written language? Thus, the
entire account from Adam and Eve to the time of David -- according to the Bible, the first 3,000 years of human history -- is based
solely on oral tradition. And the biblical accounts actually provide
significant indirect support for this assessment.

There is scant archaeological evidence for biblical events and
people prior to David and Solomon.[60] This does not mean that
Abraham, Isaac, Jacob, Joseph, and Moses did not exist, it simply
means there is no evidence that they did, other than Hebrew oral
tradition. There are, however, possible references to the "House of
David" in the archaeological record;[61] and shortly after the time of
David, Hebrew became a written language. Many subsequent
people and events mentioned in the Bible are also seen in archaeological records.[62] While there is no evidence to support biblical accounts of events before Hebrew became a written language, for
later events the biblical accounts are more reliable, on a par with
other written traditions from the region.

Intelligent design

Another theoretical perspective many evangelicals use to reconcile their views on the Bible with science is known as intelligent design, an idea that became popular in the past fifteen years. Intelligent design holds that at some point in the development of life an intelligent supernatural agent intervened. This argument derived from Michael Behe's suggestion that various biological systems and components, such as blood clotting and the cell, are irreducibly complex.[63] In other words, if any component is removed from the system, it will no longer function. An example of irreducible complexity is a mousetrap, which requires five components: the spring, hammer, catch, holding bar, and platform. If any of these components is missing, the trap will fail and the mouse will have a nice meal and live to see another day. Behe's argument is that structures such as the cell are irreducibly complex and could not have evolved by gradually adding one feature to another. If they did not evolve, then they must have been created by some intelligent designer, namely God. Though the idea certainly has its appeal, many scientists find it both flawed and somewhat short-sighted.

There is a two-part rebuttal to Behe's argument. First, some biological systems that he considers irreducibly complex can still operate with fewer parts, although that may change the function of the system. For example, studies indicate that the blood-clotting system involves the same basic proteins that were originally used in digestion, although slightly altered.[64] The blood-clotting system in and of itself appears irreducibly complex, but it may have had other purposes before a mutation altered its function. The second aspect of the rebuttal arises from the constant advance of scientific knowledge, in view of which Behe's appeal to design is premature. For example, Gregor Mendel did not know exactly how genetic traits were inherited when he made his original discoveries in the mid-1800s. Not until the 1950s did the process become clear through the discovery of the structure of DNA. Likewise, breakthrough discoveries in the future may reveal how the cell developed. Furthermore, while testifying at the Dover, Pennsylvania trial in 2005, Behe admitted that systems that appear irreducibly complex may have developed over time through completely natural processes.[65] Thus, appeals to an intelligent design for the cell or for other biological systems may be premature.

Many evangelicals who claim to accept the intelligent design perspective seem not to understand what it actually purports. They think it supports the ideas that evolution is impossible and that the biblical account of a creator God, Adam, and Eve is literally correct. This position is not consistent with the argument of intelligent design, which holds that because the cell is irreducibly complex it must have been designed, but then life evolved from that first cell, possibly under God's guiding hand.[66] In other words, intelligent design is not a critique of whether or not evolution happened, but simply a view of how life began and *how* evolution proceeded. It counters Darwinian evolution by allowing that supernatural input was needed for life to begin and perhaps to direct the evolutionary process. Intelligent design proponents differ about how much influence the designer had in the evolution of life. Loren Wilkinson states that "In the intelligent design debate ... the principle [sic] difference seems to be whether God set all of the conditions right at the very first instant, or whether God intervenes occasionally to insert new design elements in the flow of 'natural' events."[67]

Intelligent design is consistent with the evolution of life from an original cell and therefore contradicts the Genesis accounts of the origins of humans. Thus, the perspective still poses problems for those who base their worldview, including their view of human nature, sexual or otherwise, on a literal Bible. Because many evangelicals are not well-versed in scientific theory, they think that because intelligent design counters Darwin's version of evolution, it therefore goes against the entire concept of evolution, which it does not. Once again, the distinction between fact and theory comes into play. Science considers evolution to be a fact. *How* evolution proceeded is explained through Darwin's theory. It is possible that Darwin was wrong about evolution as a completely natural process that happens gradually; perhaps it is instead a supernaturally guided process that occurs in spurts. Because we cannot test whether the supernatural is guiding evolution, Darwin's theory remains the best scientific explanation for the origins of humans. In any case, intelligent design and Darwinian evolution are both contrary to the biblical account of the origins of humans.

Reconciling evangelical beliefs and science

The intent of this discussion is not to cause a crisis of faith for the evangelical believer, but to illustrate the problems that arise from taking the Bible literally. As many highly respected Christian authors and leaders do not practice biblical literalism, it clearly is not compulsory for the Christian faith. Instead of a literal interpretation, it is important to place the biblical writings in their cultural and historical contexts to determine the underlying meaning, and thereby try to understand what the passages meant for the ancient Israelites. Many evangelicals, however, generally do not interpret the Bible this way because they believe it is independent of cultural bias.

However, many Christians, including some evangelicals, do not have a problem reading Genesis figuratively. For instance, the many influential books of C. S. Lewis, including *Mere Christianity*,[68] highlight what is and is not essential to Christian belief as he understood it. Lewis did not believe that "God-inspired" meant every word of the Bible is scientific and historical truth. Instead, he argued that the Bible "carries the Word of God" and that only by studying scripture can we discern what God desires, "not by using it as an encyclopedia or an encyclical but by steeping ourselves in its tone or temper and so learning its overall message."[69]

Anthropologists have demonstrated that oral traditions are carriers of a society's morals and values which help people understand their place in the world and their relationship with the supernatural.[70] Viewed in this context, the creation stories tell us that there is a higher power to which we are accountable. The story of the flood tells us that immoral behavior has consequences. Even if we reject the notion that sin entered the world through a historical Adam and Eve, it does not mean sin does not exist. Also, how sin originated has no bearing on whether people love God with all their heart, soul, strength and mind nor on whether they love their neighbor as themselves, which Jesus said summed up the entire code of behavior that God would have us follow.[71] Thus, even though evangelicals would reject the story detailing the *origin* of sin, its dismissal would have no bearing on the *existence* of sin, and therefore the need for Jesus from an evangelical perspective. Treating the Genesis stories as oral traditions that are not historically true does not violate the apostle Paul's exhortation that "All Scripture is inspired by God and profitable for teaching, for reproof, for correction, for training in righteousness."[72] Just as Jesus used fictional stories to teach people about the kingdom of heaven and how we are supposed to live, so too the Genesis stories could be inspired in the sense that they teach people how to live in accord with God's will. Thus, the stories, although not historical, could still be used for teaching, for establishing blame or criticism (reproof), for correcting behavior and for training in righteousness. Accepting the limitations of the Bible does not require that evangelicals abandon their faith.

One additional problem that many evangelicals have is that they have been told there are only two options for how humans came to be: either God created us according to the literal interpretation of the Bible, or Darwinian evolution is true. These black or white possibilities ignore the potential shades of gray. The possibility that God used evolution to bring humans and nature into their present forms is unscientific because it brings the supernatural into the process, but it is nonetheless possible. It is unscientific because science attempts to explain everything, including human origins, in natural terms. This is a limitation of the scientific method: any explanation invoking the supernatural cannot be tested and therefore cannot be disproved. This does not mean it is untrue, just not scientific. The view that God, or some supernatural force, designed the universe and created humans through a process of directed evolution is accepted by some scientists and most Christians who do not rely on a literal Bible. Certain physicists believe the universe appears to have been designed because of the seemingly endless number of "coincidences" that had to occur for life, as we know it, to exist on earth.[73] Thus, contrary to what creation science adherents argue, there are explanations for our existence beyond the poles represented by the biblical account on one hand, and Darwinian evolution on the other.

It is certainly possible that many scientists are wrong when they say no supernatural intervention took place during the evolution of humans. God, or some other supernatural force, could have established the universe in order for humans to evolve from an ape-like ancestor. Perhaps the role God played was similar to that of a computer programmer who might have written the entire program encoded in the laws of nature, started the process, and watched the results develop over time.[74] Perhaps God was intimately involved and caused mutations in the genetic code, which eventually led to creatures that are creative, can communicate in abstract ways, and can penetrate the mysteries of the universe: in other words creatures in the image of God. Perhaps instead of instantaneous creation, God molded us into our present forms as a potter molds the clay. This concept is consistent with the biblical portrayal of God as seen in the book of Jeremiah.[75] Thus, it is entirely possible that God created humans by means of evolution.

It is important to understand that a literal interpretation of the Bible cannot be reconciled with scientific evidence. This does not, however, mean that the Bible has no value for Christians. If the Bible is understood symbolically or allegorically, it provides a context for understanding the universe and our place within it. Although the Bible has mistakes and contradictions, those do not mean a Christian must abandon his or her faith: science and faith can be reconciled.

The evangelical understanding of the Bible has significant ramifications for how homosexuals perceive themselves and how evangelicals respond to them. Based on their view of scripture, evangelical leaders create false hopes that one's sexuality can be changed. This approach can be devastating to the homosexual who seeks "God's will" and whose attempts to change his or her sexual orientation have failed. Evangelical attitudes toward scripture also create an atmosphere of prejudice and potential violence against homosexuals. An atmosphere of intolerance that arises from the idea that God rejects homosexuals is perpetuated by evangelicals who actively work to prevent homosexual equality. These attitudes make it necessary to investigate specifically what the Bible says about homosexuality and what evangelicals *think* the Bible says about it. In order to do this honestly, we need to establish the Bible's historical and cultural contexts so that our examination is not flawed by an ethnocentric orientation.

---

[1] Ray Comfort (no date).

[2] Andrew Jacobs (January 30, 2004).

[3] American Anthropological Association (December 2004). Also see the National Center for Science Education web site at www.natcenscied.org.

[4] American Anthropological Association (December 2004, 23).

[5] Steve Jones (1997, 21).

[6] John 1:1-14.

[7] James Dobson (1997, 513).

[8] Genesis 1:26-27.

[9] Southeast Christian Church (Winter 2004).

[10] Mike Haley (2001, 10).

[11] Gilbert Herdt (2006).

[12] Simon LeVay (1993, 121). See also Byne *et al.* (2001).

[13] Charles Roselli *et al.* (2002).

[14] The evidence is discussed more fully in Chapters 6 and 7.

[15] J. Michael Bailey and Richard C. Pillard (1991).

[16] J. A. Y. Hall and D. Kimura (1994) and B. S. Mustanski, J. M. Bailey and S. Kaspar (2002).

[17] Bruce Bagemihl (1999).

[18] Charles Darwin (2004).

[19] Michael Alan Park (2006).

[20] Ibid. (209).

[21] Lincoln D. Stein (October 21, 2004).

[22] This belief is demonstrated by an analogy, frequently used by supporters of creation science who compare evolution to a tornado blowing through a junkyard and creating a fully functional Boeing 747.

[23] Michael Alan Park (2006, 119-121).

[24] Donald Johanson and Maitland Edey (1990).

[25] Anonymous (2000, 11).

[26] In addition to species that are ancestral to humans, there are also many related species with mixed ape and human characteristics that were not ancestral to humans. "Dead ends" in the evolutionary process, they appeared after the ape-human split and became extinct, leaving no modern descendants.

[27] For accessible articles on evolution, see Douglas H. Chadwick (November 2001), Rick Gore (April 2003), David Quammen (November 2004), Christopher P. Sloan (November 2006), and Carl Zimmer (November 2006).

[28] Radiocarbon dating is not used to date most of the ancient fossils.

[29] David Shackelford (June 1999).

[30] Antony F. Cambell and Mark A. O'Brien (1993) and John Shelby Spong (1991).

[31] Antony F. Campbell and Mark A. O'Brien (1993, 22-23).

[32] This is my attempt to divide the Genesis account into two separate stories. For a scholarly rendition of the passages see Antony Campbell and Mark O'Brien *Sources of the Pentateuch (1993)*. Note the different writing styles and subject matter of the two stories. In the first version only the traditional Hebrew name for God, Yahweh, translated as "the LORD," is used. In the second version, every translation of "God" is from the Hebrew Elohim. The text for both stories is from the New American Standard Bible. Small portions of three verses have been omitted because they appear to be later interpolations.

[33] Ian Shaw (2000b, 328-329).

[34] Antony F. Campbell and Mark A. O'Brien (1993).

[35] Leviticus 16:1-10.

[36] See Exodus 12:1-13 and Leviticus 22:18-20.

[37] David Shackelford (June 1999).

[38] While ancient Israelite *society* relied on a patrilineal system for social identity and lineage membership, the modern Jewish *religion* traces identity through the matrilineal line.

[39] While this view of procreation was common in many agrarian societies, not all of the societies were patrilineal. Many agrarian and horticultural societies in the Americas and the Pacific were matrilineal.

[40] The text is from the *New Revised Standard Version* (2001).

[41] Most of the information on creation science beliefs derives from www.icr.org and www.answersingenesis.org.

[42] Paul Davies (1999, 158) and Michael Alan Park (2006, 119).

[43] Philip J. King and Lawrence E. Stager (2001) and Ian Shaw (2000a).

[44] Brian M. Fagan (2001, 301).

[45] Genesis 8:11.

[46] Genesis 5.

[47] Genesis 6:3.

[48] Genesis 11:24-25.

[49] Genesis 25:7.

[50] Deuteronomy 34:7.

[51] *National Geographic* (August 2004).

[52] Antony F. Cambell and Mark A. O'Brien (1993).

[53] For information on ancient Egypt I recommend Ian Shaw (2000a).

[54] Archaeologists discovered the source for the legendary Tower of Babel in the early 1900s. The tower, located in the ancient city of Babylon (also known as Babel), was a seven-level ziggurat that rose almost 300 feet high. Jean Bottéro and Marie-Joseph Stève (1993, 93).

[55] Jean Bottéro and Marie-Joseph Stève (1993), Glenn E. Markoe (2000) and Ian Shaw (2000a).

[56] Ian Shaw (2000b, 328-329).

[57] Ian Shaw (2000a).

[58] For more information on the Phoenicians, see Glenn E. Markoe (2000).

[59] For more information on the culture and history of early Israel from a scholarly perspective, see Philip J. King and Lawrence E. Stager (2001).

[60] See Philip J. King and Lawrence E. Stager (2001).

[61] A. Biran and H. Shanks (1994) and André Lemaire (1994).

[62] Philip J. King and Lawrence E. Stager (2001).

[63] Michael Behe (1996, 39-45).

[64] For scientific rebuttals of creation science and intelligent design see John Rennie (July 2002) and www.natcenscied.org.

[65] Michael J. Behe (October 2005).

[66] Michael J. Behe (February 7, 2005).

[67] Loren Wilkinson (1999, 169).

[68] C. S. Lewis (1943).

[69] C. S. Lewis (1958, 111-112).

[70] Paul Sillitoe (1998, 229-248).

[71] Matthew 22:34-40 and Mark 12:29-30. Compare with Deuteronomy 6:5 and Leviticus 19:18.

[72] 2 Timothy 3:16.

[73] For example, see Paul Davies (1999).

[74] Michael Denton (1998) argues the supernatural, not necessarily the Judeo-Christian god, orchestrated the laws of nature so that humans would evolve.

[75] Jeremiah 18:1-12 discusses how God can mold and shape nations. The illustration is not a reference to human biology but does convey the image of God seeing humanity as "a work in progress."

4 THE BIBLE: CULTURE AND HISTORY

> *With 200 homosexuals staring me in the face last Saturday, I accentuated the biblical position that homosexuality is sin. I also cautioned everyone attending that meeting that my position would never falter. I will never presume to counter God's Law.*

> — Jerry Falwell[1]

Jerry Falwell, a former evangelical minister, approached the Bible in a black and white fashion: the Bible contains God's law and it is relevant to all people everywhere. Everything in the Bible can be taken at face value: we understand its words and concepts as they were understood in the past, in spite of historical and cultural differences. If the Bible states that homosexuals are going to hell, that is God's will on the matter.

A different approach, employed by most contemporary biblical scholars, acknowledges that culture shapes our interpretation of reality; the historical-critical method examines the Bible's historical and cultural contexts in order to discern its actual meaning and intent.[2] As an anthropologist, I accept the historical-critical approach because I know that culture determines how a society views the world around it. In addition, each society has different cultural assumptions that form the basis of its code of behavior. Assuming that another culture has the same understanding of the world that we have is ethnocentrism, one of the greatest "sins" in the anthropological world. Ethnocentrism leads to misunderstanding and error. For example, many Westerners view the veil worn by Muslim women as a symbol of oppression. Anthropologists Elizabeth and Robert Fernea, however, indicate this derives from a Western misunderstanding. For many Muslim women, "the veil signals honor, personal protection, the sanctity and privacy of the family, wealth and high status, and city life."[3]

Many people read the Bible through the veil of ethnocentrism. They assume that the ancient Hebrews shared our understanding of the world and do not examine the cultural context in which the biblical passages were written. Furthermore, they overlook the universal problem of ethnocentrism which was also demonstrated by the ancient Israelites, who disparaged the rituals and customs of other societies, attributed to their enemies a less than honorable ancestry,[4] and viewed themselves as God's chosen people. An understanding of these attitudes is necessary to appropriately interpret the biblical texts.

We have seen that many evangelicals subscribe to a supposedly literal interpretation of the Bible. However, as Daniel Helminiak explains,

> the literal reading claims to take the text simply for what it says. This is the approach of Biblical Fundamentalism. It claims not to be interpreting the text but merely to be reading it as it stands. Clearly, however, even Fundamentalism follows a rule of interpretation, a simple and easy rule. The rule is that a text means whatever it means to somebody reading it today.[5]

A literal reading of the Bible ignores the dangers of ethnocentrism. It assumes that a modern reader can interpret what the text says with little or no knowledge of the historical and cultural milieu in which the text was written. To understand the Bible's historical and cultural contexts and to understand why the literal approach is rooted in error, it is important to first examine how the Bible came to exist.

Origins of the Bible according to evangelicals

The origins of the Bible comprise a highly controversial subject. Discussing the origins of a text that is foundational to one of the largest religions in the world can easily offend the sensibilities of many on both sides of the discussion. On one extreme we have many evangelicals who argue that the words of the Bible were directly and verbatim inspired by God. On the other extreme we have scholars who see a more human touch. They argue that perhaps God inspired people to write about their understanding of the spiritual world, their beliefs about God's desires, and so forth. Because many evangelicals believe that God directly inspired the words of the Bible, it must therefore be completely accurate in every detail. Because Jesus attributed the Torah to Moses,[6] most evangelicals believe that Moses wrote the entire Torah, from the creation accounts through the exodus from Egypt to the Deuter-onomical laws. Other biblical books were also supposedly written under God's direct inspiration and are, therefore, regarded as completely reliable.

Biblical inerrancy

Many evangelicals circumvent the problems of biblical error and contradiction by stating that the *original* texts of the various books were without error; the errors entered the texts over the course of time. For example, popular evangelical apologist Josh McDowell states that

> the Bible claims to be inspired by God. And if it is from God, then we can logically assume that the Bible is without error, or inerrant. . . . Inerrancy means that when all the facts are known, the Scriptures in their original autographs, properly in-terpreted, will be shown to be wholly true in everything they affirm, whether this has to do with doctrine or morality or with the social, physical, or life sciences.[7]

Unfortunately, we do not have the original texts so no one can authoritatively say what they actually state. This begs the question as to how evangelicals can trust anything in the Bible: if they do not know what the error-free original version actually says, there is no way to be sure that a passage has not been changed from its original form. This view also ignores that the Bible is not one book but a collection of writings that were assembled into one volume around the fourth century AD.

The evangelical view of a literal Bible is actually a relatively re-cent doctrine. No creedal statement from the early church re-quired belief in the inerrancy of scripture in its literal sense. At that time, the Bible had yet to be canonized and the authority of many of its books was still under debate. Bruce Bawer indicates that the belief of the inerrancy of a literal Bible, so prevalent among evangelicals today, was first stressed as church doctrine at the Niagara Bible Conference in 1895,[8] although it had previously been advocated by the Princeton Theological Seminary in 1881.[9]

Early Christian interpretations of the Bible

In spite of their insistence on maintaining a "traditional" view of scripture, evangelical leaders are actually not interpreting the Bible in a manner similar to earlier Christians. Early Christians normally treated the Old Testament as allegory and did not necessarily read it in the modern literal sense.[10] For example, Yale historian John Boswell[11] demonstrates that the apocryphal Epistle of Barnabas, which most prominent early Christian leaders regarded as authoritative, treats the kosher food laws in Leviticus and Deuteronomy as allegorical commentary on sexual behavior.[12] The epistle's author interprets the ban on eating rabbit as if it were actually an allegorical taboo on sexual relations between a man and a boy, later interpreted as a taboo on all homosexual behavior. The reasoning was based on the incorrect belief that rabbits develop a new anus each year. The taboo on eating rabbits was allegorically a prohibition on male same-sex behavior, particularly anal sex. The Epistle of Barnabas also states that hyenas are taboo because they allegorically represent adulterers. Hyenas were believed to change their sex annually and therefore would engage in sex with many others, inevitably committing "adultery."[13] Finally, the Epistle of Barnabas states that the weasel is a prohibited food in the Levitical laws because it gives birth through its mouth, a common belief in the ancient Mediterranean world.[14] Thus, the inclusion of the weasel in the kosher laws symbolically demonstrates that oral sex is sinful. These allegories are based on an understanding of nature that is not scientific and seem outlandish to the modern reader. However, to early Christians these allegories made sense because of their limited understanding of nature and their interpretation of the Old Testament. Prominent Christians regularly cited these passages as authoritative scripture that condemned homosexuality, adultery, and oral sex. In fact, Clement of Alexandria, writing in the 2nd century, used the food taboos as a primary source for his arguments that all same-sex behavior was sinful.[15] John Boswell demonstrates that these interpretations were maintained by Christians into the Middle Ages and served as a backbone for those who opposed homosexuality. Ironically, Boswell also highlights that the two Leviticus passages used today to condemn homosexuality were also treated allegorically and were thought to have no connection to a condemnation of same-sex behavior. While early Christians treated the biblical texts as authoritative, they generally did not read them in the modern literal sense.

Origins of the Old Testament according to scholars[16]

Scholars believe the various books of the Bible, the number of which varies in the Catholic, Eastern Orthodox, or Protestant traditions, came to exist in their present forms through a long process. For example, many scholars believe that the Torah was written as four separate documents during four different periods by four different authors or groups. Over time the four documents were collated, edited, and arranged into their present forms as the first five books of the Bible. The four original source documents are known as the J, E, D, and P texts.

The J-source

The J-source refers to God by the name of Yahweh, Jahweh in German, and was probably written in Jerusalem during the reign of King Solomon (about 960 – 920 BC). The J-source image of God is very anthropomorphic: God walked in the garden, made a partner for Adam through a process of trial and error, and used natural materials to make humans. The J-source text begins with the second creation story (Genesis 2:4-4:26) that details the origins of Adam and Eve, the parents of all humanity and, thereby, indicates that God is the god of all people. This view of God was important at a time when there were many gods, each tribe having its own deity or deities. Thus, the author of the J-source is declaring the universality of God. The author explains how the Jewish nation rose from slavery to an independent kingdom at the crossroads of the Middle East, stressing the importance of the Jerusalem temple and the monarchy as the twin pillars of ancient Mediterranean society.

The E-source

After the J-source was written, the death of Solomon provoked a rebellion in ancient Israel. The civil war resulted in a divided kingdom: rebellious Israel in the north and Judah in the south. Judah was home to the temple and the royal line of David. Thus, the northern kingdom of Israel needed to justify its rebellion against "church" and state. This led to the formation of the E-source of the Torah, which was written in the middle of the 9th century BC.

The E-source refers to God as Elohim and diminishes the importance of the Davidic dynasty and the royal priesthood. It indicates that God's covenant with Israel was made directly with the people and not with Moses, who symbolically represented the temple and priests. Episcopal bishop John Shelby Spong argues that the E-source portrayed the establishment of the Israelites' covenant with God before Moses became the mediator. Unlike the J-source, where the people were excluded, the people participated in the making of the covenant.[17] Because God's covenant was made with the people themselves, and not with the leaders, the leaders could be removed from power if the people so decided; hence, the justification for the civil war.

The E-source of Israel's history focuses heavily on Jacob, the grandson of Abraham. It recounts how Jacob had two wives: the beautiful and favored wife Rachel, from whom the favored son Joseph and the dominant tribe of the northern kingdom derived, and homely Leah, the mother of Judah, the ancestor of the dominant tribe in the southern kingdom. As is common in stories, the tales incorporate societal values. The symbolic portrayal of Rachel and Leah reflects the emerging northern kingdom's desire to "rewrite" history in its favor and to further justify its rebellion against the south. To counteract the loss of the Jerusalem temple, the author of the E-source repeatedly associates the Jewish patriarchs of Abraham, Isaac, and Jacob with various shrines in the northern kingdom. In place of the anthropomorphic J-source portrayal of God, who walks and talks with people in gardens and who is generally not very omniscient or omnipresent, the E-source presents a god who communicates with people through dreams.

The D-source

The late 7th century BC witnessed the next important contribution to the Torah. 2 Kings 22:8 recounts the discovery of a "lost" scroll of the law when repairs were being made to the Jerusalem temple. The scroll is believed to have consisted of the majority of the book of Deuteronomy and represents the D-source. Bishop Spong indicates that

> this sacred text was, not surprisingly, completely responsive to the prophetic tradition of Hosea, Amos, Isaiah, Micah, and especially Jeremiah, who was alive and at work when this new book was "discovered." This book called for the kind of religious reform the prophets had been calling for, and it rekindled a kind of national pride that helped to keep this soon-to-be-conquered nation intact through the period of exile.[18]

The authors of the D-source stress worship, the temple, and a desire to rid the nation of foreign influences, which is not surprising: at that time Israel was under constant threat from its neighbors. Shortly after the scroll's discovery, about 621 BC, the J, E, and D sources were combined into one volume with some editing to better harmonize them, and the books of Joshua, Judges, 1 and 2 Samuel, 1 and 2 Kings and various prophetic books were also written. Therefore, by the time of the Babylonian conquest of Judah, about 596 BC, a large part of the Torah had been formed. However, there was still one major source to come.

The P-source

Scholars believe that the P, or Priestly, source was written during the Jewish exile in Babylon. Typically, the Babylonians assimilated conquered peoples into their nation, causing them to lose their ethnic identity. However, the Jewish nation resisted, using religion to keep separate. Religious tradition is a powerful unifier, and the Jewish leaders seized upon it to strengthen the Jewish sense of identity and separateness. In particular, the Sabbath, circumcision, and the purity laws kept the Jews from being assimilated into Babylonian society. During this time, what we consider to be the first creation account in Genesis 1:1-2:3 was written, stressing the six days of creation and God's resting on the seventh day (the Sabbath). This creation account does not mention Adam and Eve but, instead, only mentions that God created humans on the sixth day. In addition, in the original Hebrew the text does not say that only one man and one woman were part of the original creation, but simply that God created humans male and female. Much of the book of Psalms and portions of Leviticus and Deuteronomy were also written during this time, including the sections detailing the kosher food laws. A second account of Noah's flood was written, and the list detailing the Ten Commandments was modified to include the observance of the Sabbath. The modification explains why there are actually eleven commandments in the "Ten Commandments."[19] By the end of the Babylonian captivity, most of the Old Testament was in its current form. Several additional books now found in the Old Testament, such as Ruth, Ezra, Nehemiah, Esther, Job, and Daniel, were written after the Babylonian exile. Thus, the Old Testament came about through a long and complex process, nor were the books immune to political influences in ancient times. Not surprisingly, the development of the New Testament is also not as simple as one might expect.

Origins of the New Testament according to scholars

Most people are aware that four gospels in the New Testament recount events in the final year or years of Jesus' life. However, many people are unaware that scholars do not believe the four gospels were written as independent texts. One clue as to how the gospels developed is the similarity of material found within the synoptic gospels (Matthew, Mark, and Luke) and their dissimilarity from John's gospel. Specifically, 600 of Mark's 661 verses are found in Matthew's gospel, sometimes expanded or slightly altered in grammar. However, Luke uses only about half of Mark's verses. When the Markian verses are removed from Matthew and Luke, a substantial number of verses, around 200, are found to be in both of those gospels but absent in Mark's gospel. It is thought that Matthew and Luke borrowed these 200 verses from a yet-to-be-discovered text that scholars call "Q," from *Quelle*, which means "source" in German. Matthew and Luke also include material that is unique to each of them and highlight events they considered important. The similarities in the synoptic gospels suggest that Mark's gospel is the oldest, as both Matthew and Luke borrow from it.

While the synoptic gospels focus on the life and ministry of Jesus, John's gospel encompasses a more explicit theological presentation and is considered representative of beliefs about Jesus held by one particular Christian community at the end of the first century AD. John's gospel stands apart from the synoptic gospels in terms of original material and tone. Bruce Bawer notes that the few verses attributed to Jesus that can be interpreted as doctrinal or theological statements are mostly found in John's gospel. These statements "are philosophically and tonally at odds with everything else that he says and does" and may be later additions to the text that reflect the early church's changing theology.[20]

Gospel contradictions

To illustrate the differences in Jesus' teachings in the gospels we can examine what Jesus says about gaining eternal life. Most evangelicals believe the answer is found in John 3:14-16. This view is "salvation by faith" and is also found in the letters of Paul and Peter.[21] However, the synoptic gospels present a different means of salvation. In Luke 10:25-28 and Matthew 22:34-40, a lawyer asks Jesus what he must do to gain eternal life. Jesus responds by instructing him to love God with all his heart, soul, strength, and mind, and to love his neighbor as himself. This view is consistent with the Old Testament. There is nothing in these passages about faith or atoning death, just simple obedience to the two great commandments. An evangelical acquaintance argued that the difference results from Jesus' telling the lawyer how to get to heaven under the Old Covenant (the Jewish law), while John's gospel has Jesus recounting the details of the New Covenant (salvation by faith). However, this implies that Jesus, supposedly knowing he would die and that the Old Covenant would no longer be in effect, intentionally deceived the lawyer on an issue that, according

> And as Moses lifted up the serpent in the wilderness, even so must the Son of Man be lifted up; that whoever believes may in Him have eternal life. For God so loved the world, that He gave His only begotten Son, that whoever believes in Him should not perish, but have eternal life.
> – John 3:14-16

to evangelicals, would determine the fate of his soul. This would be a strange thing for Jesus to do, especially if we accept the evangelical view that he was God and knew all things, even in his human mind.

There are numerous other problems in reconciling the different gospels if one takes a literal approach to them. For example, John indicates that the account of Jesus clearing the temple was at the beginning of Jesus' ministry, but the synoptic gospels place it during the final week.[22] Also, the synoptic gospels suggest Jesus' ministry lasted about one year while John's gospel implies three years.[23]

Other irreconcilable differences in the gospels occur in Jesus' genealogy, discussed in the previous chapter, and in the resurrection and post-resurrection accounts. The details of the events surrounding the resurrection differ and are sometimes mutually exclusive: Who went to the tomb? When did they arrive? Who did they meet? Where were the individuals they met located? And who did they tell about their encounter? Scholars believe the differences result from the different emphases of local churches and "Jesus movements" in the first century.[24] Those early Christians did not have the benefit of a written Christian tradition, mainly because Jesus did not write any texts. No canon, or collection of books recognized as authoritative, had yet developed. Most people were illiterate and would not have been able to read the canonized books had they existed. Thus, oral reports spread throughout the region, with the result that discrepancies developed among the traditions that would eventually become the four gospels.

The rest of the New Testament

The New Testament also includes a number of letters to churches and individuals. Various letters, particularly those of Paul, are believed to predate the gospels. Paul's letters were probably written between AD 48 and 62, shortly before Nero put him to death. Paul's letter to the Galatians highlights some of the early controversies in the Christian churches, particularly those between Christians who wanted Gentiles to abide by Jewish customs and those who found that unnecessary. This is relevant to the discussion of homosexuality and occurs in some of Paul's other letters as well, including the letter to the Romans.

During the first few centuries of the Christian era, believers argued about which books were authoritative enough to be considered canonical. Some books, such as James, Revelation, and the letter to the Hebrews, were considered controversial. The collection of books that make up the New Testament was finally agreed upon at the end of the fourth century: some important texts, such as the Gospel of Thomas and Epistle of Barnabas, were excluded from the list of authoritative works.[25]

We now have a basic understanding of the development of the Bible according to scholars. If nothing else, the sacred book that is revered by Christians has a long and complex history. Scholars believe that understanding this history provides considerable insight into what the authors of the various texts intended to convey through their writings. As we saw when examining the four sources of the Torah, if texts are to be properly understood they cannot be separated from their historical context: understanding the Bible's cultural context is also important.

Culture and the Bible

Many evangelicals only recognize the Bible's cultural context when specific commands or taboos directly affect them. For example, Leviticus 19:19 declares wearing clothing made from two different fabrics to be a sin. However, evangelicals dismiss this law as relating solely to the purity aspects of Jewish law, a law that Christians need not follow. The Bible also states that long hair on men is unnatural and is to be avoided; that women are forbidden to speak in church, braid their hair, and teach men; and that women must keep their heads covered.[26] Many evangelicals qualify these biblical teachings by alluding to their cultural context.

However, most evangelicals consider that any reference to homosexuality transcends culture, even if the types of same-sex relationships practiced in biblical cultures were different from what we recognize as homosexuality in Western society today. The evangelical double standard creates an interesting situation. Many evangelicals argue that homosexuality goes against nature, referencing a comment by the apostle Paul in Romans 1:26-27. However, as we will see, this is not an appropriate translation of the Greek. In the original Greek, Paul uses identical wording in 1 Corinthians 11:14-15 to state that long hair on men is also against nature. Most evangelicals dismiss the latter as a view that is culturally bound, but the comment on homosexuality supposedly is not. Therefore, we have a situation in which one statement by Paul is interpreted in the context of culture while an equivalent statement is seen as God's own thoughts on the matter, transcendent of the cultural context.

> For this reason God gave them over to degrading passions; for their women exchanged the natural function for that which is unnatural, and in the same way also the men abandoned the natural function of the woman and burned in their desire towards one another, men with men committing indecent acts and receiving in their own persons the due penalty of their error. – Romans 1:26-27
>
> Does not even nature itself teach you that if a man has long hair, it is a dishonor to him, but if a woman has long hair, it is a glory to her? For her hair is given to her for a covering? – 1 Corinthians 11:14-15

Understanding a cultural context is not a simple matter. The basic cultural assumptions of contemporary American society are very different from those of ancient Israel. To understand another culture, the assumptions of one's own culture must be put aside -- otherwise our assumptions can affect our understanding of how ancient Mediterranean cultures viewed topics such as family, marriage, and sex.

Ancient Israelite culture[27]

Archaeologists demonstrate that the kingdom of Israel arose from a semi-nomadic past. The ancient Israelites began as pastoralists who tended animals in the Palestinian hill country. Thanks partly to favorable climatic changes in the 13th and 12th centuries BC, the Israelite tribes gradually became more powerful. The result was the creation of the Kingdom of David and Solomon around 1000 BC. As the population increased, agricultural practices became more important, although the Israelites never forgot their pastoral roots.

Family. In pastoral societies tribal membership is held in high importance, as is the extended family group.[28] Due to the society's belief about procreation, membership in a particular tribe or lineage is determined solely through the male line. Behavior is regulated through an honor/shame system because a person's actions affect the entire family. Therefore, individualism is seen as a destructive force, so in all social interactions emphasis falls on the community rather than the individual. The focus on the community also places the family head and tribal leaders in positions of power. Not surprisingly, because membership is determined solely through the paternal line, the head of the family is the oldest male. Thus, power is limited to males, and only in very rare instances does a woman have any significant power or influence.

Marriage. Pastoral and agrarian societies are frequently polygynous.[29] One way of gaining status in these societies is to accumulate wealth, represented by material goods as well as the acquisition of wives. The more wives a man has, the more social, economic and political ties he has with other families, and the more powerful and wealthy he becomes. The political use of marriage can be seen in numerous royal marriages arranged as alliances, including Solomon's marriage to the pharaoh's daughter.[30] A man can manipulate the social and political relationships he attains through marriage to his advantage. In addition, the more wives a man has, the more children he can have. This is important because women and children are a source of labor, and the children will provide for the parents in old age. Having more people working for him allows the man to increase his wealth through the production of more goods and resources. Thus, women were seen as important social, economic, and political commodities for a man. Within this cultural framework, it is not surprising that women were essentially viewed as property in the Bible. The Ten Commandments demonstrate this view: the wife is placed among a man's possessions in Exodus

> You shall not covet your neighbor's house; you shall not covet your neighbor's wife or his male servant or his female servant or his ox or his donkey or anything that belongs to your neighbor. – Exodus 20:17

20:17. Under the patriarchy of ancient Israel, there was no prohibition of coveting a neighbor's husband.

Given that women were essentially the man's property and that society was centered on the male, divorce was a serious threat to a woman's survival. If a woman was divorced, she was considered damaged or used goods. She could hardly remarry and she had few options for livelihood -- except prostitution -- because access to goods and resources came through her husband. Thus, it is not surprising to find that divorce was a serious issue in the Bible. Of interest, in Old Testament law only the man could initiate divorce.[31] This arrangement placed a woman at a serious disadvantage. It required that she be obedient to her husband in everything, lest her husband divorce her and she lose all reliable access to things necessary for survival.

Sex. The view of women as property also affected cultural laws governing sexual relations. Not surprisingly, many of the Old Testament laws violate Western notions of justice. For example, Old Testament law dictates that if a woman is not a virgin at the time she is married, she is to be stoned to death.[32] There is no such penalty for men, of course. Also, Deuteronomy 22:28-29 explains what happens to a girl who is raped: she loses her economic value when she loses her virginity.

> If a man finds a girl who is a virgin, who is not engaged, and seizes her and lies with her and they are discovered, then the man who lay with her shall give to the girl's father fifty shekels of silver, and she shall become his wife because he has violated her; he cannot divorce her all his days. – Deuteronomy 22:28-29

Thus, the man who seized her must pay her father, and the couple must remain together for the rest of their lives. The girl has no ability to divorce him, and he is not allowed to divorce her because he has destroyed her economic value. The reason he must pay her father 50 shekels of silver is that normally, when a man married, he would pay an agreed-upon bride price. From a Western perspective, forcing a woman to marry her rapist, while the man's punishment is to pay a fee to her father, is a complete mockery of justice. However, when viewed in its cultural context the punishment makes sense because the law ensures that the woman will be provided for throughout her life.

Another important consideration is that the Old Testament defines adultery solely by the marital status of the woman.[33] This makes sense when one remembers that pastoral and agrarian societies are normally polygynous. If a man were not allowed to have sex outside of his first marriage, he could never marry a second wife. Thus, a married man's having sex with a single woman, including a prostitute, is not considered adultery. The only way a man can commit adultery is if he has sex with another man's wife. Many of the Old Testament patriarchs, including Abraham and Jacob, and other biblical heroes such as David and Solomon, had concubines, women with whom they could have sex even though they were not legally married to them. The view of women as property is a significant component for understanding the Old Testament views on sex and marriage. Another is the ancient Israelite understanding of procreation.

Procreation. Agrarian societies had a different outlook on procreation than modern industrial societies, which base their view on science. As mentioned in the previous chapter, to the ancient Israelites procreation consisted of a man placing his seed in the woman. Anthropologists hypothesize, according to this cultural view, that if semen was not placed in the womb, and was consequently "destroyed," various sexual behaviors would be considered immoral, including masturbation, oral sex on a male, male homosexuality (but not female, for no seed would be involved), and male bestiality.[34] Female bestiality would be wrong because the result would be the animal's "seed" being planted in a woman, instead of her husband's. This view of procreation explains why adultery would be considered wrong: when a married woman had sex with a man who was not her husband, another man's seed was being placed in her. The husband's wealth could be passed on to another man's child, thereby "stealing" the wealth that should be given to his legitimate descendants.

Biblical scholars disagree with this anthropological assessment of which sexual behaviors would be considered moral and immoral in ancient Israel. For example, Robert Gagnon argues that it does not explain all of the items prohibited in Leviticus 18, and that some behaviors that would also be condemned due to the seed being wasted are not mentioned, including masturbation.[35] However, Gagnon ignores that behavior considered improper or immoral is not always encoded within a society's laws. For example, although adultery is generally considered immoral in American society, it is no longer seen as illegal behavior.

Understanding ancient Mediterranean cultures and avoiding the dangers of ethnocentrism are important in understanding what the Bible says about homosexuality. However, before examining what specific passages in the Bible say about it, we must examine how homosexuality was expressed in the ancient eastern Mediterranean world.

Homosexuality in biblical cultures

To understand what types of same-sex behavior existed in the biblical world, from the Middle East to ancient Greece and Rome, we must turn to the biblical texts, early Greek and Roman literature, and archaeology. These sources demonstrate that common forms of same-sex behavior included prostitution, the sexual use of slaves, relationships factored by economics, and pederasty, which was a more complex relationship between a man and an adolescent.

In ancient Greece, both young bachelors and married men entered into pederastic unions -- erotic and often sexual relationships -- with youths whom they also loved and mentored.[36] The existence of pederasty as a culturally important form of same-sex relationships in ancient Greece, and to a lesser extent in Rome, is historically well established, although Boswell argues it was not as common as some have thought.[37] In Rome, wealthy citizens kept slave boys as catamites, sexual partners for older males. In both Greece and Rome, boy brothels were common and legal, often staffed by the enslaved sons of conquered peoples.

The eastern Mediterranean. Temple prostitution centered on fertility cults associated with Astarte (also known as Ishtar) in Near Eastern religions. A man could go to the temple or shrine and engage in sex with a male or female prostitute as part of his worship. Archaeologist Glenn E. Markoe notes that there is compelling evidence for temple prostitution from the area around Lebanon and

Cyprus.[38] One Bible study reference alleges that

> prostitution received official sanction from the Canaanite relig-
> ion which made reproductivity part of its *summum bonum* (the
> highest or chief good). There were seasons of sexual orgy asso-
> ciated with Astarte. The temple precincts became an inglorious
> brothel (Hos. 4:13, 14). This idea of unnatural and wicked
> abasement of sex, along with the revolt against marriage vows,
> was used by God's prophets to show how far they had fallen
> away from God. Even in NT [New Testament] times, the ten-
> dency to identify religious fervor and sexual excitement was
> present (cf. Acts 15:20, Rom. 1:24; 1 Cor. 6:9).[39]

Male temple prostitution was an important expression of same-
sex behavior in the eastern Mediterranean during Old Testament
times and is one of the types of homosexuality mentioned in the
Old Testament.[40] Other than two episodes of attempted same-sex
gang rape of visitors, there is no other explicit mention of same-
sex behavior in the Old Testament.

Male and female temple prostitution was also involved in the
worship of the Greek goddess Aphrodite, whose main temple was
in Corinth, the destination of two of Paul's letters and the place
from which Paul wrote the letter to the Romans. I mention these
locations because the letter to the Romans and the first letter to the
Corinthians are the primary New Testament passages evangelicals
use to condemn homosexuality.

Ancient Greece. Modern homosexuality, the type we see in the
United States between two freely consenting adults, also existed in
ancient Greece, as evidenced by recorded history and myths.
However, Western literature and society have suppressed explicit,
homosexual-themed myths and historical accounts.[41] To demonstrate this, we can examine one version of the story of Narcissus.[42]

Narcissus had never seen his reflection and did not know what
he looked like. One day, tired and thirsty in the forest, he found a
clear spring and bent down to take a drink. He saw a face in the
water and spoke to this beautiful apparition. The youth in the water moved his lips, but no sound came forth from them. Narcissus
tried to touch this beautiful male with whom he had fallen in love,
but every time he tried, the young man vanished. Narcissus grew

lovesick and remained by the spring to gaze at the object of his love. Gradually he pined away and died.

Today we are taught that Narcissus was a lover of self, and in a way that is true. However, Narcissus did not know that the beautiful young man that he saw in the reflection was himself. As far as he knew, Narcissus had fallen in love with another male. This myth demonstrates that age-equal same-sex romantic affection was known in ancient Greece and other places in the eastern Mediterranean. Thus, we can conclude that same-sex behavior in the ancient Mediterranean varied from institutionalized temple prostitution and pederasty to more egalitarian forms of homosexuality.

The first century AD. Victor Furnish, Professor of New Testament studies at Southern Methodist University, draws upon various first century authors to summarize ancient Mediterranean cultural beliefs about homosexuality during the New Testament period. He argues that there are four key points in understanding why Paul's contemporaries condemned same-sex behavior: first, it was believed that anyone who engaged in same-sex behavior was willfully overriding the natural desire for the opposite sex; second, it was believed that same-sex behavior resulted from yielding to an uncontrollable sexual appetite that caused an individual to lust after sex, regardless of whom it was with; third, it required one partner to engage in behavior that was suitable only for the opposite sex, given the association of aggressiveness with males and passivity with females; and fourth, it was feared that homosexuality would cause the extinction of the human race.[43] The final point is based on the belief that homosexual behavior made men sterile. However, science has demonstrated that each of the four points inherent to the ancient Mediterranean view of homosexuality is wrong. This different understanding of gender and sexuality is important in considering whether the Bible condemns homosexuals, as we understand the concept.

Rome and Europe. John Boswell documents the changing attitudes toward homosexuality in Europe from the rise of the Christian era through the 14th century. His findings are quite surprising in that there were periods of tolerance and acceptance interspersed with periods of persecution. For example, Boswell notes that Roman tolerance of homosexuality declined rapidly in the later years of the Roman Empire.[44] Evidence that the Roman Empire initially demonstrated a general acceptance of homosexuality includes a legal holiday for male prostitutes. Boswell argues that references to same-sex marriages were commonplace and that the practice was both legal and familiar among the upper classes. However, in the sixth century tolerance and acceptance of homosexuality gave way to criminalization of homosexual activity. A more tolerant attitude toward homosexuality arose once again in the 12th century. During this time homosexuality is apparently well-documented in the literature of Western Europe. However, Boswell adds that the tolerance was short-lived: by the early 14th century, homosexual activity incurred the death penalty in most of Europe.

> Slaves, be obedient to those who are your masters according to the flesh, with fear and tremling, in the sincerity of your heart, as to Christ: not by way of eyeservice, as men-pleasers, but as slaves of Christ, doing the will of God from the heart. – Ephesians 6:5-6

Culture, faith, prejudice, discrimination, and injustice

In their zeal to interpret the Bible literally, evangelicals generally overlook its cultural and historical contexts. This perpetuates ancient practices and attitudes largely derived from a tribal society and pre-scientific understanding of the world. For example, there were significant denominational splits in America, such as those among the Baptist and Methodist denominations, over slavery in 1845.[45] Southern Baptists pointed out that justification for slavery was found throughout the Bible, especially in Pauline literature, including Ephesians 6:5-6 and Titus 2:9-10. In these and other verses, the Bible legitimized slavery in ancient Israel. In this matter the importance of placing the texts in their historical and cultural contexts is clear. In the ancient Mediterranean a person could become a slave for several different reasons, in-

> Urge bondslaves to be subject to their own masters in everything, to be well-pleasing, not argumentative, not pilfering, but showing all good faith that they may adorn the doctrine of God our Savior in every respect. – Titus 2:9-10

cluding being captured in a war or entering into it at will and for a limited time due to poverty. In the United States, slavery had different historical and cultural precedents; consequently the supposed biblical justification for it is monstrous.

Once slavery, a practice now universally condemned by American Christians, was abolished, segregation took hold in the South. As with slavery, segregation was supported by many conservative Christian denominations. Philip Yancey mentions that his conservative church in Georgia used the Bible to justify segregation and explicitly argued that the Bible did not promote the notion of the fraternity of all humans. He also recounts how his church founded an all-white private school after the Civil Rights Act passed.[46] Yancey's church was not unique. Bruce Bawer explains that all-white private schools became common in the South after public schools were integrated by Supreme Court order. Bawer states: "Not to mince words, the Religious Right didn't grow out of a love for God and one's neighbor – it grew out of racism, pure and simple."[47]

> Let a woman quietly receive instruction with entire submissiveness. But I do not allow a woman to teach or exercise authority over a man, but to remain quiet. For it was Adam who was first created, and then Eve. And it was not Adam who was deceived, but the woman being quite deceived, fell into transgression. But women shall be preserved through the bearing of children if they continue in faith and love and sanctity with self-restraint. – 1 Timothy 2:11-15

Many evangelical churches also justify discrimination against women by appealing to the Bible. Once again, letters attributed by some to Paul, including 1 Timothy 2:11-15, are the primary sources. However, ancient Mediterranean cultures were patriarchal and viewed women as the property of men, contrary to modern American society.

In order to justify discrimination against blacks and women, those who support such views overlook the cultural and historical contexts of the Bible. Instead of focusing on the spirit of Jesus' teachings, which emphasize compassion and love, conservative Christians rely on a literal Bible to legitimize actions that flout both love and compassion. Philip Yancey recognizes the potential for modern evangelicals to blindly continue unjust attitudes that spring from a literal reading of the Bible. He states that

it is all too easy to point fingers at German Christians of the 1930s, southern fundamentalists in the 1960s, or South African Calvinists of the 1970s. What sobers me is that contemporary Christians may someday be judged just as harshly. What trivi-alities do we obsess over, and what weighty matters of the law – justice, mercy, faithfulness – might we be missing?[48]

To many non-evangelicals the answer is obvious: the present evangelical use of the Bible to legitimize discrimination and prejudice against homosexuals overrules considerations of justice, mercy, and faithfulness. Unfortunately, their worldview prevents many evangelicals from critically evaluating their use of scripture and their treatment of other, different people. By using a literal in-terpretation of an inerrant Bible and ignoring its cultural and his-torical contexts, evangelical leaders justify prejudice and discrimi-nation against homosexuals and propagate incorrect notions and beliefs about human sexuality. However, many biblical scholars argue that the assumed inerrancy of the Bible is not in its sup-posed historical or literal detail but in its themes and morals. For example, Daniel Helminiak indicates the Bible should not be read as a cookbook with ready-made answers to modern ethical ques-tions. Instead, he believes it provides examples of godly behavior to be applied to our individual and collective situations.[49]

Cultural beliefs and values

Scott Ross of the Christian Broadcasting Network asserts that God created humankind male and female, not homosexual.[50] The im-plication that homosexuals are neither fully male nor female is a common mistake among evangelicals. Sexual desire and the ex-pression of gender are not dependent on biological sex. Biological sex is determined by genetics and prenatal hormones; gender is culturally determined; and sexual orientation appears to be gov-erned by how the brain is hardwired, influenced by both prenatal hormones and genetics.[51] Ross incorrectly assumes that gender roles are biologically determined, contrary to sociological and anthropological findings. Stating that God made people male and female has no bearing on whether or not God "made" people homosexual. Furthermore, most cultures, including those of the ancient Mediterranean, subjugated biological sex to gender roles: if a man acted as a woman, he was considered to be a woman. This was especially true regarding sexual behavior: if a man was willing to be penetrated, he was behaving as a woman. For example, Yaron Peleg argues that Jonathan, the son of King Saul, behaved as a female in his relationship with David; because Jonathan took on the role of a female, he was no longer fit to inherit the throne.[52]

In order to understand what the biblical texts meant to the authors and their audience, it is essential to understand the cultural setting for the writings. A society's beliefs regarding the natural and cultural environment directly affect the cultural values, including what is considered proper conduct.[53] If a society has different core beliefs, the values and morals derived from them will be different. Compare modern American society with the European Middle Ages: the two societies differ significantly in their views on women and procreation. As our scientific understanding of the world developed and as women gained greater access to material wealth, and therefore greater social equality, our societal values diverged from those of the Middle Ages. Divorce is no longer scandalous, partly because women are able to earn their livings without husbands.

The view that a woman must be a virgin at marriage and that if she is not she must be killed has fallen from favor. Virginity may still be an ideal among many, especially those with strong religious backgrounds, but it is not as important as it once was. Societal views on masturbation and oral sex have also changed dramatically from those held in the Middle Ages, and even from the 19th century. There is no sound reason, other than personal feelings or appeals to the supernatural, still to consider them wrong. We know now that semen does not contain the entire child that needs to be nourished in a woman's womb so "spilling" the semen does not destroy a potential child.

Modern American views on adultery are largely consistent with those of the ancient Mediterranean, but for different reasons. In Mediterranean societies as well as most societies of the world, the family arranged a child's marriage. Marriage was a social, economic, and political arrangement between two families;[54] decisions about an appropriate partner were too important to be left to young people. A woman who committed adultery created the possibility of another man's child inheriting her husband's possessions; this compromised the economic relationship between the families, and was therefore considered wrong. In modern Western society, however, marriage is normally based on love, trust, and fidelity. Adultery violates these foundations and remains a societal taboo.

In light of the changing Western worldview it is not surprising that beliefs about homosexuality are also changing. The societal understanding of exactly *why* it is considered wrong for two males or females to have sex has lost its foundation. In opposing this shifting view, evangelical leaders can only maintain that homosexuality is wrong because they believe the Bible says so. They cannot reasonably explain *why* it is wrong.

---

[1] Jerry Falwell (no date).

[2] For more on the contrast between the literal and historical-critical approaches to the Bible see Daniel A. Helminiak (1999).

[3] Elizabeth W. Fernea and Robert A. Fernea (2003, 253).

[4] See Genesis 19:30-38 for one example.

[5] Daniel A. Helminiak (2000, 33).

[6] For example, see Mark 10:5.

[7] Josh McDowell (1999, 338).

[8] Bruce Bawer (1997, 88-90).

[9] Michael Ruse (2005, 160-161).

[10] David F. Wright (1990, 103-106).

[11] Many evangelical leaders completely dismiss all of Boswell's research given some questionable statements he has made, even though his book

Christianity, Social Tolerance and Homosexuality was awarded the 1981 prize for history book of the year. For example, Glenn Stanton and Bill Maier (2004, 42) suggest that "John Boswell cannot be taken seriously as a reasonable historian." It is true that Boswell appears to have ignored some ancient documents that contradicted his main premise that homosexuality was tolerated or accepted by early Christians, and that he mistranslated a number of key terms in a later book. However, Boswell's research is not entirely faulty and makes an important contribution to the understanding of homosexuality in the early Christian era of Western society.

[12] John Boswell (1980, 137-143).

[13] For one example of the belief that hyenas changed their sex see Ovid (2005, 299).

[14] Some translations include the weasel in Leviticus 11:29, otherwise the weasel would be included in the group of animals mentioned in Leviticus 11:27.

[15] John Boswell (1980, 163).

[16] Information on the scholarly view of the Bible derives from Antony F. Campbell and Mark A. O'Brien (1993), Gordon McConville (1996) and John Shelby Spong (1991).

[17] John Shelby Spong (1991, 49).

[18] Ibid (50).

[19] The eleven are as follows: 1) You shall have no other gods before me; 2) You shall not make for yourself an idol, or any likeness of what is in heaven above or on the earth beneath or in the water under the earth; 3) You shall not worship them or serve them [the idols]; 4) You shall not take the name of the LORD your God in vain; 5) Remember the Sabbath day; 6) Honor your father and your mother; 7) You shall not murder; 8) You shall not commit adultery; 9) You shall not steal; 10) You shall not bear false witness against your neighbor; 11) You shall not covet your neighbor's house; you shall not covet your neighbor's wife or his male servant or his female servant or his ox, or his donkey or anything that belongs to your neighbor.

[20] Bruce Bawer (1997, 41).

[21] For example, see Ephesians 2:8-9 and 1 Peter 1:5.

[22] Compare John 2:13-17 with Matthew 21:12-13, Mark 11:15-19 and Luke 19:45-48.

[23] John Shelby Spong (1991, 85).

[24] K. C. Hanson and Douglas E. Oakman (1998) and Bruce J. Malina (2001).

[25] Larry W. Hurtado (1990).

[26] 1 Corinthians 11:6, 14; 14:34 and 1 Timothy 2:9, 12.

[27] Readers interested in exploring the cultural context of ancient Israel and Palestine are encouraged to examine K. C. Hanson and Douglas E. Oakman (1998), Philip J. King and Lawrence E. Stager (2001) and Bruce J. Malina (2001).

[28] Daniel G. Bates and Elliot M. Fratkin (2003, 188-189).

[29] Ibid (213). Both polygyny (one man with more than one wife) and polyandry (one woman with more than one husband) are found among pastoral and agrarian societies, although polygyny is more common and was the form of polygamy practiced in ancient Israel.

[30] 1 Kings 7:8. See Stephanie Coontz (2005, 53-142) for more on the political aspects of marriage throughout history.

[31] Deuteronomy 24:1-4.

[32] Deuteronomy 22:13-21.

[33] For example, see Deuteronomy 22:22.

[34] L. William Countryman (1988, 26) regards the bestiality prohibitions as part of the purity code prominent in ancient Israel that prohibited the mixing of kinds. I believe that the moral code based on the importance of semen and the one based on not mixing kinds reinforce one another. From his discussion of Philo's comments, Countryman appears to share this view (1988, 60-63).

[35] Robert A. J. Gagnon (2001, 132-134).

[36] For example, see David F. Greenberg (1988, 106-110).

[37] For more information see John Boswell (1980), Louis Crompton (2003) and David F. Greenberg (1988, 106-110).

[38] Glenn E. Markoe (2000, 120).

[39] Spiro Zodhiates (1994, 2360).

[40] Louis Crompton (2003:40-43).

[41] This is addressed in greater detail by John Boswell (1980) and Andrew Calimach (2002).

[42] The general outline for the myth is well known. I used the format presented in M. V. Seton-Williams (1993). Andrew Calimach (2002) discusses the homosexual elements in a number of Greek myths.

[43] Victor Paul Furnish (1994, 25-27).

[44] John Boswell (1980, 73).

---

[45] Bruce Bawer (1997, 82).

[46] Philip Yancey (1997, 131).

[47] Bruce Bawer (1997, 144).

[48] Philip Yancey (1997, 201).

[49] Daniel A. Helminiak (1999).

[50] Scott Ross (2003).

[51] B. S. Mustanski, M. L. Chivers and J. M. Bailey (2002).

[52] Yaron Peleg (2005).

[53] Michael Alan Park (2003, 145-152).

[54] James Peoples and Garrick Bailey (2000, 121-122) and Stephanie Coontz (2005, 69).

5 FADE TO GRAY:
THE BIBLE AND HOMOSEXUALITY

It's time Christian conservatives accepted the fact the Bible's laws against homosexuality, like its laws permitting slavery, monarchy, and genocide, are archaic and no longer applicable to the current age.

— Steve Kangas[1]

Don Schmierer is mistaken when he concludes that the Bible "clearly states that homosexuality is wrong;"[2] on this issue there is considerable gray. Specifically, only one passage in the entire Bible, Romans 1:24-27, possibly mentions female homosexuality. Contrast this with the number of passages that indicate lending money at interest to be wrong, despite which evangelicals fail to denounce modern banking.[3] However, even with the one passage that possibly discusses female homosexuality, disagreement arises as to whether it unequivocally condemns the behavior, once the context is considered. Unfortunately, most evangelicals believe leaders such as Jerry Falwell who, after quoting Romans 1:24-27 and arguing that it condemns homosexuality, incorrectly states that "other similar verses abound."[4]

In *Solid Answers* James Dobson highlights the biblical passages that he believes condemn homosexuality.[5] In most cases the passages do involve an *aspect* of same-sex behavior, but they arguably do not condemn general homosexuality. It is worthwhile to examine these passages to see what the Bible does and does not say on the subject. I argue that due to their historical and cultural contexts, the biblical passages relating to homosexuality are not relevant to a discussion of modern homosexuality.

The Old Testament

Sodom

No biblical passage or city is more often associated with homosexuality than Sodom. Sodom has traditionally been so closely identified with homosexuality that the act of two males having

sex is still sometimes called sodomy. However, there is disagreement among Christian scholars about whether the biblical
condemnation and destruction of Sodom was due to homosexuality. For example, Cardinal Ratzinger, now Pope Benedict XVI,
said "the deterioration due to sin continues in the story of the
men of Sodom. There can be no doubt of the moral judgment
made there against homosexuality."6 Former Jesuit priest John
McNeill counters this argument: "Every time Jesus refers to
Sodom he identifies the sin of that city as inhospitality to strangers."7

> Before they lay down, the men of the city, the men of Sodom, sur-
> rounded the house, both young and old, all the people from every
> quarter; and they called to Lot and said to him, "Where are the
> men who came to you tonight? Bring them out to us that we may
> have relations with them." But Lot went out to them at the door-
> way, and shut the door behind him, and said, "Please, my broth-
> ers, do not act wickedly. Now behold, I have two daughters who
> have not had relations with man; please let me bring them out to
> you, and do to them whatever you like; only do nothing to these
> men, *inasmuch as they have come under the shelter of my roof.*"
> [Emphasis added.] – Genesis 19:4-8 (Sodom)

> While they were making merry, behold, the men of the city, cer-
> tain worthless fellows, surrounded the house, pounding the door;
> and they spoke to the owner of the house, the old man, saying
> "Bring out the man who came into your house that we may have
> relations with him." Then the man, the owner of the house, went
> out to them and said to them, "No, my fellows, please do not act
> so wickedly; *since this man has come into my house*, do not com-
> mit this act of folly." Here is my virgin daughter and his concu-
> bine. Please let me bring them out that you may ravish them and
> do to them whatever you wish. But do not commit such an act of
> folly against this man. [Emphasis added.] – Judges 19:22-24 (Gibeah)

Given these disparate views, we will examine the passage in
question along with a passage from the book of Judges. The latter
focuses on events in the town of Gibeah, and is almost identical
to the Sodom account.

In both passages the men in the town demand to have sex with male visitors to a household (in Sodom the visitors were angels). The hosts refuse, but instead offer females to the townsmen. In Sodom the females are Lot's virgin daughters, while in Gibeah one of the women is the host's virgin daughter and the other is the guest's concubine. In Sodom the two daughters are not actually delivered to the men, but in Gibeah the concubine is subsequently raped and dies.

Of relevance, the Bible declares Lot to be righteous in God's eyes even though he is willing to give his two virgin daughters to the men of Sodom.[8] Later, Lot's daughters have sex with their father after getting him drunk. Genesis 19:30-38 indicates that Lot's daughters became pregnant, and the resulting children became the founders of two enemy tribes of Israel. From a 21st century perspective, it is a very strange standard that declares a man righteous when he offers to give up his own daughters to be raped by a group of men and later fathers their children. To understand why Lot is declared righteous, we must understand the cultural context.

In ancient Mediterranean cultures being a good host was an extremely important value. Ensuring the safety and well-being of a guest brought honor to a family; letting harm come to the guest damaged the family's honor and standing in the society. Because the honor/shame system was one of the most important aspects of ancient Mediterranean culture, it was necessary to protect a guest at any cost.[9] The Bible encodes this value: "When a stranger resides with you in your land, you shall not do him wrong. The stranger who resides with you shall be to you as the native among you, and you shall love him as yourself; for you were aliens in the land of Egypt: I am the LORD your God."[10] With this background, consider the response of the host in the two accounts: the reason why the same-sex rape would be wrong is that the visitors had come into the host's house and were his guests. The host was, therefore, responsible for the guests' well-being. The passages imply that the host would not object to the rape if the men were not *his* guests. Louis Crompton places the threat of rape in cultural context, indicating that "such assaults are seen not as illicit pleasure but as a means of warding off intruders – just as Roman gardens sported phallic statues of the god Priapus inscribed with threats of rape to ward off thieves and trespassers."[11] This highlights that other factors were involved in what was considered acceptable and unacceptable behavior in ancient Israel: only by understanding ancient Mediterranean cultures can one interpret biblical passages correctly.

Ezekiel 16:48-50 and most other biblical passages that mention the doomed city cite aspects of inhospitality as the sin of Sodom. Isaiah 1:10-17 encourages the people of Sodom and Gomorrah to repent of their behavior and defend orphans and widows, the two groups that were the most easily abused and in greatest peril in ancient Mediterranean societies. Amos 4:1-13 states that God overthrew Israel because the Israelites oppressed the poor and crushed the needy, as did the people of Sodom and Gomorrah. Zephaniah 2:8-11 compares Sodom to the ancient tribes of Moab and Ammon, the two tribes fathered by Lot with his daughters, specifically highlighting arrogance as their sin. The apocryphal book of Wisdom 19:13 states that the sin of Sodom was a hatred of strangers and enslaving guests. Finally, in Matthew 10:15 and Luke 10:12, Jesus mentions Sodom in the context of people who do not demonstrate hospitality. While most of these items are explicitly mentioned as the sins of Sodom in Ezekiel 16, nowhere in the Bible is homosexuality indicated as such.

> "As I live," declares the Lord GOD, "Sodom, your sister, and her daughters, have not done as you and your daughters have done. Behold, this was the guilt of your sister Sodom: she and her daughters had arrogance, abundant food, and careless ease, but she did not help the poor and needy. Thus they were haughty and committed abominations before Me. Therefore I removed them when I saw it." – Ezekiel 16:48-50

Jude. Many evangelicals point to Jude 7 to connect the sin of Sodom with homosexuality.[12] The evangelical assumption is that the "strange flesh" implies homosexuality. However, this is not consistent with the original Greek text. The passage compares the men of Sodom and Gomorrah with angels who left heaven to live on earth and have sex with humans.[13] Thus, "strange flesh" is a reference to the Sodomites wishing to have sex with the angelic visitors, not a reference to homosexuality. This is demonstrated in that "strange" is translated from the Greek word *heteros*, which means of a different kind, nature or class; not of the same type (*homos*). In this context the Greek word *heteros* indicates something of a different nature from humans, specifically angels. If the author is referring to homosexuality, then the Sodomites would be going after the same flesh, not "strange flesh." Thus, when Jude 7 is read in the context of Jude and other ancient Hebrew writings, such as the first book of Enoch, it does not associate Sodom with homosexuality. The passage indicates that just as angels left heaven and came to earth to have sex with women, so in the same way those in Sodom went after strange flesh to have sex with angelic visitors.

Abomination. Some evangelicals attempt to link homosexuality to the unspecified abominations mentioned in Ezekiel 16:48-50.[14] The argument is based on the Hebrew word *to'evah*, translated "abominations" in the Ezekiel passage, because *to'evah* is found in

> Just as Sodom and Gomorrah and the cities around them, since they in the same way as these indulged in gross immorality and went after strange flesh, are exhibited as an example, in undergoing the punishment of eternal fire. – Jude 7

other passages that evangelicals use to condemn homosexuals. However, in the early Hebrew texts *to'evah* is used in connection with religious purity, including human sacrifices, eating pork and other ritually unclean animals, sacrificing blemished animals, engaging in occult activities, and practicing temple prostitution.[15] Thus, the connection to general homosexuality is unwarranted.

Inhospitality, not homosexuality. The passages discussing the events in Sodom and Gibeah cannot be used as general condemnations of homosexuality, much less monogamous homosexuality, for several reasons. First, the homosexual act discussed in the passages refers to gang rape. Logic dictates that condemnation of a specific behavior is not a condemnation of a more general behavior. Alice Ogden Bellis furthers this argument by indicating that rape is more about power than sex, and that the intent of the rape was to humiliate the intruders by treating them in a degrading manner.[16]

Robert Gagnon, associate professor of the New Testament at the Pittsburgh Theological Seminary, denies the relevance of Bellis' argument, suggesting that

> the logic sounds convincing until one stops to reflect on the historical and literary contexts for the narrative in Judges 19-21. The Deuteronomistic History ... takes a clear stance against homosexual intercourse as an abominable violation of God's standards for human sexual expression. It is itself dependent on the Deuteronomic law code for its moral valuation of various acts, a work which also takes a demeaning view of homosexual intercourse (referring to homosexual cult prostitutes as "dogs").[17]

However, contrary to Gagnon's assertion, all other references to homosexual behavior in both the Deuteronomistic history (which includes the books of Joshua through 2 Kings) and the Deuteronomic law code focus only on temple prostitution. There is not a single reference in any of these passages to other types of same-sex behavior. Thus, the passages do not take "a clear stance against homosexual intercourse," because only temple prostitution is mentioned. Thus, Gagnon's objection is without substance.

The second reason the passages should not be used to condemn homosexuality is that in both cases women are offered to the angry mob. In Gibeah the woman is raped and murdered, implying that the men are either bisexuals or heterosexuals who engage in homosexual behavior (which would not be surprising given that rape is about power, not sex). Third, God had already declared that Sodom was to be destroyed *before* the attempted rape occurred, not *because* of it.[18] Fourth, the cultural context indicates that inhospitality, not homosexuality, was the reason why the behavior of the Sodomite men was deemed wrong. Finally, Ezekiel 16:48-50, a passage that discusses why God destroyed Sodom and Gomorrah, does not include homosexuality as one of Sodom's sins, but states that Sodom was destroyed for arrogance, abundant food, careless ease, and not taking care of the poor and needy.

Contrary to then Cardinal Ratzinger's views, most scholars accept that the crime of Sodom was inhospitality, a serious issue in the ancient Middle East. As Daniel Helminiak notes,

> there is a sad irony about the story of Sodom when understood in its own historical setting. People oppose and abuse homosexual men and women for being different, odd, strange or, as they say, "queer." Lesbian women and gay men are just not allowed to fit in; they are made to be outsiders, foreigners in our society. They are disowned by their families, separated from their children, fired from their jobs, evicted from apartments and neighborhoods, insulted by public figures, and then beaten in the schools and killed on the streets and in the backwoods of our nation. All this is done in the name of religion and supposed Judeo-Christian morality.

> Such wickedness is the very sin of which the people of Sodom were guilty. Such cruelty is what the Bible truly condemns over and over again. So those who oppress homosexuals because of the supposed "sin of Sodom" may themselves be the real "sodomites," as the Bible understands it.[19]

We can safely conclude that the passages relating to Sodom in no way involve or condemn general homosexuality.

Deuteronomy and Kings

James Dobson believes that five Old Testament passages in Deuteronomy, 1 Kings and 2 Kings condemn homosexuality. However, it is apparent that, in light of the original Hebrew, the passages deal only with male temple prostitution. The Hebrew word used in these passages, *qadhesh*, refers to "male temple prostitutes." Strangely, this word is translated "sodomites" in 1 Kings 22:46 in the New American Standard Bible and in all five of these passages in the King James Version. This is curious given that the Hebrew texts only reference male temple prostitutes. Furthermore, the word translated "abomination" in 1 Kings 14:24 is *to'evah*, which, as already indicated, is primarily used in the context of religious purity. Such use is consistent with the subject of temple prostitutes, given their association with idolatry. Thus, it is apparent that these passages do not condemn homosexuality, but instead condemn temple prostitution. As with gang rape, logic dictates that condemnation of male temple prostitution does not imply condemnation of general homosexuality, just as the passages that condemn female temple prostitution do not imply a condemnation of heterosexuality.

> None of the daughters of Israel shall be a cult prostitute, nor shall any of the sons of Israel be a cult prostitute. – Deuteronomy 23:17

> And there were also male cult prostitutes in the land. They did according to all the abominations of the nations which the LORD dispossessed before the sons of Israel. – 1 Kings 14:24

> He also put away the male cult prostitutes from the land, and removed all the idols which his fathers had made. –1 Kings 15:12

> And the remnant of the sodomites who remained in the days of his father Asa, he expelled from the land. – 1 Kings 22:46

> He also broke down the houses of the male cult prostitutes which were in the house of the LORD, where the women were weaving hangings for the Asherah. – 2 Kings 23:7

Leviticus

This brings us to the two Old Testament passages that many evangelical leaders suggest are the most explicit in their condemnation of homosexuals: Leviticus 18:22 and 20:13. In fact, Louis Crompton argues that these verses are the foundation for European and European-influenced laws that mandated the death penalty for homosexuality until the end of the eighteenth century.[20] Actually misrepresenting the biblical teachings, Pat Robertson presents the passages to his followers in this way: "The Bible says that it is an abomination for a man to lie with a man as with a woman, *or a woman to lie with a woman as with a man* (see Leviticus 18:22, 20:13)"[21] [emphasis added]. He states that the two Leviticus passages specifically condemn women having sex with women. They do not. Robertson actually changes what the passages say to make them condemn all homosexuals.

Daniel Helminiak indicates that the lack of a prohibition on female homosexuality in Leviticus results from the female's anatomical inability to sexually penetrate another female as a male does. This means that neither woman violates the female's role as the penetrated partner by acting as a penetrating male.[22] However, when a male is penetrated by another male, he assumes the role of the female gender and violates the society's standard for sexual behavior, thus the mention of a man lying with a male in Leviticus. As Saul Olyan and Daniel Boyarin have shown, the concern of Leviticus is male-male penetrative sex, and not general homosexuality.[23]

> You shall not lie with a male as one lies with a female, it is an abomination. – Leviticus 18:22

> If there is a man who lies with a male as those who lie with a woman, both of them have committed a detestable act; they shall surely be put to death. Their blood guiltiness is upon them. – Leviticus 20:13

Robert Gagnon argues that even though the passages in Leviticus only specify homosexual males, the author actually implies that all homosexuality is an abomination to God. He argues that homosexuality confuses the genders by violating "the anatomical and procreative complementarity of male and female," destabilizes the family as presented in Genesis 1-3, and endangers the survival of the species.[24] Gagnon's first reason derives from a literal interpretation of Genesis, although Gagnon himself states "I cannot be a biblical literalist or fundamentalist and still retain intellectual integrity."[25] Furthermore, sociologists have demonstrated that homosexuality does not destabilize the integrity of the family nor does it affect the survival of the human race: only a small portion of humans is homosexual or inclined to engage in same-sex intercourse. Thus, Gagnon's explanation for considering homosexuality an abomination does not withstand scrutiny. He does not satisfactorily explain why, if homosexuality mixes "things that were never intended to be mixed,"[26] lesbianism receives no comment whatsoever in the Old Testament.

William Countryman believes that the purpose of the prohibition on male-male sex is not an ethical or moral one, but as part of the Hebrew purity regulations, it is designed to help keep Jewish

identity strong.[27] Daniel Helminiak compares the religious prohibition to one found in the Catholic church:

> There used to be a church law that forbade Roman Catholics to
> eat meat on Fridays … That church law was considered so se-
> rious that violation was a mortal sin, supposedly punishable
> by hell. Yet no one believes that eating meat was something
> wrong in itself. The offense was against a religious responsibil-
> ity: one was to act like a Catholic.[28]

This is evident in that the same Hebrew word used to describe
the behavior in the Leviticus passages as an "abomination" or
"detestable act," *to'evah*, is used to describe various foods as ritually unclean, such as eating camels, rabbits, and pigs.[29] This word
is rarely used in the context of sexual behavior that is inherently
immoral, although it is used to condemn male temple prostitution. *Zimmah* is typically used to discuss sexual immorality.[30] Furthermore, while other sexual behaviors that are considered inherently immoral are mentioned elsewhere in the Old Testament,
male homosexuality is not. Given that the focus is solely on ritual
and social purity, Helminiak argues that the prohibition on male
homosexuality is no longer important. Christian tradition has
viewed the purity concerns and regulations in Leviticus as irrelevant.[31]

John Boswell criticizes those who use the Leviticus passages to
condemn homosexuals, given that Leviticus also condemns many
things that are not considered wrong by evangelicals, including
tattoos, wearing garments made of two types of cloth, and eating
pork.[32] As Boswell notes,

> their extreme selectivity in approaching the huge corpus of
> Levitical law is clear evidence that it was not their respect for
> the law which created their hostility to homosexuality but
> their hostility to homosexuality which led them to retain a few
> passages from a law code largely discarded.[33]

While the passages in Leviticus may have condemned aspects of
male homosexual behavior, there is no indication that they condemn all homosexuality, or that the condemnation had any moral
implications. The Levitical condemnation was rather a response
to issues of ancient Israelite culture and identity.

The Old Testament and homosexuality

Robert Gagnon argues that an encounter between Noah and his son Ham also condemns homosexuality. Genesis 9:20-27 mentions that Ham saw his father's nakedness. Gagnon's interpretation has it that Ham raped his father and that God subsequently cursed Ham's son, Canaan, for the immoral behavior.[34] Even if the story is interpreted as an incident of incestuous rape, it certainly should not be considered a condemnation of general homosexuality. From an anthropological perspective, the story simply justifies the Israelite's view of their Canaanite neighbors. It was not uncommon in cultures around the world to demean neighboring enemies by attributing to them a less than respectable ancestry. For example, Genesis 19:30-38 indicates that two of Israel's neighbors, the Moabites and Ammonites, arose from an incestuous encounter between Lot and his daughters. If Gagnon's interpretation is correct, then the story simply portrays an Israelite accusation that the Canaanite tribe descended from an ancestor who tried to usurp his father's power and authority by raping him. Given the context, the situation simply should not be applied as a general condemnation of homosexuality.

We have now examined all of the Old Testament passages that supposedly condemn homosexuality. There is no condemnation of general homosexuality anywhere in the Old Testament. When the passages are examined in their cultural, historical, and scriptural contexts, there is no clear condemnation of general male homosexuality, nor is there any mention of female homosexuality. Thus, to find the supposedly clear biblical condemnations of homosexuality promised to us by evangelical leaders, we turn to the New Testament.

The New Testament

Letters to Corinth and Timothy

James Dobson and many other evangelical leaders proclaim that three New Testament passages are clear in their condemnation of homosexuality.[35] Notably, 1 Corinthians 6:9 and 1 Timothy 1:10 are the only passages in which some modern translations of the Bible use the term "homosexual."

> Or do you not know that the unrighteous shall not inherit the king-
> dom of God? Do not be deceived; neither fornicators, nor idolaters,
> nor adulterers, nor effeminate [*malakoi*], nor homosexuals [*arseno-*
> *koitai*], nor thieves, nor the covetous, nor drunkards, nor revilers,
> nor swindlers, shall inherit the kingdom of God.
> – 1 Corinthians 6:9-10

> But we know that the Law is good, if one uses it lawfully, realizing
> the fact that law is not made for a righteous man, but for those
> who are lawless and rebellious, for the ungodly and sinners, for the
> unholy and profane, for those who kill their fathers or mothers, for
> murderers and immoral men and homosexuals [*arsenokoitai*] and
> kidnappers and liars and perjurers, and whatever else is contrary to
> sound teaching. – 1 Timothy 1:8-10

Malakoi. Surprisingly, there is very little consistency in how
two key Greek words are translated in different versions of the
Bible. *Malakoi* (Table 2) literally means "soft" or "pliable" and is
the same word Jesus used to talk about clothing.[36] Predating Paul,
Aristotle defines *malakoi* as "[Someone who] gives way without a
struggle to pleasures and pains that most people can resist."[37]
Men of this disposition were considered effeminate because
women were considered unable to resist temptation as well as
men, hence the translation in some Bibles. Notably, Paul does not
use the ancient Greek word for effeminate, *truphe.*

Some argue that "effeminate" was used in Greek society as a
metaphorical term for males who were the passive partner in a
homosexual act. However, John Boswell indicates that there was
no exclusive association between homosexual men and effeminate men in the ancient world, given the cultural focus on gender
roles rather than sexual orientation. Ancient authors labeled
many heterosexual men as effeminate, but homosexual men were
not considered effeminate unless they expressed feminine characteristics.[38] Thus, in 1 Corinthians 6 *malakoi* could mean weak-
willed, or it could be interpreted as a euphemism for effeminate,
but in either case, it does not refer to homosexuality.

Some Bible translations say "male prostitutes" as an appropriate English translation for *malakoi.* The verses following 1 Corin-

Table 2: Malakoi

Bible version	Translation
Tyndale (1525)	Weaklings
King James (1611)	Effeminate
Darby (1890)	Those who make women of themselves
American Standard (1901)	Effeminate
Goodspeed (1939)	Sensual
Jerusalem (English, 1968)	Catamites
New American (1970)	Boy prostitutes
New American Standard (1971)	Effeminate
New Jersusalem (1973)	Self indulgent
New International (1978)	Male prostitutes
New Revised Standard (1990)	Male prostitutes

thians 6:9-10 discuss immorality and Christians joining themselves with prostitutes, possibly referring to temple prostitutes in Corinth, the center of Aphrodite worship. This might indicate that Paul was concerned with male temple prostitution in Corinth and was specifically referring to it here.

The difficulty in translating *malakoi* implies that it is not as clear-cut a condemnation of homosexuality as many evangelical leaders believe. In fact, it probably has nothing to do with homosexuality. The word is used in so many different contexts in ancient Greek literature that it is unclear what the apostle Paul intended. John Boswell argues, "So many people are denigrated as [*malakoi*] in ancient literature, for so many reasons, that the burden of proof in this case must be on those who wish to *create* a link with gay people"[39] [emphasis in original].

Arsenokoitai. Unfortunately, the meaning of *arsenokoitai* is no clearer (Table 3). At least in modern English Bibles, the various translations all center on a common theme, but this is misleading, as the German and French translations show. *Arsenokoitai* is a composite of two Greek words that mean "male" and "bed," but the term is not found in any Greek writing prior to Paul.[40]

Because this word is included in a list of items, there is no context to help decipher its meaning. What can be determined, however, is that it involves male sexuality: *arsen* is never used to refer to males and females as "mankind" or "humankind" is used in the collective sense in English. Thus, while the word's specific meaning is unknown, it clearly does not include lesbians. There is no justification for translating the word to condemn all homosexual behavior.

Table 3: Arsenokoitai

Bible version	Translation
King James (1611)	Abusers of themselves with mankind (1 Cor 6:9) Defile themselves with mankind (1 Tim 1:10)
Darby (1890)	Abuse themselves with men (1 Cor 6:9) Sodomites (1 Tim 1:10)
American Standard (1901)	Abusers of themselves with men
Jerusalem (French, 1966)	Men with infamous desires (*gens de mœurs infâmes*)
Jerusalem (English, 1968)	Sodomites
Jerusalem (German, 1968)	Boy molestors (*knabenschänder*)
New American (1970)	Homosexuals
New American Standard (1971)	Homosexuals
New International (1978)	Homosexual offenders (1 Cor. 6:9) Perverts (1 Tim. 1:10)
New Revised Standard (1990)	Sodomites

An indication of what is intended by *arsenokoitai* may be gar-nered from the few other times it appears in early Greek litera-ture. The first extant Christian writers to use the term understood *arsenokoitai* as male prostitutes who slept with females or as other sexual behavior involving money.[41] This translation of *arsenokoitai* appears accurate, given that the author's attention turns from this word, included in a list of those who will not inherit the kingdom of heaven, to prostitution in 1 Corinthians 6. If *arsenokoitai* derives from the Greek translation of Leviticus 20:13, as some scholars be-lieve,[42] then it could refer to male temple prostitutes engaging in male-male penetrative sex. They were common in Corinth, were considered *to'evah* in 1 Kings 14:24, and would have been in-cluded in the Leviticus prohibition.[43]

John Boswell demonstrates that no early Christian writer used *arsenokoitai* to refer to homosexuals. He writes that

> Clement of Alexandria uses at least thirteen different expres-sions for 'homosexual,' 'sodomite,' and 'sodomy,' but none of them is [*arsenokoitai*]. Yet he clearly knew the word, since he quoted the passage from Corinthians (in a different context) in several of his works.[44]

A second influential Christian of the time, Saint John Chry-sostom, was very public in his condemnation of homosexuality. Yet Chrysostom never used *arsenokoitai* in reference to same-sex behavior, even though he wrote extensively on the subject, and provided detailed discussions of every passage in the Bible in which he could find any hint of same-sex behavior. Chrysostom discusses the two passages that use *arsenokoitai* and are seen to-day as explicit condemnations of homosexuality, 1 Corinthians 6:9 and 1 Timothy 1:10, but he makes no mention of same-sex be-havior.[45] Boswell notes that prior to its ever being translated as "homosexuals," *arsenokoitai* was interpreted by Christian writers as a reference to child molestation and anal sex between a hus-band and wife.[46] Thus, it is apparent that early Christians did not associate *arsenokoitai* with same-sex behavior and that the actual meaning of this term is unknown.

A popular modern argument is that the two words *malakoi* and *arsenokoitai* refer to the receiving and giving partners in male anal sex.[47] The males in the passive role were sometimes catamites, young boys who were used for sexual purposes, while in some other cases the males were boy prostitutes or slaves.[48] Some argue that *arsenokoitai* refers to the men who had sex with these individuals. Indeed, in the 1st century Roman Empire, attractive boys were sometimes kidnapped and sold into slavery to be used as catamites. This could explain why the author, in the letter to Timothy, mentions kidnappers immediately after *arsenokoitai*.[49] This interpretation raises the question of whether the passage is really a condemnation of abusive male-male sexual practices rather than of all male homosexuality. Regardless, John Boswell indicates that the translation of the two Greek words as the receiving and giving partners in male homosexual sex is "fanciful and unsubstantiated by lexicographical evidence."[50] First, *malakoi* does not occur with *arsenokoitai* in 1 Timothy; furthermore, the two terms are *never* known to be used in this way anywhere else in Greek literature on homosexuality. Second, as late as the 12th century, when theologians discussed all the potential biblical references to homosexuality, neither 1 Corinthians nor 1 Timothy were included. Thus, it is unlikely that the two words reference the receiving and giving partners in male homosexual behavior.

Because *arsenokoitai* does not occur in ancient Greek literature, there is no way to know for sure to what it refers. Nonetheless, it is highly unlikely that it refers to homosexuals, mainly because *arsenokoitai* was not used in ancient Greek society to describe them. Once again, we find that what evangelical leaders state is a clear black and white condemnation of homosexuality turns out to be a shade of gray. While the passages may condemn *some* aspect of male homosexuality, they give no evidence that all homosexual behavior is condemned.

Letter to the Romans

This brings us to the only passage in the Bible that clearly mentions male homosexuality and possibly mentions female homosexuality, Romans 1:24-27. When read in isolation from the context of the entire letter to the Romans and without reference to the context of ancient Mediterranean cultures, the passages could be interpreted to condemn all homosexuality. However, if they are read in the context of Paul's entire letter and the cultural milieu of Paul's time, a different conclusion emerges.

> Therefore God gave them over in the lusts of their hearts to impurity, that their bodies might be dishonored among them. For they exchanged the truth of God for a lie, and worshiped and served the creature rather than the Creator, who is blessed forever.
> Amen.

> For this reason God gave them over to degrading [*atimia*] passions; for their women exchanged the natural function for that which is unnatural [*para physis*], and in the same way also the men abandoned the natural function of the woman and burned in their desire towards one another, men with men committing indecent [*aschemosyne*] acts and receiving in their own persons the due penalty of their error.
> — Romans 1:24-27

Richard Hays, Professor of New Testament at Duke Divinity School, argues that Romans 1 clearly condemns homosexuality, but Paul's intent is to give a diagnosis of the human condition, with homosexuality one example of behavior Paul believes is contrary to God's natural created order. According to Hays, Paul's intent is not to outline a code of sexual ethics, but to use homosexuality as an example of conduct he believes is offensive. This is similar to the situation in 1 Corinthians 11:14, in which, during a discussion of the context of proper worship, Paul mentions that it is against nature (*physis*) for men to have long hair. Yet, 1 Corinthians 11 is seldom seen as an explicit condemnation of all men with long hair, given the context.

Ancient ethnocentrism. Culture shaped the ancient Mediterranean world's understanding of homosexuality: an understanding that is scientifically incorrect. Anthropologists recognize that a culture will generally regard its habits and customs as being natural, and consider the habits and customs of others unnatural. This stems from an ethnocentric understanding of what is natural: habits and customs that have been practiced since birth will always seem natural. For example, Americans consider it natural for a woman to cover her breasts with clothing when in public,

given their supposedly inherent erotic quality. In some Micronesian societies women do not feel obligated to cover their breasts
but, instead, take great care to hide the inside of their knees, for
the area is considered to be highly erotic, whereas breasts are
not.[51] What is natural in some Micronesian societies seems
strange and unnatural to Americans. Similarly, Paul's mention of
male hair length in the context of proper worship in 1 Corinthians 11:14 is culturally pre-
scribed and is, therefore, not a
clear condemnation of men with
long hair. Likewise, on the basis
of the mistaken and ethnocentric
view that what is typical for a
culture is also natural, Paul's
mention of homosexuality in
Romans is also culture-bound. If Hays is correct in his view that
Paul mentioned homosexuality as an example to illustrate his
point, and that the example is based on ethnocentrism, Romans 1
cannot be seen as a clear condemnation of homosexuality.

> Does not even nature *[physis]*
> itself teach you that if a man has
> long hair, it is a dishonor
> *[atimia]* to him, but if a woman
> has long hair, it is a glory to her?
> For her hair is given to her for
> a covering. — 1 Corinthians 11:14-15

Unnatural or unusual. Robert Gagnon argues that Paul understood and used the term *physis*, "nature," to mean the natural
world, not cultural preferences.[52] He argues that Paul specifically
focused on genitals to determine that homosexuality is unnatural:
"Paul in effect argues that even pagans who have no access to the
book of Leviticus should know that same-sex eroticism is 'contrary to nature' because the primary sex organs fit male to female,
not female to female or male to male."[53] Gagnon's view of what
Paul considers "natural" creates an interesting situation in that
homosexuality is widely found in nature,[54] a fact Gagnon does
not acknowledge.[55] Thus, according to Gagnon's argument, nature itself acts in a way that is unnatural, even though by definition that is impossible.

It is significant that modern Bibles have Paul saying that homosexual attractions are "unnatural." As mentioned, the Greek
words used to describe "unnatural" acts, *para physis*, are based on
the same word Paul uses to discuss male hair length in 1 Corinthians 11:14. Paul's use of *physis* to argue that long hair in men is

against "nature" simply reflects an ethnocentric view. He is saying that long hair in men is not the custom, it is atypical or unusual. Likewise, Paul's use of *para physis* in the context of homosexuality is grounded in Jewish ethnocentrism. Homosexuality
was not considered appropriate or typical behavior for Jews. It
was a behavior that other people engaged in, but one that was
not consistent with Jewish purity concerns. According to Boswell,
the translation of *para physis* as "atypical" or "unusual" is consistent with Paul's usage of those words elsewhere.[56] For example,
scholars note that *para physis* is also used to describe God's behavior in Romans 11:24.[57] If *para physis* means immoral, then we
must conclude that God acted immorally, contrary to the Judeo-
Christian understanding of God. Clearly, to describe something
as *para physis* does not imply a moral judgment.[58]

If *para physis* is defined as "atypical" or "unusual," then Romans 1:26 may not actually refer to lesbianism at all. Instead, the
passage simply refers to female sexual behavior that was uncommon in the Jewish context. For example, Leviticus 18:19 re-
stricts a female from having sex during her menstrual period.
Thus, Romans 1:26 could simply be a commentary on women
who violate that prohibition.[59] An argument against this interpretation is that Paul continues by stating "and in the same way also
the men abandoned the natural function of the woman and
burned in their desire towards one another." However, Paul may
simply be stating that just as females engaged in sexual behavior
that is atypical, so did the men. For Daniel Helminiak this is possible because "a figure as important, sex-negative and homophobic as Saint Augustine did not think Romans 1:26 referred to lesbian sex. And there is ongoing discussion among scholars today
on this very point."[60]

Immoral or improper. William Countryman argues that Paul's
mention of homosexuality in Romans 1:24-27 carries no moral
connotations, but instead focuses on purity concerns.[61] This argument is strengthened by other terms used in Paul's discussion
that imply social disapproval rather than ethical or moral viola-
tions. For example, Paul refers to "degrading (*atimia*) passions"
and "indecent (*aschemosyne*) acts." In 2 Corinthians 6:8 and 11:21

Paul says that he is *atimia* because of his passion for following Jesus, while in 1 Corinthians 11:14 he states it is *atimia* for men to have long hair. Based on his writings, it is clear that Paul uses the term for things that are socially unacceptable, unusual, dishonorable, or not highly valued. Thus, interpreting *atimia* as a moral condemnation is inconsistent with Paul's use of the word. Likewise, *aschemosyne* implies something that is unseemly. In 1 Corinthians 13:5 Paul uses it in the context of love, to suggest that "love does not act *unbecomingly*," while in 1 Corinthians 12:23 it refers to genitals. This clearly indicates that no moral connotation is implied, given that Paul's terms refer to public opinion and social considerations; he avoids using words that imply moral considerations. This is reminiscent of Leviticus 20:13 where the author uses a term that simply implies a purity violation (*to'evah*) instead of a moral one (*zimmah*). In fact, whenever aspects of homosexuality are mentioned in the Bible, the terms used relate to purity or social concerns, not moral ones.

Romans in context. Additional evidence for this view comes from the context of Romans. In Romans, Paul writes to the believers in Rome, both Gentile and Jewish; the latter held themselves in high regard due to their heritage. When one reads Romans 1:24-27 in the context of the entire letter it becomes evident that Paul's concern is not with homosexuality but with the debate among early Christians about those of Jewish heritage being favored over Gentiles. Paul addresses this issue in other letters, including Galatians.

In the first few chapters of the Letter to the Romans Paul is setting up his argument to impress upon the Jews that the purity and holiness codes of the Jewish tradition are no longer relevant.[62] After making his introductory comments, Paul highlights a variety of behaviors that are condemned for one reason or another in the Old Testament. Paul establishes that people have turned from God and engaged in idolatry, indecency, and other socially unacceptable ways that were common practice in Rome. In so doing, he gains the attention of the Jewish believers and humbles the Gentile ones. As such, Paul uses homoerotic acts as an example of Gentile impurity. Helminiak argues that

At this point Paul appears to be sympathizing with the common Jewish feeling that the Gentile culture is unclean, the Gentiles are dirty. It sounds like Paul is taking part in a petty name-calling bout. He seems to be playing a game of we're-better-than-you. In fact, that's just what is happening. Paul is quoting Jewish prejudice precisely to counter and reject it.[63]

Robert Gagnon supports Helminiak's argument that Paul is attempting to elicit a visceral response by the Jews toward Gentiles.[64]

In chapter 2 Paul turns the table on the Jewish believers by pointing out that the Jews do the very same things for which the Gentiles are condemned: thus, not only are the Gentiles deserving of God's wrath, but so are the Jews. Paul is establishing that the Jewish believers are not better than the Gentile ones. However, in chapter 3 Paul reassures the believers that while all stand in God's judgment, faith is able to reconcile people to God, regardless of ancestry. He furthers this argument in chapter 4 by highlighting that the traditional Jewish symbols of righteousness or acceptance by God, circumcision and adherence to the Old Testament laws, are meaningless. The important thing, according to Paul in chapters 5 and 6, is that both the Jewish and Gentile believers have been reconciled to God by faith. As such, he encourages them in chapters 7 and 8 to focus on God and not on matters pertaining to the flesh, telling the believers that they will be able to overcome immoral behavior through God's help.

Paul then turns his attention to the Jewish unbelievers in chapters 9 and 10, reminding the believers that having Jewish ancestry does not mean that God holds them in higher regard than non-Jews. Instead, Paul highlights how the Jewish people had turned from God and were not living by faith as were some Gentiles. After humbling the Jewish believers, Paul turns his attention back to the Gentile believers in chapter 11, encouraging them to not be arrogant about their adopted status as God's heirs at the expense of the non-believing Jews. Then, in chapters 12 and 13, Paul reminds all believers to be humble, recognizing that they are equals, and that they should help and encourage one another: they should humbly engage in behavior that is honorable and does not encourage others to stumble. As such, in chapter 14, Paul reminds the Jewish believers that the old purity regulations that the Jews and Gentiles fought over are unimportant: "I know and am convinced in the Lord Jesus that nothing is unclean in itself; but to him who thinks anything to be unclean, to him it is unclean."[65] Finally, before making his closing comments, Paul once again encourages the Gentile and Jewish believers to live in harmony, encouraging one another as fellow believers.

From the context of the letter we see that Paul's comments in Romans 1:24-27 are simply one part of his larger argument. The intent of his comment on homosexuality was not to make a moral condemnation, but to use it as an example of a behavior for which the Jewish people looked down on the Gentiles: from the Jewish perspective it was unseemly, not socially acceptable, and against Jewish purity considerations. Daniel Helminiak argues that "Paul structures his Letter to the Romans so that he can win the favor of both the Jewish and Gentile Christians. He tries to appeal to both while keeping them in harmony with one another."[66] The notion that Paul was attempting to condemn homosexuality is refuted by his own comments in Romans 14:14, that *nothing* is unclean in and of itself. In Romans, Paul dismisses the purity concerns and restrictions of male same-sex behavior found in Leviticus. He acknowledges that homosexuality violates Jewish social norms and decency standards, but, given his use of words that carry no moral connotations, he acknowledges that homosexuality, in and of itself, is not immoral. Thus, those who use Romans 1:24-27 to condemn homosexuality are taking the passage out of the context of the letter.

Some evangelical leaders use Romans 1 as "proof" that homosexuality is a choice.[67] For example, Paul says the men *abandoned* the natural use of the woman and instead lusted after other men. They argue that this implies men who *chose* to sleep with other men *instead* of women, in the sense that they once preferred women but then switched. However, this statement simply does not describe many homosexuals, including myself. Richard Hays argues that the passage is simply referencing the "fallen condition of the pagan world" and that it is not referring to individual life-decisions, an interpretation that seems consistent with the context of the passage. Thus, Romans 1 should also not be used as a statement that homosexuality is a choice.

Additional considerations

We now have the cultural and historical basis for understanding what the Bible does and does not say about homosexuality. We have also addressed every passage in the Bible that is said to discuss aspects of homosexuality. The results do not support the evangelical opinion that the Bible is clear in its condemnation of homosexuality. This leads us to several additional considerations.

What did Jesus say?

First, while Jesus discusses adultery, he does not mention homosexuality. Instead, Jesus was more concerned with wealth, justice, and even demonic possession. Robert Gagnon argues that Jesus' silence on homosexuality is evidence that he condemned the practice. Gagnon explains why he believes that Jesus was silent on the subject: "The obvious answer is that Jesus did not encounter any openly homosexual people in his ministry and therefore had no need to call anyone to repentance for homosexual conduct."[68] Of course, this argument simply assumes that Jesus believed homosexuality was sinful and ignores that it is possible, based on the historical context, that the Roman centurion in Matthew 8 and Luke 7 engaged in same-sex intercourse, and that the sick servant he held in high regard was his sexual partner.[69]

Gagnon also mentions that "Since Jesus upheld the law, his silence on the issue of homosexuality indicates his acceptance of the teachings of Hebrew Scripture, which as we have seen is unanimous in its rejection of same-sex intercourse."[70] However, the only specific examples of same-sex behavior in the Old Testament are in the context of sexually violating strangers and temple prostitution, both of which would be considered wrong even without their homosexual aspects. Included in the scripture Gagnon suggests Jesus would have used to condemn homosexuality is the story of Sodom's destruction:

Jesus' likely awareness of the homoerotic dimension to the sins of Sodom is confirmed not only by the presence of Gen 19:4-11 in his scriptures but also by the fact that the two most prominent Jewish writers of the first century C.E., Philo and Josephus, interpreted Gen 19:4-11 to refer explicitly to homosexual acts.[71]

Notwithstanding, Gagnon fails to demonstrate that Jesus was aware of this interpretation, which is first evident in the writings of Philo,[72] who was probably contemporary with Jesus, while Josephus, who lived between AD 37–100, would not have written anything until long after Jesus' death. When Jesus refers to Sodom it is in the context of inhospitality to strangers.[73] Thus, Gagnon's assertion that Jesus would have condemned homosexuality based on the Sodom account is unsupported.

Silence is condemning

Some evangelicals argue that homosexuality is sinful because the Bible does not have any positive images of it.[74] However, many biblical scholars have argued that in the original Hebrew the Old Testament does present positive images of homosexual behavior.[75] Boswell indicates that the relationships of Saul and David, David and Jonathan, and Ruth and Naomi "were celebrated throughout the Middle Ages in both ecclesiastical and popular literature as examples of extraordinary devotion, sometimes with distinctly erotic overtones."[76] Yaron Peleg comments that David and Jonathan's relationship is based on the ancient Mediterranean heterosexual model, with Jonathan taking the subservient female role and David the dominant masculine role. Peleg further notes that "the frequent reference, manipulation, and substitution of gender roles in this story draws attention to their very existence and carries a clear sexual meaning,"[77] explaining why David and Jonathan are often seen as lovers.

Regardless, many things not mentioned in the Bible are nonetheless considered moral by most. The Bible does not mention healing by doctors, which does not make it wrong. Some groups believe all healing must be based on faith because that is the only type of healing presented in the Bible. Birth control is not discussed positively in the Bible, but is not considered wrong by many, the Roman Catholic church excluded. There are no clear-cut positive images of left-handed people in the Bible and many allusions to the left side as being evil.[78] Left-handed people were formerly considered inherently evil and burned at the stake for their orientation, but Christians today accept them, although many other cultures and religions do not.[79] The argument based on silence does not stand up to logical scrutiny.

God made Eve, not Steve

A third argument is that because God only created heterosexuals, homosexuality is wrong. The argument is similar to the argument from silence. It is based on the premise that God created Adam and Eve, but not "Adam and Steve." This is equivalent to stating that because God only made Adam and Eve, presumably Semites, those of other ethnic groups are outside of God's creation.

The "Adam and Steve" argument relies on a literal interpretation of the Bible, specifically of the creation account. The assumption is that 6,000 years ago God created two humans; they were heterosexual and we all should be as well. This argument makes little sense but is consistent with the evangelical worldview. Focus on the Family's booklet *When a Loved One Says, "I'm Gay"* tells the story of John Paulk's conversion "to Christianity from homosexuality."

> One day this pastor asked if he could visit John. . . . So, the pastor came to visit, and their conversation led right into a discussion of the Scriptures. But, instead of talking about Romans 1 or 1 Corinthians 6, this pastor began talking about the first two chapters of Genesis and God's original plan for man and woman. Then the pastor read Genesis 1:26, "And God made man in His own image. In the image of God, He created them male and female." Then they read Genesis 2:18, "Then the Lord God said, It is not good for the man to be alone. I will make a helper suitable for him, And he created woman." It was one of those divinely empowered moments when the scales fell off John's eyes. He realized that homosexuality was not God's intent for him. Within weeks, John became a Chris-

tian, and this pastor and his wife supported him in leaving homosexuality behind.[80]

From this story we see the importance of the literal Adam and Eve story to many evangelicals in condemning homosexuality. We also see a somewhat dishonest use of scripture. Genesis 2:18 actually says "Then the LORD God said, 'It is not good for the man to be alone; I will make him a helper suitable for him. '" This verse does not say that God then created a woman. The following verse states that in the search for a suitable helper, God first created animals. However, none of the animals were seen as being suitable for the man, so God then took one of Adam's ribs and made Eve. This passage creates trouble for biblical literalists who view God as omniscient and omnipotent because it shows God engaging in trial and error to create a companion for Adam. In any case, the context of the passage indicates that only another human is a suitable companion for a human: an animal is not. Certainly a female would have to be created for procreation, but that does not imply all people have to be heterosexual.

Evangelical leaders believe that this "literally true" story indicates that God created woman to be man's companion. For example, Richard Hays observes that

> from Genesis 1 onwards, scripture affirms repeatedly that God has made man and woman for one another and that our sexual desires rightly find fulfillment within heterosexual marriage (see, for instance, Mark 10:2-9, 1 Thess. 4:3-8, 1 Cor. 7:1-9, Eph. 5:21-33, Heb. 13:4).[81]

Hays says scripture *repeatedly* affirms that our sexual desires only find fulfillment within heterosexual marriage, but he only cites the New Testament. The Old Testament actually has no prohibition on a man having sex with a woman outside of a marital relationship, so long as she is not a temple prostitute nor married. Nonetheless, evangelical leaders believe that any man who takes another man as his companion is violating God's intent and is sinning, as is any woman who takes a woman as her companion. The assumption is that because the first people were heterosexual, all people must be heterosexual: God did not give Adam and

Eve any genes or other factors that could naturally cause homosexuality in subsequent generations.

Once again, this argument from silence is based on how evangelical leaders view God and scripture. From an anthropological perspective, the Adam and Eve story explains why the different sexes exist, why humans mate with and marry other humans (usually a man with at least one woman), and it helps to justify male dominance in that particular culture: women were created specifically for man's benefit, not vice versa. There are myths in most other cultures that explain these same things in different ways. There is no scientific evidence to believe that the Genesis story is literally true and plenty of evidence to indicate that it is not. There is also no reason to believe it was intended to condemn homosexuality.

Evangelicals and scripture

Before we discuss evangelical views on whether or not homosexuality is an inborn characteristic and the evangelical response to same-sex marriage, let us review evangelical leaders' statements and conclusions about the biblical passages discussed above. As mentioned earlier, Jerry Falwell presents Romans 1:24-27 and asserts that "other similar verses abound" throughout the Bible, when they do not. Don Schmierer argues that the Bible clearly condemns homosexuality, based on Romans 1:26-27, 1 Corinthians 6:9, Leviticus 18:22 and Jude 1:7, and that any suggestion to the contrary is simply a valiant effort to reinterpret scripture.[82] Schmierer's comment is interesting, in that no biblical translation prior to 1952 translated 1 Corinthians 6:9 to condemn all homosexuals. Contrary to Schmierer's view, it is actually modern evangelical leaders who reinterpret the Bible to make it fit their views on sexuality. Pat Robertson inserts his own views into Leviticus 18:22 to make it condemn lesbians. Robertson also reminds his readers that God utterly rejects homosexuals and that execution was an appropriate judgment for them in the Old Testament.[83] This is a serious matter in view of hate-crimes against homosexuals.

Pat Robertson's influence at the Christian Broadcasting Network is apparent in writings from others in the organization, including Scott Ross. After accepting Robertson's revised translation of the Leviticus passages, Ross expands on 1 Corinthians 6:9-11:

> 'Don't fool yourselves; people who are immoral, or who worship idols or are adulterers or homosexual perverts, or who steal or are greedy or are drunkards or who slander others or are thieves, none of these will possess God's Kingdom.' (1 Corinthians 6.9). Lest I am accused of discrimination, notice that it is not only homosexuals who are under judgment. I wonder how long it will be before we have a demand for equal rights for drunks? A greed demonstration? A slander protest? And a parade for thieves?[84]

Ross' "parade for thieves" analogy highlights an important point in his perspective, which he shares with many other evangelical leaders: he believes that homosexuality is not biological in nature and is equivalent to criminal behavior. Consider Ross' statement: "While some say that one can be born a homosexual, the Bible indicates that an individual has a free choice and chooses to be a practicing homosexual."[85] Ross confuses the distinction between an individual's sexual *orientation* and sexual *behavior*. It is true that one can choose to be a practicing homosexual, as opposed to a celibate homosexual, but this has no bearing whatsoever on the inborn orientation.

Not all evangelicals, however, engage in such rhetoric and some even criticize the views and statements presented above. Tony Campolo expresses concern over such statements in *Speaking My Mind:*

> Beyond any arguments over what the Bible says or does not say about homosexual behavior is my concern about the meanness and ugly, untrue rhetoric that gay men and lesbians have to endure from many Christians. ...

> I am not saying that we in the church have deliberately condoned violence against homosexual people. But there is little doubt in my mind that misguided persons have taken some

things that preachers have said in the church, in the name of preaching the gospel, as permission to do terrible and evil things to gay men and lesbians.[86]

Campolo demonstrates that, even if a person opposes homosexuality, he or she can extend love and compassion to them by working to ensure their safety and well-being.

Walter Wink, professor of biblical interpretation at Auburn Theological Seminary and United Methodist minister, highlights that while many evangelicals appeal to the Bible to condemn homosexuality, they ignore what it says on other matters, including the biblical command that a man marry his brother's childless widow.[87] Thus, we see that many evangelical leaders contradict themselves by appealing to a literal interpretation of the Bible when condemning homosexuality, but ignoring it on matters that directly affect many within their churches. Wink asks "What makes the one [homosexuality] so much greater a sin than the other [divorce], especially considering the fact that Jesus never even mentioned homosexuality but explicitly condemned divorce?"[88] Data from the United Nations indicate that the United States, seen as the stronghold of evangelicalism, may have the highest divorce rate in the world.[89] Research also indicates that divorce rates are actually higher in "Bible-belt" states than in the more liberal states:[90] they are also higher among conservative Protestant denominations, including evangelicals, as compared with mainline Protestants, Catholics, and Jews.[91] Thus, the groups most likely to condemn homosexuals and claim a literal adherence to the Bible are the ones most likely to divorce, contrary to Jesus' explicit teachings on the matter.

The black and white fades to gray

Evangelical leaders boldly proclaim that the Bible is clear in its condemnation of homosexuality. However, we find that the promised black and white biblical condemnations of homosexuality have faded to gray. In short, the Old Testament says absolutely nothing (positive or negative) about general homosexuality. The three New Testament passages supposedly condemning homosexuality are very difficult to translate due to the cultural, historical, and scriptural contexts. The key words used by Paul and generally translated as condemning homosexuals are either not found in other early Greek writings or have a wide range of possible meanings. Purity or social concerns, rather than moral ones, are the foundation of Paul's view of homosexuality. As Bruce Bawer notes,

> the point that emerges, then, from a careful study of the Biblical passages that are invoked in attacks on homosexuality is that one cannot divorce them from their historical and textual settings. The unfortunate fact is that anti-gay bigots have had their own motives for wrenching certain lines out of context, with the consequence that the idea of homosexuality as a violation of Christian teachings has in recent centuries become deeply ingrained in the minds of most people in the Western world.[92]

Many evangelical leaders condemn homosexuals, even in the absence of scriptural, historical, or logical justification. There is considerable gray on this subject, much more than there is for divorce, lending money at interest, overeating, or being wealthy.

---

[1] Steve Kangas (1999, 21).

[2] Don Schmierer (1999).

[3] For example, see Exodus 22:25, Leviticus 25:36-37 and Deuteronomy 23:19.

[4] Jerry Falwell (no date).

[5] James Dobson (1997, 514-516).

[6] Joseph Cardinal Ratzinger (1994, 41).

[7] John J. McNeill (1994, 54). Biblical references for Jesus' comments about Sodom come from Matthew 10:15 and Luke 10:12.

[8] 2 Peter 2:7.

[9] Philip J. King and Lawrence E. Stager (2001, 186). Also see Bruce J. Malina (2001, 27-56) for a discussion of honor in ancient Mediterranean.

[10] Leviticus 19:33-34. Also see Exodus 22:21.

[11] Louis Crompton (2003, 39).

[12] For example, see Timothy J. Dailey (2004, 2) and James Dobson (1997, 515).

[13] See Jude 6 and Genesis 6:2.

[14] Timothy J. Dailey (2004, 2).

[15] Biblical passages include Deuteronomy 12:31, 14:3-8, 17:1, 18:9-14 and 1 Kings 14:23-24, respectively. Also see Spiro Zodhiates (1994, 2380). The term is also generically used in Proverbs (for example 6:16-19 and 24:9) to represent evil-doers and in Psalms 88:8 to represent those who are deformed, which violated the Hebrew purity code.

[16] Alice Ogden Bellis (1999, 129).

[17] Robert A. J. Gagnon (2001, 95).

[18] God declares Sodom will be destroyed in Genesis 18:20-33, while the attempted rape occurs in Genesis 19:4-11.

[19] Daniel A. Helminiak (2000, 49-50).

[20] Louis Crompton (2003, 34).

[21] Pat Robertson (2001).

[22] Daniel A. Helminiak (2000, 59-60).

[23] Saul M. Olyan (1994) and Daniel Boyarin (1995).

[24] Robert A. J. Gagnon (2001, 348).

[25] Ibid (345).

[26] Ibid (135).

[27] L. William Countryman (1988, 30-32, 110-123). Also see Daniel A. Helminiak (2000, 47).

[28] Daniel A. Helminiak (2000, 47).

[29] Some scholars interpret to'evah as relating to idolatry. If we accept this definition then, as J. D. Douglas (1982, 488) explains, the Leviticus condemnations "apply to homosexual activity conducted in the course of idolatry, but not necessarily more widely than that." Thus, regardless of whether one defines to'evah as a purity or idolatry violation, the result is the same: the Leviticus passages do not condemn male homosexuality.

[30] Examples of zimmah include Leviticus 18:17, Job 31:11, Ezekiel 16:27 and Ezekiel 22:9, 11. The behaviors discussed in these passages include having sex with a mother and daughter, adultery, incest and sex with foreign prostitutes (not temple prostitutes).

[31] Daniel A. Helminiak (2000, 132).

[32] Leviticus 19:28, 19:19 and 11:7-8, respectively.

[33] John Boswell (1980, 105).

[34] Robert A. J. Gagnon (2001, 63-71)

[35] For example, Timothy J. Dailey (2004, 9-13), James Dobson (1997, 515) and Ronnie W. Floyd (2004, 102-107).

[36] See Matthew 11:8 and Luke 7:25.

[37] Aristotle (1976, 243).

[38] John Boswell (1980, 339).

[39] Ibid (340).

[40] John Boswell (1980, 341) and Daniel A. Helminiak (2000, 109-115).

[41] John Boswell (1980, 350-351) and Dale B. Martin (1996).

[42] Robin Scroggs (1983, 108).

[43] J. D. Douglas (1982, 488).

[44] John Boswell (1980, 346-347).

[45] Ibid (347).

[46] Ibid (347).

[47] Robert A. J. Gagnon (2001, 338). Also see Gordon Robertson (2003).

[48] The original Greek words used in Matthew 8 and Luke 7 (*pais* and *doulos*), indicate that the Roman Centurion's servant may have been a catamite.

[49] Daniel A. Helminiak (2000, 113).

[50] John Boswell (1980, 341).

[51] Martha Ward (2005, 35).

[52] Robert A. J. Gagnon (2001, 256-257).

[53] Ibid (254).

[54] Bruce Bagemihl (1999), Robert Epstein (February 2003), Charles E. Roselli *et al.* (2002) and Dinitia Smith (February 7, 2004).

[55] Gagnon (2001, 180) does include one oblique reference to homosexuality in animals while discussing a passage in Pseudo-Phocylides. Gagnon argues that homosexuality is unnatural because animals do not engage in it, but in the instances where they do practice homosexual behavior it is obviously morally inferior and thus humans are right for condemning it. In his response to Pseudo-Phocylides and throughout his book Gagnon uses circular reasoning in his arguments that homosexuality is wrong by first assuming it is wrong.

[56] John Boswell (1980, 112-113), also see Daniel A. Helminiak (2000, 77-80).

[57] "For if you were cut off from what is by nature a wild olive tree, and were grafted contrary to nature [*para physis*] into a cultivated olive tree, how much more shall these who are the natural branches be grafted into their own olive tree?"

[58] L. William Countryman (1988, 113-114) and Daniel A. Helminiak (2000, 77-83).

[59] Daniel A. Helminiak (2000, 86-90).

[60] Ibid (2000, 87).

[61] L. William Countryman (1988, 117).

[62] L. William Countryman (1988, 110-117) and Daniel A. Helminiak (2000, 92-104).

[63] Daniel A. Helminiak (2000, 76).

[64] Robert A. J. Gagnon (2001, 265).

[65] Romans 14:14.

[66] Daniel A. Helminiak (2000, 101-102).

[67] *The Parsonage* (1999).

[68] Robert A. J. Gagnon (2001, 187).

[69] See Daniel A. Helminiak (1999).

[70] Robert A. J. Gagnon (2001, 191).

[71] Ibid (91).

[72] Louis Crompton (2003, 136).

[73] Matthew 10:15 and Luke 10:12.

[74] Lisa Sowle Cahill (1994, 71).

[75] See Yaron Peleg (2005).

[76] John Boswell (1980, 105).

[77] Yaron Peleg (2005, 188).

[78] For example see Ecclesiastes 10:2 and Matthew 25:33. However, many would consider Ehud in Judges 3 to be a positive image of a left-handed individual because he was a leader in Israel. However, he achieved that position by murdering a king in cold blood, an act that certainly is contrary to "biblical morality."

[79] See Karl G. Heider (2001, 59).

[80] Bob Davies (2002, 33).

[81] Richard B. Hays (1994, 10).

[82] Don Schmierer (1999).

[83] Pat Robertson (2001).

[84] Scott Ross (2003).

[85] Ibid.

[86] Tony Campolo (2004, 70-71).

[87] Walter Wink (1999, 43).

[88] Ibid (41).

[89] United Nations (2001).

[90] Stephanie Coontz (2005, 287).

[91] Norval D. Glenn and Michael Supancic (1984).

[92] Bruce Bawer (1993, 134).

6 GENDER CONFUSION?

Modern scientific research indicates that sexual orientation is largely determined by the time of birth, partly by genetics, but more specifically by hormonal activity in the womb arising from various sources.

— Glenn Wilson and Qazi Rahman[1]

In anthropology courses, I sometimes give unusual but revealing assignments. Once, some of my students were asked to develop questions they could ask homosexual men. Their responses included the standards such as "Do you think you were born this way?" and "When did you realize you were like this?" Then I instructed them not only to ask homosexual men those questions but also to ask heterosexual men the same questions. The students immediately said that would feel stupid asking a heterosexual man if he was born that way, or when he realized he was straight. To the students, it was apparent that people are born heterosexual, for no one ever questions that assumption. We discussed why they thought it would be different for a homosexual. Feeling rather awkward and uncomfortable, my students bravely headed out and completed their assignment.

The results surprised all of us. A typical response from homosexual informants was as expected, "I was born this way." The response from heterosexuals was not. The informants, usually males between the ages of 18 and 25, laughed, did not take the questions seriously, or became defensive and somewhat upset that anyone would seemingly "challenge" their heterosexuality. One student observed that the same questions started long, meaningful conversations with homosexuals but short, uncomfortable, and defensive exchanges with heterosexuals. The students concluded that while society accepts the inborn nature of sexuality, it does so only for heterosexuals. The double standard is also revealed by the scientific search for the cause(s) of homosexuality: very few scientists are working on the causes of heterosexuality.

Nonetheless, the search for specific cause(s) of homosexuality continues and many possibilities have been suggested: genetics, prenatal hormones, bad parenting, peer labeling, being molested as a child, choice, and combinations of these. The cause of homosexuality is an important issue in the debate about marriage for homosexuals. If homosexuality is a learned behavior, then it can be changed and the homosexual who desires to marry and have children has hope. If homosexuality is an inborn orientation, however, then change is unlikely and discrimination becomes an issue: why should certain civil rights and privileges be withheld from some people simply because of their biological characteristics?

It is not surprising that most scientists favor biological explanations, while most evangelical leaders prefer social ones that describe homosexuality as a learned behavior, a view that is consistent with their interpretation of the Bible. For example, Don Schmierer says

> Many people, even many Christians are surprised to learn that no solid scientific evidence exists to indicate that there is a homosexual gene. The complex causes of homosexuality occur over the period of time from birth through adolescence. Later in life, as these factors converge, they play a strategic role in the choices people make involving their sexual relations.[2]

Schmierer's statement not only simplifies genetics but demonstrates an ignorance of basic biology, especially about how biological characteristics are determined.

Scientists base their understanding of genetic inheritance on the work of Gregor Mendel. In 1856 Mendel, a monk from what is now the Czech Republic, began a series of experiments that led to the discovery of the basic laws of genetics. His experiments on pea plants demonstrated that genes determine many of our biological characteristics. However, more recent experiments show that many biological traits are not the result of only one gene. Many such traits, including skin color, are *polygenic*: multiple genes, sometimes influenced by the environment, determine how the trait is expressed. If sexuality is polygenic, as some scientists have recently indicated, it would make identifying the responsible genes difficult.[3] Thus, one would not necessarily expect to find a gene responsible for homosexuality because it could be caused by the combination of many genes, and it could be difficult to identify the right combination of some 25,000 genes in the human body.[4] Therefore, simply because a homosexual gene has not been found does not mean that homosexuality is not genetic. The trait could result from the cumulative effects of many genes.

Schmierer and other evangelical leaders also incorrectly assume that biological traits must necessarily be *entirely* caused by genes; they believe that if a gene is not found for a trait, it is not biological. While genetics is an important factor in determining our biological traits, it is not the only component. The prenatal environment, completely ignored by Schmierer, is an important influence on the development of many biological traits. It explains why identical twins do not have identical fingerprints, even though they have the same genetic code for fingerprints. It also explains why they do not always have the same handedness. Though most people accept that handedness is an inborn biological characteristic, it cannot be entirely genetic because there is not a 100 percent concordance in handedness between pairs of identical twins.[5] Thus, many scientists believe that both genetics and the prenatal environment play a significant role in the development of the trait.[6] The influence of the prenatal environment for twins is different even though they are "womb-mates" (if I may borrow a term from the movie *Zorro: The Gay Blade*). The twins do not absorb nutrition or hormones in exactly the same measure. However, the differences in the prenatal environment are much less in twins than in non-twin siblings, an important distinction, as we will see.

Of interest, a number of studies demonstrate that homosexuals are more likely to be left-handed than heterosexuals.[7] This does not imply that all left-handers are homosexual, just that homosexuals tend to be left-handed much more often than heterosexuals. This association can be explained by theories about hormones in the prenatal environment, but not by social factors. For example, it appears that both traits are influenced by hormones released between the second and sixth months of pregnancy which affect the brain.[8] The hormones influence both sexuality and handedness, increasing the likelihood that homosexuals will be left-handed more often than heterosexuals.

Homosexuality may also be epigenetic in its origin. Epigenetic traits tend to be dichotomous and are expressed only if the combined genetic and environmental "loading" passes a threshold level, which can vary from individual to individual. The trait is not manifested if the threshold is not surpassed. It is also possible that homosexuality may be inborn even if it is not genetic: not all biological traits are determined by genes. For example, women are encouraged not to drink alcohol or smoke while pregnant because birth defects, which are non-genetic inborn biological traits, may result from these prenatal influences.

These possibilities illustrate why it is difficult to prove biological explanations for traits like homosexuality. They also demonstrate that human biology is much more complex than the simplistic scenarios offered by evangelical leaders who base their views on incorrect understandings of biological inheritance. When evangelical leaders question the biological basis of homosexuality, claiming that science has never found a gene for it, scientists respond that their argument lacks substance because it demonstrates no understanding of basic biological principles. The equivalent statement would be to proclaim that left-handedness is not biological because scientists have not yet found a gene that completely determines it.

Biology and homosexuality

This brings us to the question of what scientists and evangelical leaders say causes homosexuality. Just as the favored explanation for homosexuality varies between evangelical leaders and scientists, the reasoning behind the respective conclusions also vary. James Dobson acknowledges that homosexuality may be an inborn characteristic, although he quickly dismisses the biological explanations for homosexuality in favor of social ones:

> There could be inheritable tendencies (which does not make homosexuality "involuntary") in some individuals. … It could also result from the presence or absence of hormonal "spik-

ing" that typically occurs before birth. It is more likely to be related to one or more of the following: (1) confusion of role models seen in parents, including, but not limited to, a dominant mother and a weak or absent father; (2) serious family dysfunction that wounds and damages the child; (3) early sexual abuse; (4) the influence of an older homosexual during a critical period of adolescence; (5) conscious choice and cultivation; and/or (6) homosexual experimentation, such as mutual masturbatory activity, by boys in early adolescence.[9]

Dobson's comment that even if homosexuality is inherited, that does not make it involuntary indicates that he defines homosexuality solely as a behavior, not an orientation.

Dobson's objections

In *Solid Answers* Dobson presents four reasons for denying that homosexuality has biological causes. He relates those reasons to genetics, natural selection, the Bible, and his view of God. Underlying his arguments are several important assumptions which he and other evangelical leaders make on this question.

Genetics. Dobson argues that if homosexuality results specifically from genetics, then identical twins would always be concordant in their sexual orientation.[10] Dobson is correct that if homosexuality is *specifically* (that is, entirely) genetically determined, then the sexual orientation of identical twins would always be similar. Dobson overlooks the fact that our biological traits derive from the interplay of our genetic code and environmental influences. Consequently, there is no reason to expect that identical twins would have identical sexual orientations. However, if homosexuality is caused *partly* by genetics, we would expect similar sexual orientation to occur more frequently in identical twins than in fraternal twins and non-twin siblings.

Twin studies: Michael Bailey and Richard Pillard examined this question in one of the most informative studies on the causes of homosexuality.[11] They studied the rates of homosexuality among male identical twins, fraternal twins, and non-twin siblings, including adopted siblings. At least one of the individuals in each category was homosexual. The results are fascinating: if one identical twin is homosexual, the concordance rate for his twin brother is 52 percent.[12] For fraternal twins, the concordance rate is 22 percent; and among non-twin biological siblings and non-twin adopted siblings it drops to about 10 percent.[13] Dobson and others claim that this study conclusively refutes a genetic cause for homosexuality, because the concordance rate of that orientation in identical twins is not 100 percent. Bailey and Pillard's study, however, actually provides evidence that *both* genetics and the prenatal environment *are* major causal factors, while the social environment is *not*.

The significantly higher concordance rates for identical compared to fraternal twins, and for fraternal twins compared to non-twin siblings, indicate that both genetics and the prenatal environment play significant roles in the development of homosexuality. If genetics had no role whatsoever, we would see no difference in the rates between identical and fraternal twins because they would not have significantly different social or prenatal environments. While twins may not receive nutrition or hormones in equal measure, there is no evidence that identical twins receive more or less nutrition or hormones than fraternal twins. However, the concordance rate of identical twins is more than twice that of fraternal twins. Neither the social nor prenatal environment can explain this significant difference. The only variable at play is the different genetic code of fraternal twins compared to the identical genetic code of identical twins. This demonstrates that genes are important factors in determining sexuality.

The results also show that other factors are important in the development of homosexuality. The comparison of fraternal twins and non-twin siblings reveals a significant difference, even though both groups have equivalent levels of genetic variability. The principal difference between them is the prenatal environment. Fraternal twins share the prenatal environment, they are womb-mates, while non-twin siblings are not. The fact that the homosexual concordance rate for fraternal twins is more than twice that of non-twin siblings shows that the prenatal environment is also a significant factor in the development of homosexuality.

Bailey and Pillard's study provides evidence that homosexuality is biological, the result of both genetic and prenatal influences. While Dobson does not explicitly deny this, his argument is based *solely* on a genetic cause. He dismisses genes as the *sole* cause of homosexuality, as well as the prenatal environment. His insistence that homosexuality is a learned behavior is based on his interpretation of the Bible. Because of this bias Dobson and other evangelical leaders deny the biological causes of homosexuality and discredit Bailey and Pillard's study.

The main evangelical criticism of Bailey and Pillard's study relates to the matters just discussed. Focus on the Family's *Love Won Out* series[14] comments: "Another troubling factor was that only about half of the identical twins examined were both homosexual. For this study to be valid, they would have both needed to be homosexual in every case."[15] In his book *Outrage* Peter Sprigg illustrates this point:

> If you did a study of identical twins, you would find that one hundred percent of black identical twins would be black, one hundred percent of male identical twins would be male, one hundred percent of redheaded identical twins would be redheads, and one hundred percent of blue-eyed identical twins would have blue eyes. Remember, identical twins (known to scientists as "dizygotic," [sic[16]] meaning that they come from the same fertilized egg) have a completely, one hundred percent identical genetic makeup. Therefore, a study showing that 52 percent of the identical twins of homosexuals are also homosexual proves only one thing – that homosexuality is not genetic.[17]

This argument highlights the all-or-nothing mentality for biology held by many evangelical leaders. They incorrectly assume that because some of the identical twins had differing sexual orientations, homosexuality is therefore not genetic.

A number of evangelical publications also criticize Bailey and Pillard's study for lacking a control group. For example, Mike Haley argues:

> Their study had a major flaw: All of their twins grew up together. These researchers failed to compare their findings with

a control group of twins raised apart. If they had, they would have discovered other influencing factors, such how [sic] their family dynamics and their relationships with their parents affected who they were.[18]

This criticism is actually irrelevant to the discussion of whether or not genes play a role in causing homosexuality. If parental relationships and other family dynamics were important factors, then they would have affected the two types of twins in equivalent ways. But because the concordance rates for identical twins and fraternal twins are significantly different, especially when compared to non-twin siblings, there is little reason to believe that social factors had any effects on the study. The only difference between the two types of twins is the level of genetic similarity. Therefore, the finding that identical twins are more likely to both be homosexual illustrates that genes are a causal factor. In addition, there are statistical tests that provide a way of measuring the respective importance of the genetic code, the prenatal environment, and the postnatal environment on the development of a trait such as homosexuality. The statistical analysis from Bailey and Pillard's study reveals that while genes play a significant role in the development of homosexuality, the importance of the postnatal (social) environment as a causal factor was slight to none. Once again, the *only* variable that is different in the comparison between the identical twins and fraternal twins is the genetic code. It is interesting how confidently Haley asserts that "they *would have discovered* other influencing factors" [emphasis added]. There is no evidence to suggest this is the case. The only imaginable possibility that would support this view is if the postnatal environment for identical twins is fundamentally different than the postnatal environment for fraternal twins. However, there is no evidence to support this possibility. Certainly a study that does have a control group of twins raised apart would be interesting, but it is not necessary for demonstrating that homosexuality does have *both* a genetic and non-genetic biological component in its causation. What such a study would contribute is whether or not social factors play a role in how the individual's homosexuality is *expressed*, or if social factors lead to same-sex

behavior for a small minority of those who self-identify as homosexual. Furthermore, contrary to Dobson's assumptions, there is
no solid psychological or sociological evidence that indicates bad
parenting determines or significantly affects a child's sexual orientation.

A second twin study challenges some of the findings in the
Bailey and Pillard's research. Scott Hershberger examines sexual
orientation among twins from Minnesota to establish rates of
homosexuality in the overall population and to determine
whether genetics are important in the development of sexual orientation.[19] Hershberger argues that while sexual orientation appears to be affected by genetics, the "significant genetic effects
were found for self-identified female homosexuality, but not for
male homosexuality, in both the twin and extended family analy-
ses."[20] He also suggests that environmental effects play an important role in determining sexual orientation. However, Hershberger's study has some serious methodological problems.

First, the individuals included in the study were all born between 1936 and 1955. People within this group are generally not
as open about their homosexual orientation as the younger generation. Second, not all of the co-twins participated in the study.
This means that the self-reported sexual orientation was not
available for some of the participants. Instead, Hershberger relied
on the twin's assessment of "the *perceived* sexual orientation of
the co-twin, as well as the *perceived* sexual orientation of non-twin
brothers and sisters"[21] [emphasis added]. The assumption that
each individual knows the other twin's sexual orientation is questionable due to the stigmatized nature of homosexuality and the
reluctance of many to disclose their orientation to others. Third,
the study primarily focuses on unmarried individuals in the
Minnesota Twin Registry, and assumes that they are most likely
to be homosexual. However, this assumption ignores that many
homosexuals born between 1936 and 1955 actually married: in
one national survey, 42 percent of men who identified themselves
as homosexual or bisexual were married to women.[22] Thus, many
homosexuals who married women were not included in this
study. In addition, the sexual orientation reports based on the

perceptions of a sibling are flawed because the co-twin could be assumed to be heterosexual simply because he or she was married.

A similar issue arises in a study of Australian twins by Bailey and his colleagues.[23] The same general pattern of concordance for homosexuality among twins that Bailey and Pillard found in the earlier study emerged, although the frequencies are considerably lower than in the study based on American twins. The lower frequencies, suggested by Stanton Jones and Mark Yarhouse as evidence against a partial genetic basis for homosexuality,[24] are not surprising given the greater acceptance of homosexuality in the United States as compared to Australia. Considering that homosexuality is a stigmatized condition, the influence of cultural attitudes should not be dismissed when interpreting data derived from an informant's self-disclosure.

In another study by Bailey and his colleagues, there were concordance rates of 48 percent for female identical twins both being homosexual, 16 percent for female fraternal twins and 14 percent for non-twin biological sisters.[25] However, evangelical psychologists Stanton Jones and Mark Yarhouse argue that these results are not valid due to yet another female twin study.[26] The latter, which focuses on twins reared apart, suggests that the concordance rate for female identical twins is zero.[27] That study, however, was based on only four sets of twins, so the results are not statistically reliable. In order to conduct a valid statistical analysis the sample should include at least 30 sets. The interpretation of Jones and Yarhouse, that these results contradict the other studies, arises from the small sample which cannot generate a scientifically acceptable result.

One interesting conclusion in a study of female twins by Bailey and Benishay[28] is that there may be separate factors that cause male homosexuality and female homosexuality. Given that this finding is consistent with the statements of James Dobson and others who focus on social causes for homosexuality, it is surprising that Focus on the Family uses it to denounce the biological findings.[29] Regardless, there is no reason to believe that the genes would affect males and females in the same manner, even if homosexuality is entirely genetic. What causes an individual to be attracted to a male may be different than what causes an individual to be attracted to a female; this could explain why some people are attracted to both.

The research on twins comprise two of the five studies suggesting that homosexuality is biological that are criticized in the *Love Won Out* series from Focus on the Family. A third study, relating to differences in the inner ear of heterosexual and homosexual females, has garnered little attention from the scientific community and does not require further comment here.

Family studies: The fourth study highlighted by the series focuses on the X chromosome as the possible source for male homosexuality. Dean Hamer and Peter Copeland found that a higher than expected percentage of homosexual brothers had the same genetic sequence in a particular region of the X chromosome, although it was not associated with any particular known gene on the chromosome.[30] The conclusion is that this region of the chromosome may be important in the development of a homosexual orientation, a conclusion that has since been supported by additional research.[31] The study is criticized on three fronts by Focus on the Family.[32] First, they argue that a Canadian research team failed to replicate the study. This is an important objection and a point that requires further scientific investigation. Second, they argue that the authors confined their search to the X chromosome because their studies seemed "to reveal a disproportionately high number of male homosexuals on the mothers' sides of the family."[33] Why does Focus on the Family object to this? If a biological trait is found in a higher proportion of males on the mother's side of the family than on the father's side, it is normally the result of the X chromosome, which males inherit only from the mother. Thus, Hamer and Copeland's focus on the X chromosome is warranted. Finally, Focus on the Family questions the statistical significance of the results, which rely on an estimate that only two percent of the population is homosexual, stating that if a different estimate is used the results are no longer statistically significant. This is questionable: Focus on the Family repeatedly estimates the number of homosexuals in the American population at about two percent.[34] Notwithstanding, Hamer and Copeland's study is of interest, but certainly not conclusive about the role of the X chromosome in the development of male homosexuality.

Brain research: The neurohormonal theory of sexual differentiation suggests that the brain in all humans begins as "female" and must then be "masculinized" in males.[35] This is accomplished by exposure to testosterone during critical periods of fetal development during the second trimester of pregnancy: specific regions of the brain may have different critical periods. In the absence of testosterone or other androgens, or if the brain does not have the receptors to absorb the available testosterone, the brain remains unaltered.

The anterior hypothalamus is a small region at the base of the brain that is known to affect sexual impulses. Although the brain masculinizes, the anterior hypothalamus may remain unaltered due to the timing of the hormonal release or a lack of androgen receptors in the region, explaining male homosexuality.[36] In addition, if the hormones are not present in sufficient amounts, an intermediary orientation may arise, explaining bisexuality. Likewise, androgens found in females may influence the development of the female brain. If androgens are released in significant amounts, the anterior hypothalamus may masculinize, leading to a homosexual orientation in females.

The neurohormonal theory has received considerable support from studies on animals, including ferrets, rats, hamsters, dogs, and pigs in which testosterone levels were manipulated and the resulting offspring demonstrated homosexual behavior.[37] Thus, the neurohormonal theory, which incorporates the role of the genes in the production of hormones, is one of the leading views on the development of homosexuality. This is demonstrated by the fifth study criticized by Focus on the Family in the *Love Won Out* series: Simon LeVay's study of the hypothalamus.[38]

LeVay found that the nucleus of cells within the third interstitial nuclei of the anterior hypothalamus (INAH-3) differs in size between heterosexual males and females. The size of the nucleus is on average two to three times larger in heterosexual males than it is in females. Interestingly, in homosexual males the average size of the nucleus is the same as in females. This is particularly significant because this region of the brain is important in regulating sexual behavior. For example, researchers have found a direct correlation between the size of the nucleus and sexual behavior in rats. Rats with a large nucleus tend toward the aggressive or dominant role in sexual behavior, while those with a smaller nucleus tend toward a more passive role, although the size of the cells' nucleus does not explain the entire sexual behavior of rats. LeVay comments that the size of the nucleus is determined by the level of circulating testosterone during a critical period of fetal development. Referencing a study on monkeys, LeVay notes that increased prenatal testosterone increased aggressive behavior in females and decreased it in males. Similar effects have been found in humans.[39]

Thus, we see that in animals the differences in the size of INAH-3 cells in the hypothalamus are directly associated with aspects of sexual and non-sexual behavior, and that these size differences appear to be caused by the levels and absorption of testosterone in the prenatal environment. The implication is that because human biology is similar to that of animals, this might be the case for us as well. It is important to provide a cautionary note on the effects of testosterone on human social behavior: while the hormone may affect human behavior, it alone does not determine it. Thus, it is not uncommon to find a range of variation in aggressiveness or passivity among both homosexual males and females.

Recent studies of sheep support LeVay's findings concerning the significance of the INAH-3 cells. Charles Roselli and his colleagues demonstrate that approximately six to ten percent of rams exhibit an exclusive preference for other males.[40] Studies focusing on hormonal levels found that homosexual rams have lower levels of circulating testosterone than heterosexual rams. In addition, examination of the size of the nucleus in cells located in the medial preoptic region of the hypothalamus, which corresponds to the INAH-3 in humans, produced results comparable to LeVay's: the average size of the nucleus in homosexual rams was the same as in ewes, and both were considerably smaller than the average nucleus in heterosexual rams.

Stanton Jones and Don Workman, evangelical proponents for non-biological causation of homosexuality in humans, acknowledge the studies of animals that connect homosexuality with abnormal hormone levels in the prenatal environment.[41] However, Jones and Workman dismiss the studies as irrelevant to humans, even though our general anatomy and physiology are the same as other animals, simply because of their belief that humans are made in "God's image." In the absence of that bias, there are no reasons to believe that humans are significantly different from animals in a strictly biological sense, nor that being made in "God's image" refers to biology.

LeVay's study provides evidence that the size difference in the nucleus of INAH-3 hypothalamus cells could be a direct or indirect cause of homosexuality. However, Focus on the Family's *Love Won Out* series criticizes the study in three ways.[42] First, because many of LeVay's small sample of homosexual subjects had died of AIDS, they object that differences in size of the INAH-3 cell nuclei could have resulted from the disease. They fail to mention that in the heterosexual subjects there were no differences between the cell nuclei of those who had the disease and those who did not. Thus, there is no reason to believe that AIDS caused the cell nuclei to be smaller in homosexual males but not in heterosexual males. In addition, LeVay mentions that after his study was complete he studied four additional cadavers, including one homosexual who died of lung cancer. The results were consistent with his original findings and have since been supported by further independent research.[43]

The second criticism is the legitimate concern that one cannot discern whether the smaller nuclei of INAH-3 cells was the cause or the effect of homosexual behavior in humans: LeVay raises this consideration himself. He notes, however, that preliminary studies of animals indicated the size of the cell nuclei is determined during early fetal development and remains unchanged thereafter. Therefore, the size of the nuclei does not appear to be affected by sexual behavior.

Finally, Focus on the Family objects that "The area of the brain LeVay was measuring (the INAH3) was quite small – smaller than snowflakes."[44] Exactly why they think this is a significant or valid objection is bewildering. Scientific technology routinely measures things considerably smaller than snowflakes with tremendous accuracy. However, additional support for the significance of differences in the anterior hypothalamus region of the brain between homosexual and heterosexual males is found in recent studies of potential human pheromones.

Pheromone studies: Chemical signals, known as pheromones, are important sexual stimulants in animals; they are increasingly thought to be significant in humans as well. Savic and colleagues found that the anterior hypothalamus region of the brain in homosexual men and heterosexual females responds similarly to a progesterone derivative (AND) found in male sweat; there was no such response in heterosexual males (Table 4).[45] When stimulated with an estrogen-like steroid (EST) found in female urine, the response in homosexual males was again similar to that of heterosexual females: the anterior hypothalamus did not react to EST, although the olfactory regions did. Meanwhile, in heterosexual males it was the anterior hypothalamus that reacted to EST. Thus, the anterior hypothalamus region of the brain in both homosexual males and heterosexual females responds to a putative pheromone compound produced in much higher quantities in males than in females and does not respond to a compound produced in females.

Table 4: Activation of the anterior hypothalamus

	Progesterone derivative (AND)	Estrogen-like steroid (EST)
Heterosexual females	yes	no
Heterosexual males	no	yes
Homosexual females	no	yes
Homosexual males	yes	no

Hans Berglund and his colleagues obtained similar results in a study of homosexual females, with one important difference.[46] In heterosexual males EST activates the anterior hypothalamus while AND activates the olfactory regions. However, in homosexual females EST activates both the olfactory region and the anterior hypothalamus, while AND does not activate the anterior hypothalamus. This implies that female homosexuality differs from male homosexuality, a hypothesis supported by studies of male brothers.

Fraternal birth-order effect: One observation established in studies of male homosexuality is that the number of older brothers is a predictive variable for homosexual orientation. This is known as the fraternal birth-order (FBO) effect; it explains homosexual orientation in about 15 percent of homosexual males.[47] Until a recent study by Anthony Bogaert on 944 Canadian males,[48] researchers were unable to determine whether the FBO effect is due to postnatal factors, including child rearing, or to prenatal ones.

Bogaert first examined the FBO effect by statistically comparing the impact on a male's sexual orientation of the number and sequence of his siblings: older brothers (biological and non-biological), younger brothers, older sisters, and younger sisters. If postnatal factors underlie the FBO effect, then the number of older non-biological brothers should be predictive of sexual orientation. If prenatal factors are the cause, then only the number of biological older brothers should be predictive. The results indicate that prenatal factors underlie the FBO effect: the number of biological older brothers is predictive of homosexual orientation, while the numbers of non-biological older brothers, younger brothers, older sisters, and younger sisters are not.

It is possible that the results could be affected if the length of time reared with biological older brothers was significantly longer than the length of time reared with non-biological older brothers. Bogaert compared the amount of time reared with older biological and non-biological brothers but found this variable was not predictive. The important factor is the number of biological older brothers, not how much time was spent being reared with them, regardless of whether the older brothers were biological or not.

As a further test of influences on the FBO effect, Bogaert also studied biological brothers who were not reared together. If postnatal factors are important in the FBO effect, then the number of biological older brothers with whom the male was not reared should *not* be predictive of sexual orientation. However, the results indicate that the number of biological older brothers *is* predictive, whether or not the brothers were reared together: this demonstrates conclusively that the FBO effect is the result of prenatal factors.

It is also significant that the birth-order effect only applies to males, not females. This can be explained by the maternal immune response theory: during pregnancy, a male fetus produces androgens, and the mother's immune system responds by producing antibodies. With each successive male fetus the mother produces additional antibodies and their accumulation affects the sexual differentiation of a male fetus' developing brain. Because a female fetus does not normally produce hormones foreign to the mother's body, the number of older sisters has no effect on the sexual orientation of male or female children.[49]

Intersexuals: A recent study by the CDC in Atlanta of more than 100,000 people indicates that about 90 percent of Americans identify as heterosexual.[50] Additional studies indicate that about one percent of the American population has combinations of genitals and chromosomes that do not follow the majority patterns. These intersex individuals provide considerable insight into what determines a person's sexual orientation.[51]

Some intersex individuals, medically known as hermaphrodites, are born with the genitals of both sexes. It is not uncommon in American society for doctors to perform an operation on a newborn intersex individual to "fit" them into the traditional male or female categories. Until genetic testing was available, surgery did not always align the genitals with the individual's chromosomal pattern. Sometimes surgery would provide a newborn with female anatomy, even though the chromosomal pattern was male, or vice versa. Significantly, these genetically-male intersex individuals are ordinarily attracted to females, while the genetic females are attracted to males, regardless of how they were assigned.

When a boy's penis is damaged around the time of birth, as may happen during circumcision, the solution is known as *ablatio penis*, or removal of the injured organ. Thus the child's gender is surgically reassigned, so he appears as a female, and is usually raised as one. In the few instances that have been studied, the individuals are attracted to females.

Cloacal exstrophy is a disorder of embryogenesis that causes poor differentiation of the genitals but not the brain. Thus, genetic males are frequently raised as females because that is how their genitals appear. Nonetheless, the vast majority of these individuals are attracted to females.

Congenital adrenal hyperplasia (CAH) is a recessive trait that causes production of testosterone in genetic females. This results in masculinization of the genitals and of the brain in varying degrees. According to the neurohormonal theory, we would predict a dramatic increase in attraction to females among these individuals compared to other genetic females, and such is the case: 50 percent of CAH genetic-females are attracted to other females. This example highlights the importance of genetics in determining sexual orientation through the production of hormones.

Androgen insensitivity syndrome (AIS) is an X-linked genetic mutation that makes genetic males insensitive to androgens so neither their brains nor their genitals masculinize. Again, the neurohormonal theory would predict a dramatic increase in attraction to males among these individuals when compared to other genetic males. In fact, virtually all AIS genetic-males are attracted to males.

The information gained from the study of intersexuals is further evidence that sexual orientation is determined *in utero* by both genetics and the prenatal environment, and is not the result of learned behavior.

Fly studies: Of additional interest are studies of homosexuality in animals. One discovered that a mutation in a particular gene affects the brains of fruit flies, causing homosexual behavior under particular environmental circumstances.[52] At about 66 degrees Fahrenheit, fruit flies with the mutation demonstrate heterosexual behavior. However, as the temperature increases to 86 degrees, the male fruit flies, but not the females, increasingly engage in homosexual behavior even when females are available for mating. Obviously the situation is different for humans, but the example illustrates that homosexual attraction in some nonhuman species is dependent on both genetics and environment. Likewise, the available evidence indicates that homosexuality in humans also depends upon genetic and prenatal conditions.

Thus, we see that Dobson's first reason for denying a genetic or biological causation for homosexuality is wrong and that scientific data do, in fact, point to biological causes for homosexuality.

Natural selection. Dobson's second reason for denying a biological cause for homosexuality centers on Darwin's theory of natural selection, popularly known as "survival of the fittest." According to the theory, traits that help an organism to survive and reproduce are passed on to future generations in greater numbers than those that do not. Traits that hinder survival or reproduction are selected against and may eventually disappear. This theory has become a foundation of evolutionary biology. At the time he presented his idea however, Darwin was not aware of Mendel's discovery of the basic principles of genetic inheritance and could not have considered the crucial role of recessive and dominant traits.

To explain why dominant and recessive traits are important I will briefly explain three genetic concepts: phenotype, genotype, and alleles. The *phenotype* is the observable characteristic of the genetic code. For example, in the ABO blood group, a person can have one of four blood types: A, B, O, or AB.[53] The four basic blood types are the *phenotypes* for the ABO blood group, the observable results of the underlying genetic code. The *genotype* is the underlying genetic code for a particular trait; it is

Table 5: ABO Blood Group

Genotype	Phenotype
OO	O
AO	A
AA	A
BO	B
BB	B
AB	AB

comprised of two *alleles*, or alternate expressions of a gene, one from each parent. For example, someone who has type O blood, representing the phenotype, does so because the underlying genetic code, the genotype, is OO (Table 5). Each "O" in this genotype represents one of the two *alleles* for the trait. Someone who has type A blood has one of two genotypes: AA or AO. The O allele is *recessive* to the *dominant* A allele. If an individual has one recessive and one dominant allele, the dominant allele will manifest as the phenotype. So a person who has one A allele and one O allele, resulting in an AO genotype, has type A blood (the phenotype), as does someone with an AA genotype.

Unfortunately, things are not always so straightforward. For example, even though there is a demonstrable genetic basis for fingerprints, there is also an environmental component for it: influences in the mother's womb. Thus, the phenotype is actually the result of interplay between the genotype and the environment. Mathematically, this can be expressed as

$$genotype + environment = phenotype$$

Various environmental factors such as nutrition, hormones, and the physical environment can influence the phenotype. This is why identical twins do not always have identical features, even though the traits may be primarily genetically based.

With this understanding of genetic inheritance we can examine why dominant and recessive traits are important in natural selection. We can also examine Dobson's second reason for not accepting a biological basis for homosexuality. Dobson argues that because homosexuals reproduce less than heterosexuals, natural selection would eliminate any "homosexual gene." He then argues that because there is no evidence homosexuality is in decline, it therefore cannot be genetic.[54]

There are four main issues with this assertion. First, what data does Dobson have that show no indication that numbers of homosexuals are in decline? To my knowledge there has never been, except in modern times, any study to determine how many homosexuals there are. Thus, there can be no way of knowing if homosexuality is increasing, decreasing, or remaining constant.

Second, I question Dobson's use of natural selection. It is true that Darwin's theory of natural selection states that if a trait is not conducive to survival or reproduction it will be selected against. However, Darwin was not aware that recessive alleles, even harmful ones, can linger in populations without ever disappearing. The only way recessive alleles can be selected against by natural selection is if an individual gets two copies of the allele in his or her genotype. If there is only one allele present, it can be passed on to some or all of that individual's offspring without causing any effects. Thus, it may never disappear from the gene pool. This is actually the situation with a number of traits, including hemophilia and albinism.[55] These traits are recessive and are selected against if they are manifested. However, their recessive nature helps them persist in the population because an individual with one copy of the recessive allele can pass it on to succeeding generations. Once again, Dobson's assumption is not consistent with basic biological principles.

Third, while homosexuals in modern Western society are not as likely to be married to someone of the opposite sex, this has not always been the case. Traditionally, homosexuals have married members of the opposite sex and have had children through those marriages. In fact, many did not have a choice because in most cultures, including Western society until recent times, marriages were arranged and heirs were virtually required. Thus, homosexuals had to engage in heterosexual behavior and frequently produced children. While homosexuals *may* reproduce less at this point in time, there is no indication this has always been the case. This is a further reason to believe that natural selection is not a relevant issue when discussing frequencies of homosexuality throughout history.

Finally, Dobson's comment once again assumes a solely genetic explanation for homosexuality. However, even if other factors are required for homosexuality to develop, such as varying testosterone levels in the fetal environment, which do not occur during the development of a particular individual, that individual may be heterosexual but could still pass on a gene, or several genes, that would predispose the offspring to homosexuality.

Therefore, Dobson's second reason for denying a biological cause for homosexuality is unscientific and not based on the evidence.

The Bible. Unlike the first two reasons Dobson presents for not accepting biological explanations for homosexuality, the third avoids scientific arguments. Dobson states that the Bible, specifically Romans 1:26-27, mentions "epidemics" of homosexuality.[56]

Nowhere does the Bible indicate that frequencies of homosexuality dramatically increased over time in any culture. There is also no evidence that we are experiencing an "epidemic" of homosexuality today. What we do see today is that people are more open about their sexuality. This does not mean that there are greater numbers of homosexuals than 100 years ago but only that there are greater numbers of homosexuals who are out of the closet. A similar situation probably existed in ancient Greece and Rome, given that those societies were more accepting of differing expressions of sexuality.[57] Dobson's comment also illustrates that many evangelical leaders view homosexuality as if it were a disease, even though the American Psychological Association has rejected this view.[58] Furthermore, in his discussion Dobson treats sexually transmitted diseases as God's punishment for homosexuals, a point he alludes to elsewhere in his book, ignoring that heterosexuals get the same diseases.[59]

God's character. This brings us to Dobson's final reason for not accepting a biological basis for homosexuality: God would not condemn homosexuality and refer to it as an "abomination" if it were biological.[60] However, we have seen that the Bible does not explicitly discuss general homosexuality, nor is general homosexuality ever referred to as an "abomination." Thus, because the foundation of Dobson's basic premise is in error, we can dismiss this reason for homosexuality not being an inborn characteristic.

Of interest, Pat Robertson states that "God does not form each human being by a special act of creation, but by natural biological processes."[61] Homosexuality is common in nature and all the evidence indicates that it is the result of natural biological processes in humans as well. Thus, either Robertson or Dobson is wrong in their view of how God does things. On this point I side with

Robertson, especially because none of Dobson's reasons for not accepting a biological basis for homosexuality are reliable; furthermore, the evidence indicates homosexuality is a natural and inborn variant of sexuality in both humans and animals.

We have now examined some of the reasons why many scientists support a primarily biological explanation for homosexuality and the reasons why many evangelical leaders do not accept these explanations. The reasons presented by evangelical leaders are based on misunderstood scientific principles and on attempts to protect their worldview.

However, as Dobson demonstrates, most evangelical leaders prefer social explanations for homosexuality. These include the peer-labeling and psychoanalytical theories. Therefore, it is worthwhile to investigate these theories in greater depth.

Sociology and homosexuality

The traditional sociological approach to homosexuality, the peer-labeling theory, sees it as a learned behavior.[62] Homosexuality may result from how a child is socialized and whether he or she accepts a "homosexual" label from others during the "critical period" of developing gender identity, normally before the age of five. This view emphasizes four primary agents of socializing the young child into the accepted role of a man or woman: parents, peers, education, and the media. If the bond with the same-sex parent is weak, the young child may not learn the proper role and thus find him- or herself more comfortable identifying with the roles of the opposite-sex parent. This leads to labeling by same-sex peers, which the individual internalizes as a homosexual identification. For example, if a young boy is a poor athlete he may be labeled a "sissy," while a girl who is athletic is labeled a "tomboy." If the child accepts and internalizes the label during the critical period, he or she may take on other roles that society associates with the identity, such as homosexuality.

The peer-labeling theory accepts stereotypes of gays and lesbians and fails to explain why homosexuality develops in those who do not conform to them. For example, many homosexual men are masculine and excellent athletes. A number of retired professional football, basketball and baseball players have publicly acknowledged their homosexuality,[63] as have athletes in other team sports such as rugby. Meanwhile, many sensitive and effeminate men are heterosexual. In addition, many women who are tomboys are heterosexual, while many feminine women are lesbian. There is no demonstrable causal relationship between sexuality and these behavioral characteristics. There is also no way to measure the degree to which humans internalize the four primary agents of socialization. These are two of the reasons why sociologists have altered their views of and approach to sexuality.

Today, many sociologists have abandoned the peer-labeling theory for homosexuality, believing that there are multiple pathways that can lead to homosexuality in an individual. In other words, there are many factors that work together in different combinations to cause an individual to identify him- or herself as homosexual. While some have used the peer-labeling theory to argue that an individual could change his or her sexual identity, most sociologists now argue that there may be little flexibility in sexual orientation and that biology does play a role in its development.[64]

Rather than focusing on causes of homosexuality, sociologists are increasingly interested in how homosexuality is expressed in a society and in the societal response to homosexuals. They are also interested in how people construct their sexual identity, which may or may not be consistent with their sexual desires. This pertains to the situation of many homosexuals who undergo reparative therapy, for they are taught to see themselves as heterosexual even though their desires are homosexual.

Psychology and homosexuality

Of the two main non-biological explanations for homosexuality, the psychological view, specifically Freud's psychoanalytical approach, is the one considered most important by many evangelical leaders.[65] It suggests that a weak father or domineering mother is responsible for a boy's eventual homosexual attraction, while female homosexuality is a response to a weak mother. An additional important factor is whether the child experienced sexual abuse, which distorts normal sexual development. It is argued that a child's unmet emotional needs may eventually be expressed in homosexual attraction. Supporters of this view generally assume *a priori* that the poor parental relationship is the cause and homosexuality the effect. As evidence, supporters highlight findings that homosexual males tend to have poor relationships with their fathers.[66] However, Robert Epstein, the general editor for *Psychology Today*, notes that the view's supporters

> attribute virtually all male homosexuality to poor father-son relationships, failing to present any hard data to support their assertion and ignoring the possibility that fathers avoid effeminate sons – in other words, that *homosexual tendencies cause bad father-son relations and not vice versa.*[67] [Emphasis added.]

To elaborate on Epstein's point, homosexual tendencies do not cause bad father-son relations but, as sociologists point out, the *attitudes* of both parties toward those tendencies do. Additional blows to the psychoanalytical theory are that it fails to explain why many males who had poor relationships with their fathers develop a heterosexual attraction.

The American Psychological Association does not support Freud's psychoanalytical theory for the causes of homosexuality:

> Various theories have proposed differing sources for sexual orientation, including genetic or inborn hormonal factors and life experiences during early childhood. However, many scientists share the view that sexual orientation is shaped for most people at an early age through complex interactions of biological, psychological and social factors.[68]

This is in contrast to the predominant view of many evangelical leaders that homosexuality is caused by the social environment and can therefore be changed. Significantly, it remains plausible that while homosexuality is an inborn biological characteristic in most individuals who self-identify as homosexual, it is possible that the peer-labeling or psychoanalytical theories may explain homosexual behavior in *some*.

Neither the peer-labeling or psychoanalytical explanations consider the correlations between homosexuality and various other biological traits, such as smaller nuclei in specific hypothalamus cells in both humans and sheep. They also fail to explain the differences between the frequency of homosexuality in identical and fraternal twins, the correlation between homosexuality and handedness, and the presence of homosexuality in animals.

Evangelicals and homosexuality

James Dobson focuses on role model confusion, dysfunctional families, the influence of an older homosexual during childhood, sexual abuse, conscious choice, and cultivation as explanations for the causes of homosexuality. Of interest, the same book that presents Dobson's explanation includes a letter to him from a homosexual man.[69] Significantly, the writer addresses virtually every one of Dobson's causal explanations for what makes a person homosexual, yet not one applies to him. In fact, he was raised in an environment that Dobson and other evangelicals epitomize as one that would prevent homosexuality.[70] Dobson's response to the letter is quite interesting. Even though the letter completely refutes what Dobson says earlier in his book about the causes of homosexuality, he ignores the contradiction and simply defends Focus on the Family's attempts to deny homosexuals equal rights. He admits that biblical scholars argue the Bible is inconclusive on the morality of homosexuality.[71] He then bemoans the amount of money being spent on AIDS research to argue that the homosexual community is not an oppressed minority and states that "AIDS is only one avenue by which sickness and death befall those who play Russian roulette with God's moral imperatives."[72] Unfortunately, Dobson and other evangelical leaders place their beliefs above everything else, ignoring any and all evidence that contradicts them.

AIDS

Many evangelical leaders believe that homosexuals contract AIDS because homosexuality is "inherently sinful" and because of the supposed inherent promiscuity of homosexual males. For example, Alan Sears and Craig Osten recently criticized evangelical sociologist and author Tony Campolo for encouraging evangelical Christians to help individuals with AIDS. They mention that Campolo encouraged evangelicals to show compassion to those with AIDS when he mentioned how Elizabeth Taylor worked relentlessly for AIDS victims.[73] Sears and Osten disagree with Campolo, suggesting that one loves homosexuals by sharing the gospel with them, including the premise that homosexuality is sinful, not by promoting safe sex and equal rights.[74] Sears and Osten continue by further condemning Campolo and his wife Peggy, who also ministers to homosexuals: "On one hand, these evangelicals say, 'Don't do this wicked thing,' and yet call homosexual activists 'my friends' and attack those who are trying to take a stand for righteousness."[75]

This view is further enforced by Ronnie Floyd, evangelical pastor and author of *The Gay Agenda*, who argues that "the person who affirms and enables a person in the gay lifestyle in reality hates him."[76] From their comments it appears that these evangelical leaders do not understand the nature of Jesus' ministry. Jesus regarded the prostitutes, adulterers, lepers, tax collectors, and other "undesirables" as his friends. He opposed the religious leaders who supposedly took a stand for righteousness but "neglected the weightier provisions of the law: justice, mercy and faithfulness."[77] Jesus attended to the needs of the sick, poor, outcasts, and the helpless while condemning the religious leaders for their refusal to do the same.[78] I find it unfortunate that Sears and Osten condemn the Campolos for following Jesus' example and admonition to obey the Golden Rule.

One additional factor that contributes to the view of AIDS as God's retribution is that evangelical leaders remain relatively ignorant of the development and causes of the worldwide AIDS crisis. Because they focus on the spread of AIDS in the United States, many evangelical leaders are misled into associating AIDS with homosexuals; in reality, homosexuals make up only a small portion of the worldwide population suffering from it.[79] Peter Sprigg acknowledges that in the United States the number of

AIDS cases resulting from homosexual contact is thought to be about 52 percent.[80] This means that approximately one-half of all AIDS cases in this country result from heterosexual contact, intravenous drug use, or other means of acquiring the disease.

Evangelical leaders employ a selective use of evidence, ignoring that the majority of people worldwide with AIDS are women and children.[81] The determining or crucial factor is not a person's sexuality; rather it is whether or not the sexual partner or mother is already infected. Due to the possible consequences, suggesting that heterosexuals have less risk of infection than homosexuals, as evangelical leaders do, is unethical. *Anyone* who has unprotected sex with an infected partner is at risk.

This sort of misrepresentation has serious potential consequences in AIDS policies and research funding. Robert Knight of the Culture and Family Institute states that "true compassion means ... opposing AIDS policies which have been disastrous – mostly for homosexuals."[82] Knight believes the best policy for AIDS is one advocating abstinence from sex outside of marriage, which would require life-long chastity for homosexuals.

Meanwhile James Dobson laments that the federal government spends considerably more on AIDS research than for research on heart disease.[83] He is forgetting that AIDS is an infectious disease and one that is now creating severe crises in many countries. With 39 percent of the adult population of Zimbabwe and Botswana suffering from AIDS, research and treatment are critical. Meanwhile, Florida Governor Jeb Bush remarked that "It looks like the people of San Francisco are an endangered species. That's probably good news for the country."[84] Based on such comments, we can only conclude that many conservative and evangelical leaders believe AIDS is God's punishment for homosexuals and that we should not be "wasting" our money trying to find a cure for this divine "justice." Unfortunately, it may require the deaths of millions more people before evangelical leaders recognize the significant impact of AIDS on *all* people, heterosexual and homosexual.

Evangelical explanations for homosexuality

In an article for *Focus on the Family Magazine*, Don Schmierer contradicts statements by the American Psychological Association and the American Sociological Association:

> Genetic, psychological and social research confirm that a variety of causes sets the stage for homosexual choices. But gender confusion can be reversed. Biological predisposition can be treated. Patterns of attraction and addiction can be understood and reformed. These things, in fact, should be addressed before homosexual behavior ever takes place.[85]

Schmierer's "variety of causes" that set the stage for "homosexual choices" include the list of primary factors favored by Dobson, with a few extras thrown in:

1. the individual person's self-will
2. pornography
3. media and culture
4. spousal abuse in the home
5. molestation and pedophilia
6. parental adultery
7. moral relativism
8. seduction by peers
9. chemical imbalances
10. failure of leadership.

This list seems to imply that the majority of the population should be homosexual. Unfortunately, Schmierer gives no evidence for these supposed causes of homosexuality. His list has not been subjected to scientific scrutiny, and seems to reflect things he finds problematic. Nonetheless, Schmierer is confident that "With the right information, the right strategy and God's help, we can prevent homosexuality."[86]

Focus on the Family has also produced a list of factors that supposedly contribute to homosexuality. In addition to Schmierer's, they cite the following factors for males:

1. same-sex experimentation
2. negative spiritual influences
3. personality temperament
4. negative body image

5. peer-labeling
6. fear of, or an inability to relate to females.[87]

They also add the following factors to Schmierer's list for the development of homosexuality in females:
1. physical and emotional trauma
2. unhealthy parental roles and family environment
3. personality temperament and self-concept
4. negative spiritual influences
5. relationship problems
6. public education
7. peer-labeling
8. fear of, or an inability to relate to males.[88]

The last item in both Focus on the Family lists contradicts what they say elsewhere. They suggest that in their youth homosexual males feel more comfortable with, more secure with, and are better at relating to females than to other males.[89] Yet here they state the opposite, that a fear of, or an inability to relate to the opposite sex contributes to homosexuality. If being able to relate to females can lead to male homosexuality, and not being able to relate to females can lead to male homosexuality, then how do males become heterosexual? Ironically, in Focus on the Family's booklet explaining how males become homosexual, the authors conclude: "As this booklet has made clear, *no one cause for homosexuality can be pinpointed*"[90] [emphasis added]. It is not surprising that they come to this conclusion since they ignore biological factors. Surely the better explanation, supported by the evidence, is that homosexuality is inborn and relationships with the opposite sex do not significantly impact it.

Is homosexuality a choice?

One final possibility concerning the cause(s) of homosexuality should be addressed. There are those who believe that homosexuality is a choice. While the decision to perform a sexual act, homosexual or heterosexual, is almost always a choice (rape is a notable exception), sexual orientation is not. Edward Stein argues against homosexuality as a choice:

There is also observational evidence that suggests that sexual orientations are not chosen, that is, scientific, clinical, psychological, and testimonial evidence that a person cannot change his or her sexual orientation ... Countless numbers of gay men and lesbians have attempted to change their sexual orientation through one or another kind of treatment. Attempted treatments have included lengthy psychoanalysis, prayer, hormonal injections, and electric shock treatment to name just a few. All such treatments have been dramatic failures. That most people who have tried to change their sexual orientations have failed seems to count against voluntarism about sexual orientation. Further, in places where there are no positive representations of lesbians and gay men, where homosexuals are violently repressed and severely punished, and in which social pressures push an individual to be heterosexual, there are still people who are sexually attracted to people of the same sex-gender. It seems that at least some of these people living under such conditions would choose to be heterosexuals if they could. Since they are not in fact heterosexuals, this suggests that they do not have a choice in the matter.[91]

The "choice" view is quickly falling out of favor, even among evangelicals, based partly on the testimony of some evangelicals who "struggle with homosexuality."[92]

Sinister southpaws

The current situation with homosexuality is reminiscent of a former debate on handedness. Left-handed people were once considered sinister (the word derives from the Latin *sinistra*, which also means "the left side"). Many cultures around the world still view left-handedness as abhorrent and immoral.[93] The Bible clearly associates the left side with evil and the "right hand" with good.[94] Left-handed people are mentioned twice in scripture: the first reference concerns Ehud who delivered Israel by murdering, in cold blood, the king of Moab,[95] while the second reference mentions 700 left-handed men who defended Gibeah against other Israelites.[96] The latter is from the same passage that discusses how the men of Gibeah attempted to gang rape a male visitor but instead raped and murdered a female concubine. The reference to left-handed men defending Gibeah from the other Israelite tribes is significant in that it associates left-handed people with the wicked city. In short, the only two biblical references that mention left-handed people associate them with cold-blooded murder and wickedness. Thus, it is not surprising that in the past the Bible was used to condemn left-handed people, while in the Middle Ages left-handed people were burned at the stake. Modern American society has also used a variety of techniques to force left-handed people to become right-handed. Although they were able to engage in right-handed *behavior*, their natural *orientation* never changed. Bishop Paul Egertson notes that attempting to force such change only led to additional hardships, just as it does for homosexuals and lesbians.[97]

Explanations for the cause of left-handedness have included personal choice, parental or societal influence, hormones in the prenatal environment, and partial genetic control.[98] As with homosexuality, the exact cause of left-handedness is unknown, although it is clearly biological but not entirely genetic. It may also be related to the cause(s) of homosexuality given the significantly higher frequency of homosexuals who are left-handed compared to heterosexuals.[99] The parallels between the historical and religious responses to left-handed people and homosexuals are clear.

Relying on a literal interpretation of the Bible, many evangelicals believe that the apostle Paul argues that homosexual desires are not natural. Therefore, they attempt to find explanations for homosexuality based solely on social causes, ignoring or discrediting the biological evidence because it does not fit with their beliefs. Evangelical leaders end up identifying so many potential causes that it appears as if *everything* causes homosexuality, except the most obvious possibility: biological factors.

---

[1] Glenn Wilson and Qazi Rahman (2005, 10).
[2] Don Schmierer (1999).
[3] Brian S. Mustanski *et al.* (2005).
[4] Lincoln D. Stein (October 21, 2004).
[5] Clare Porac and Stanley Coren (1981) indicate a concordance rate of 76 percent for left-handedness.

[6] For example, see Nadia Corp and Richard W. Byrne (2004), Michael Hopkin (December 7, 2004) and Clare Porac and Stanley Coren (1981).

[7] See J. A. Y. Hall and D. Kimura (1994) and Brian S. Mustanski, J. M Bailey and S. Kaspar. (2002).

[8] See Michael Hopkin (December 7, 2004), Simon LeVay (1993, 85) and Edward Stein (1999, 131-140).

[9] James Dobson (1997, 512-513).

[10] Ibid (513).

[11] J. Michael Bailey and Richard C. Pillard (1991).

[12] In the context of this discussion, the concordance rate examines the number of homosexual males who have a homosexual brother. This is not the same as likelihood: it inflates the percentage because it counts pairs of homosexual brothers twice, since each brother has a brother who is also homosexual.

[13] Traditionally, these results have been interpreted to mean that if one identical twin is homosexual there is a 52 percent chance that the other twin will be homosexual as well. Stanton L. Jones and Mark A. Yarhouse (2000, 73-77) argue that this interpretation of the results is in error, based on the manner in which the statistics were determined. Jones and Yarhouse argue, using Bailey and Pillard's data, that if one male identical twin is homosexual there is only a 34 percent chance the other will be as well. For male fraternal twins the frequency drops to about 13 percent and for male non-twin siblings the frequency is about five percent. Regardless of which estimates are correct, the overall pattern is the same with the results indicating that both genetics and the prenatal environment are important factors in determining homosexuality in males. The only change based on the revised estimates of Jones and Yarhouse is the *relative* importance of genes compared to the environment.

[14] The *Love Won Out* series includes six booklets designed to instruct evangelicals on matters such as what causes homosexuality, how evangelicals can fight the "gay agenda," and how evangelicals can understand the "myths and facts" in the homosexuality debate. The six booklets, with authors including several "ex-gays," are by Joe Dallas (1999), Bob Davies (2002), Focus on the Family (2001, 2002a, 2002b) and Mike Haley (2001).

[15] Focus on the Family (2001, 5).

[16] Identical twins are monozygotic, from one fertilized egg; fraternal twins are dizygotic. Sprigg's definition is incorrect.

[17] Peter Sprigg (2004, 39-40).

[18] Mike Haley (2001, 9).

[19] Scott L. Hershberger (1997).

[20] Ibid (221).

[21] Ibid (219).

[22] Joseph Harry (1990).

[23] J. Michael Bailey et al. (2000).

[24] Stanton L. Jones and Mark A. Yarhouse (2000, 78).

[25] J. Michael Bailey et al. (1993).

[26] Stanton L. Jones and Mark A. Yarhouse (2000, 74).

[27] Elke Eckert et al. (1986).

[28] J. Michael Bailey and Deana S. Benishay (1993).

[29] Focus on the Family (2001, 6).

[30] Dean Hamer and Peter Copeland (1994).

[31] Brian S. Mustanski et al. (2005) found that genes on the X chromosome, in addition to chromosomes 7, 8, and 10, might all be important in determining a person's sexual orientation.

[32] Focus on the Family (2002b, 6-7).

[33] Ibid (7).

[34] Mike Haley (2001, 6).

[35] For more information see Kenneth M. Cohen (2002).

[36] Glenn Wilson and Qazi Rahman (2005, 107-126).

[37] See Simon LeVay (1993), Charles E. Roselli (November 2002) and Charles E. Roselli et al. (2002).

[38] Simon LeVay (1993).

[39] Ibid (86).

[40] Charles E. Roselli et al. (2002).

[41] Stanton L. Jones and Don E. Workman (1994).

[42] Focus on the Family (2002b, 5-6).

[43] W. Byne et al. (2001).

[44] Focus on the Family (2002b, 6).

[45] Ivanka Savic et al. (2005).

[46] Hans Berglund et al. (2006).

[47] J. M. Cantor et al. (2002).

[48] Anthony F. Bogaert (2006).

[49] Ibid.

[50] William D. Mosher et al. (2002).

[51] See Brian S. Mustanksi, Meredith L. Chivers, and J. Michael Bailey (2002) for additional information.

[52] Toshihiro Kitamoto (1997).

[53] The positive and negative aspects frequently associated with these blood types, such as O+ or A-, refer to a different blood protein and are separate and unrelated aspects of blood types.

[54] James Dobson (1997, 513).

[55] Steve Jones (1997, 192-196 and 249-256).

[56] James Dobson (1997, 513).

[57] John Boswell (1980).
[58] American Psychological Association (July 1998).
[59] Victor Paul Furnish (1994, 27).
[60] James Dobson (1997, 513-514).
[61] Pat Robertson (2001).
[62] Pepper Schwartz and Virginia Rutter (1998, 28).
[63] Including former Atlanta Falcon Super Bowl defensive lineman Esera Tuaolo (2006).
[64] Pepper Schwartz and Virginia Rutter (1998).
[65] For example, see Stanton L. Jones (1994) and various publications from James Dobson and Focus on the Family.
[66] Focus on the Family (2002b, 10).
[67] Robert Epstein (February 2003).
[68] American Psychological Association (1999, 157).
[69] James Dobson (1997, 519-520).
[70] James Dobson (1997) and Don Schmierer (1999).
[71] James Dobson (1997, 522), although Dobson does not accept their findings.
[72] Ibid (519).
[73] Alan Sears and Craig Osten (2003, 129).
[74] Ibid (129).
[75] Ibid (129).
[76] Ronnie W. Floyd (2004, 30).
[77] Matthew 23:23.
[78] For example, see Matthew 23, Luke 10:30-37 and Luke 11.
[79] See Susan L. McCammon et al. (2004, 412-413, 437), www.unaids.org and www.cdc.gov. Most experts estimate that 90 percent of HIV cases in African adults result from heterosexual transmission (for example, see Per Kallestrup et al. 2003).
[80] Peter Sprigg (2004, 47).
[81] Susan L. McCammon et al. (2004, 412-413, 437) and www.unaids.org.
[82] Robert Knight, in Pete Winn (August 21, 2003).
[83] James Dobson (1997, 523).
[84] Time (November 24, 2003).
[85] Don Schmierer (1999).
[86] Ibid.
[87] Focus on the Family (2002b, 10-11).
[88] Focus on the Family (2001, 11-12).
[89] Focus on the Family (2002b, 23-24).
[90] Ibid (31).
[91] Edward Stein (1999, 260).
[92] For example see Anonymous (March 11, 2002).

[93] See Karl G. Heider (2001, 59).
[94] See Exodus 15:6; Psalm 17:7, 18:35, 63:8; Isaiah 41:10, Matthew 25:33 and Acts 2:34.
[95] Judges 3:15-23.
[96] Judges 20:16.
[97] Paul Wennes Egertson (1999, 29).
[98] For example, see Nadia Corp and Richard W. Byrne (2004), Michael Hopkin (December 7, 2004) and Clare Porac and Stanley Coren (1981).
[99] See J. A. Y. Hall and D. Kimura (1994) and Brian S. Mustanski *et al.* (2002) for additional references on homosexuality and handedness, and homosexuality and somatic asymmetry. They report left-handedness is significantly more common among male homosexuals (about 1 in every 6 are left-handed) than male heterosexuals (less than 1 in every 10 are left-handed).

7. DIVERSE SEXUALITIES: AN ANTHROPOLOGIST'S PERSPECTIVE

> *Contrary to our own view, such cultures as the Sambia see homosexuality not as a negation of masculinity but as the only means through which it is attained.*
>
> — Gilbert Herdt[1]

Anthropology, the study of humans, is the most diverse of the social sciences. Anthropologists study the origins of ancient civilizations and of humans; social organization among humans and chimpanzees; how culture affects language and biology; and they help to solve criminal cases and how the Easter Islanders made giant stone statues. If it involves humans, or our closest relatives in the animal kingdom, anthropologists are studying it. Thus, it is not surprising that anthropologists are interested in human sexuality.

Anthropologists develop insight into different marriage and sexual customs, including how homosexuality is expressed in various cultures. Thus, in the current debate on homosexuality, the anthropological approach provides a comprehensive understanding of the issues. For example, the psychoanalytical and peer-labeling explanations (Chapter 6) do not explain homosexuality in other cultures. Therefore, it is evident that many evangelical leaders are viewing the causes of homosexuality from an ethnocentric perspective. They are only looking at American society in considering what causes homosexuality and are ignoring the evidence from other cultures and from nature. When we consider the anthropological evidence, we see additional flaws in explanations of homosexuality that avoid a biological perspective.

Many evangelicals hold that only heterosexual desire is an instinctive part of God's creation. Same-sex behavior, however, is widely seen in nature and has been documented in more than 450 animal species, including both placental and marsupial mammals, insects, and more than 130 species of birds.[2] Consequently, if we define "natural" as what occurs in nature, then by definition homosexuality is natural and instinctive. Non-biological explanations for homosexuality fail to explain why it is common in animals, including the bonobo apes, which are genetically similar to humans.

The bisexual bonobos

The bonobos are well known in the anthropological community for sexual behavior that is similar to human habits. These endangered apes from the tropical forests of the Democratic Republic of Congo (formerly Zaire) are very similar to chimpanzees. These are the two animal species whose genetic makeup is most similar to humans. Scientists believe humans, chimpanzees, and bonobos share a common ancestor who lived about five to seven million years ago.[3] Although the bonobos are the least studied of the apes, they are now receiving more anthropological attention.

Bonobo sexual behavior includes many traits that are unusual in other primates, such as face-to-face mating and prolonged sexual receptiveness in females.[4] For many Americans, however, the most surprising aspect of bonobo sexual behavior is frequent same-sex activity among both males and females. Bonobo behavior can be characterized as bisexual: they frequently engage in sex with both male and female partners. Bonobo males mount one another, engage in "penile fencing," and perform oral sex on each other. Bonobo females masturbate and mimic heterosexual intercourse by rubbing their genitals against those of other females. Sexual activity is apparently a source of pleasure as well as a vital aspect of bonobo social harmony: it is a means of establishing cooperation and group cohesion. Bonobos use sex to reduce tension and conflict among group members and to create alliances. When bonobos come upon a food source they will have sex, then share the food they have found. This social dimension of bonobo sexual behavior is unusual in other animal species, but common in humans. Although it is difficult to determine whether all bonobos are bisexual or if their behavior was learned as part of their cultural heritage, same-sex behavior is widespread among them. Bonobos represent only one of many instances of homosexuality in nature.

The peer-labeling and psychoanalytical reasons for homosexuality are not universal because they do not explain why homosexuality exists throughout nature. Certainly such explanations cannot be applied to bonobos. The biological explanation has some validity because bonobo and chimpanzee biology is similar to our own. We contract many of the same diseases, including polio and HIV. In fact, it is believed that HIV moved to humans from chimpanzees. Because homosexuality is so prevalent in nature, the neurohormonal theory is the most comprehensive explanation for it. Instead of positing different explanations for different, but closely related, animal species, we have one explanation that works for all mammals and is supported by initial scientific research on both humans and sheep.

Many evangelical leaders cannot accept an explanation for homosexuality that is based on common evolutionary heritage and biological similarities between humans and other primates. In evangelical reality, humans are made in God's image, and apes are not: this belief undermines any evidence based upon observations of nature. Consequently, our critique of the comment that homosexuality is unnatural will be rejected by many evangelical leaders because they believe human nature is different from animal nature. So let us turn to other human societies to see what evidence they may provide for the peer-labeling, psychoanalytical, or biological explanations for homosexuality.

Although homosexual attraction is found throughout the world, and homosexual behavior is reportedly accepted in 64 percent of societies,[5] same-sex relationships have a variety of expressions across different societies. Gilbert Herdt groups expressions of same-sex behavior seen in traditional cultures into three categories based on gender transformation, specialized roles, and age.[6] By examining non-Western examples of homosexuality, we can learn more about our own views on sexuality, gender, and marriage.

Micronesia: gender transformation

Micronesia comprises a number of small Pacific countries and territories including the Federated States of Micronesia, the Marshall

Islands, Kiribati, Guam, and the Northern Marianas Islands. Many of these islands are small atolls with limited land and natural resources, while a handful are high volcanic islands with greater diversity in flora and fauna. Micronesian societies tend to be similar to the chiefdoms found in Polynesia: a central political power is inherited and family lineages are ranked according to their affinity to the chief's lineage. Micronesian societies tend to be matrilineal, with land ownership and other aspects of inheritance passed on through the mother's side of the family. Micronesian chiefs are typically male, but they generally reach that position as the oldest male in the maternal lineage. One benefit of a matrilineal system is that no child can be illegitimate: every child is naturally incorporated into the mother's lineage and has a place in society with full membership in the kinship system. In a patrilineal system, such as existed in ancient Israel, a child acquires identity through the father's lineage. If the father is unknown, then the child's lineage cannot be established and the child is considered illegitimate.

Children are highly valued in Micronesian societies, so much so that childless couples are often pitied and a frequent solution to infertility is adoption. Unlike American society where adoption is cloaked in secrecy, Micronesian adoption is very public and extremely common. Anthropologist William Alkire notes that about half of all the children on Lamotrek atoll during 1962-1963 had been adopted.[7] Adoption reinforces kinship ties but frequently also has as an economic purpose. For example, on the island of Butaritari, an atoll with limited resources, the family whose child is adopted receives land, a valuable commodity, in return.[8] The adopted child retains strong ties to its birth parents, and frequently continues to live with them during early childhood. Thus, adoption links two families together in an economic and social relationship bound by a spirit of cooperation.

Another significant difference between Micronesian and traditional Western societies is the attitude toward premarital sex. Micronesian societies place no stigma on premarital sex, rather seeing it as a natural feature of life that should not be discouraged. Marriage, which is frequently arranged, especially first marriages, was seen as being an important social and economic contract of cooperation between the families involved, not just between two individuals. Marriage generally did not occur until a couple had a child: prior to childbirth, there was nothing that required full cooperation between the two families. Just as Micronesian views on premarital sex differ from those of traditional Western society, their views of other aspects of marriage also differ. In certain situations, such as during the taboo on intercourse after childbirth, a married man was permitted to have extramarital sexual relations. Polygyny was acceptable, although not prevalent because it was seldom economically feasible to support a large family on land with limited resources. Divorce was also a common feature of life: on Lamotrek atoll the average person married three to four times.[9]

On islands with severely limited natural resources we might expect the society to manage its population carefully. In the Pacific, however, there are numerous islands so that when a population became too large, a number of families would colonize an uninhabited island. Although colonization of Pacific islands is relatively recent, by the time of European contact, virtually all the habitable islands were occupied. On large islands, such as Hawaii, Easter Island, and Tahiti, population growth caused increasing stratification in the political, social, and religious arenas. The population of Easter Island later decreased markedly due to over-exploitation of natural resources.[10] Among intentional "birth-control methods" in Pacific societies was prolonged breastfeeding, which results in fewer pregnancies. Infanticide was common in other societies, particularly in Melanesia, but not in Micronesia, partly due to the economic value of children and the frequency of adoptions. Same-sex marriages were not frequent and had little impact on regulating population growth, although same-sex couples often adopted children to establish a family.

Micronesian societies generally have rigid gender definitions. Women manage the household and tend to a variety of domestic chores, including cooking, cleaning, collecting shellfish, sewing, and weaving. Men generally do the fishing, work on boats, build houses, climb coconut trees and do much of the harder agricultural work. The division of labor based on gender did not always correspond to biological sex: a male could habitually perform "female" tasks, just as a female could perform "male" tasks. In these instances, though, the person was usually identified by the role performed rather than by biological sex.

Anthropologist Martha Ward's study of Pohnpei, located in the Federated States of Micronesia, includes the story of a girl who did not follow the normal gender roles.[11] This girl, Maria, engaged in what is known as "night crawling." In traditional Pohnpeian society it was inappropriate for teens who were dating each other to be seen in public because it would signify that they were married. Thus, the only opportunity for singles to meet was under cover of darkness. It was normal for teenage males to sneak out in the middle of the night and secretly call out to the girl at her parents' home, so that they might have a meeting filled with passion and romance. For boys, night crawling was accepted and expected behavior. Maria, however, also engaged in night crawling, but visited another girl. When this eventually became public knowledge, it caused no scandal: her family simply had a meeting to discuss the situation. They publicly cut Maria's hair and declared that she would now be known as Mario. Mario was accepted by the society as a man and took on all the societal expectations of that role. Mario eventually married a woman, adopted children, and raised a family.

From a Western perspective, the most surprising aspect of Maria/Mario's story is how easily the transition was made for Mario, his family, and the rest of society. There was no great fuss over the change, no public debate about morality, and no confusion about who he was. The society realized that while Mario had female genitals, his basic emotional and mental makeup was male. Therefore, instead of forcing him to live a tortured existence or be stigmatized for being different, the society simply accepted who Mario was. There were no issues about same-sex marriage, parenting, or adoption, nor was there any evidence to suggest that the resulting marriage and adoptions were harmful to the society or the children. Pohnpeian society considered the arrangement normal, treated it as normal, and as it turns out, it is normal.

The same resolution for transgender individuals and homosexuals is found elsewhere in Micronesia. Alexandra Brewis documents such a situation on the island of Butaritari in Kiribati.[12] The Butaritari people recognize individuals who change their gender to marry someone of the same sex: a *binabinaaine* (literally, to be like a woman) is a male who takes on the role, duties, and expression of a woman, while a *binabinamane* (literally, to be like a man) is a female who takes on the role and expression of a man. Thus, a male who becomes a binabinaaine dresses as a woman, grows his hair out like a woman and performs all the social responsibilities and obligations of a woman. Likewise a binabinamane dresses, talks, and acts as a man. These individuals marry someone of the same biological sex and adopt children. Although they are treated with some curiosity, they are not considered any less human, inherently immoral, nor in any way psychologically disturbed. Binabinaaine and binabinamane, however, are not considered homosexual, nor are their spouses. The binabinaaine are seen as women because they act like women and marry men. Likewise, their spouses are not considered homosexual because they are men who marry a person the society accepts as a woman, even though the partners are both of the same biological sex. The situation is similar for the binabinamane. Because the marriages are not always arranged and individuals can freely choose spouses within culturally appropriate boundaries, it is likely that at least some of the individuals married to the binabinaaine and binabinamane have what we would consider a homosexual orientation.

However, while it is acceptable, albeit rare, for a male to change his gender and become a binabinaaine or for a female to change her gender and become a binabinamane, Western expressions of homosexuality, specifically between two males or two females without either partner taking on the roles of the opposite gender, are neither accepted nor tolerated. Thus, it appears that same-sex couples were only accepted if they conformed to the heterosexual model of gender differentiation.

Actual pre-contact indigenous views on same-sex relationships can be difficult to ascertain due to the reluctance of many anthropologists to report or acknowledge such behavior, or because the

indigenous population had learned from early Christian missionaries that such information would not be acceptable to Westerners. For example, in his study of the Ulithi society of Micronesia,
William Lessa indicates that "'True' homosexuality seems to be
unknown. ... Women of mature age, usually because of involuntary continence, are said sometimes to resort to mutual masturbation, but only as a substitute for the normal sexual congress being
denied them."[13] Lessa does not mention that homosexuality via
gender transformation existed on Ulithi, although given its occurrence in other Micronesian societies it is possible that it did. Furthermore, his comment that "true" homosexuality was unknown
on the island implies that, while the European expression of homosexuality was not present (although this is contradicted by his
remark about female mutual masturbation), it is possible that homosexuality accompanied by gender transformation was present.

Micronesian societies correctly recognize that gender and sex
are different. There is an understanding and acceptance that while
a person may have masculine genitals, they may have a feminine
gender, or vice versa. Science has documented that our genitals
and our brains have different developmental causes and sometimes do not correspond.[14] A person with male genitals may have
a "feminine" brain, while a person with female genitals may end
up with a "masculine" brain. Thus, the Micronesian worldview
agrees with what science has discovered: biological sex does not
automatically determine gender, nor does biological sex automatically determine sexual orientation. There is no assumption or belief in these Pacific societies, as there is in Western society, that a
person's gender and sex must be the same, nor that all people
must be heterosexual.

Also noteworthy is that while Micronesian societies focus on
gender to determine who may or may not marry, American society emphasizes the biological sex of the individuals involved. For
example, American law allows a person who undergoes sex
change surgery to marry someone of the opposite sex. Thus, except in Massachusetts where same-sex marriage is currently legal,
two people who are born with the same genitals cannot marry
unless one of them undergoes a sex-change operation.

Samoa, Siberia, and Native America: specialized roles

Samoa

In West Polynesia we find adaptations similar to those in Micronesia. The *fa'afafine* are biological males who express the female gender.[15] They perform tasks that Samoan society attributes to women, such as nurturing children, taking care of the home, and cooking meals. Highly influenced by Western culture, contemporary fa'afafine are most visible in the entertainment sectors of Samoan society, like Western drag queens. But this was not the case in traditional Samoan culture.[16]

Formerly, fa'afafine were sometimes seen as religious specialists, able to communicate with the supernatural more readily than other individuals. This religious role for transgender and homosexual individuals is seen worldwide: individuals who range beyond societal norms of gender and sexual orientation are thought to bridge the gap between the sexes as well as the one between humans and the supernatural. What human, then, might most readily communicate with a supernatural male/female being than one who has aspects of both male and female? Thus, homosexuals, intersexuals, fa'afafine, and other transgender individuals frequently become religious specialists. Thus, fa'afafine find acceptance in their societies as well as in many Christian churches.[17] They are valued as Sunday school teachers because they nurture as females, but can discipline as males. This is dramatically different from many American churches which ostracize homosexuals or deny them positions of authority. In Samoa, social acceptance of fa'afafine allows them to live honestly, and to find fulfillment as productive members of the community.

Siberia

Another example of the religious significance of gender transformation and same-sex behavior is found among the Chukchi of northeastern Siberia.[18] Chukchi shamans are expected to change their gender from man to woman and to dress in women's clothes. Instead of performing the typical masculine roles, including hunting, the shaman becomes a nurturer. He is permitted to take male lovers and even marry them, performing the usual rituals associated with marriage. Unlike the same-sex marriages found among societies with age-structured homosexual relationships, discussed below, Chukchi same-sex marriage is for life. As is typical in societies in which a gender transformation has occurred, neither the shaman nor his husband are considered to be homosexual, even though two biological males are married and have sex together. The shaman is no longer considered a man, therefore the relationship involves a man (the partner) and a woman (the shaman).

Native America

The unique status of homosexuals and transgender individuals in societies around the world is also seen in various Native American cultures. The Native American two-spirit[19] typically is a biological male who takes on aspects of the female gender. Some Native American cultures have traditionally fully recognized marriages between a two-spirit and another male. However, while two-spirit individuals are often accepted, their specific roles in different Native American societies vary.

The two-spirit often mediates between men and women. Many Native American cultures often place the two-spirit individual in a position of religious influence. In these societies the homosexual and transgender individual is not denigrated, but is celebrated as someone with the unique ability to communicate with the spiritual world. Given their combined masculine and feminine qualities, two-spirit individuals incorporate a more complete spectrum of human qualities, blending the "aggressive male" with the "nurturing female." The apparent assumption is that only an individual who can combine the masculine with the feminine can effectively communicate with the spiritual world, in which the masculine and the feminine are also combined.

Whereas traditionally in Western society homosexuals have been denigrated for being different, in Chukchi and Native American societies they are frequently honored and seen as important members of society, even to the extent of being included in the mythology.[20] For example, Walter Williams recounts a Zuni myth that the deities created the two-spirit for a special purpose that would benefit the greater society.[21] Curiously, the Zuni incorporated a positive image of the two-spirit into their mythology, but in practice they generally ostracized two-spirit individuals.

This may reflect how their culture changed over time, perhaps as the result of Western contact.[22] The mythological aspect is important in that it helps the two-spirit individuals understand their place in the society and in nature: it destigmatizes them and removes any confusion as to why they are different -- the gods had made them so to benefit society.

New Guinea, ancient Greece, and Africa: age-structured relationships

The Sambia of New Guinea

Anthropologist Gilbert Herdt, who studied the Sambia of New Guinea, notes that 10 to 20 percent of Melanesian cultures institutionalized same-sex behavior, including at least 30 cultures in southwestern Papua New Guinea.[23] As with many other Melanesian cultures, Sambia same-sex behavior is highly structured and regulated, expressed in a manner quite foreign to Western sensibilities. In these cultures same-sex behavior was considered necessary to help boys become men.

Traditionally, many cultures in New Guinea incorporated two features that had a direct implication on institutionalized same-sex behavior: warfare and gender separation. New Guinea societies included tribes that engaged in subsistence horticulture and raised pigs as an important economic commodity. It was necessary to protect the villages, pigs, and garden plots from neighboring groups who might seize the land or steal the pigs or women. Not surprisingly, warfare was a common feature of life in New Guinea and training boys to become warriors was essential for the groups' survival.

A man's warrior mentality was both contradicted and enhanced by his fear of his wife or wives. Women were generally thought to be highly polluting, evidenced by the monthly release of "contaminated" blood. Belief in the pollution of women was widespread in traditional cultures, including ancient Israel.[24] A man could easily be contaminated by the woman's pollution, with potentially grave consequences. Therefore, it was necessary to have a strict separation of the sexes, to the point that women would use a separate path from men, would occupy a separate part of the house, and could never pass over a man or any of his belongings as that could contaminate his possessions.

Men had a second reason to fear women: villages were small and frequently comprised of related men, so they had to find wives in neighboring groups with whom they were often at war. Not only did a man's wife come from the enemy, but she also had at her disposal the means to kill him at any time: she could secretly mix some of her menstrual blood with his food. These two characteristics created serious tension and antagonism between the sexes: it was in this environment that children were raised.

The Sambia, who live in the high mountains of eastern New Guinea, separate the world into male and female realms. This extends not only to housing arrangements and what path a person may use, but also to work and the natural world. For example, although they engage in only limited gardening activities, Sambia men are responsible for raising taro, one of the most important crops, because it is considered a "male" plant: it grows vertically in the ground and is hard. The sweet potato, however, is soft and lies horizontally in the ground, so it is "female" and falls in the realm of women's work.[25] Sambia women watch over the children and do much of the gardening, while the men are mainly warriors and hunters, although they also do the heavier labor in the gardens. Thus, Sambia boys are primarily raised by women -- perceived by men as potential enemies -- and have relatively little interaction with adult men until they are about seven years old.

These separate male and female worlds also extend to biological considerations, for the Sambia believe men and women are fundamentally different in many ways. They believe that while females naturally grow into women, males do not naturally become men: femininity is natural, but masculinity must be achieved by acquiring *jerungdu*.[26] Jerungdu, found in semen, is a bodily essence that produces masculinity: it is male strength, not some abstract concept, but a tangible substance that a male must acquire in order to become a man. This belief makes sense to the Sambia, because boys who have not gone through puberty and acquired jerungdu have not yet developed the secondary sex characteristics that distinguish them from men. Thus, because the

Sambia believe that boys do not acquire jerungdu naturally, and therefore do not naturally develop into men, the men must intercede. If the men do not help the boys acquire jerundgu, the boys will forever remain feminine and would not become warriors able to protect the village from their many enemies.

Thus, at about the age of seven the boys are taken away from the world of women and begin their initiation into the men's cult. This initiation, which lasts more than 10 years, helps the boys learn tribal folklore, how to protect the village from enemies, how to hunt, proper interaction with others in the tribe and, most importantly, to become men. A boy is assigned a ritual guardian or sponsor, who is referred to as the mother's brother, the preferred but not required relationship of the guardian to the boy. It is the ritual guardian's duty to teach him the ways of the Sambia, particularly how he will become a man.

Before a boy can learn how to acquire jerungdu and become a man, he must be rid of the female pollution that hinders his growth and development. After all, he has sucked at his mother's breast, exposing his mouth and face to considerable female pollution and, for the first seven years of his life, has been regularly exposed to her menstrual pollution. Thus, it is essential that the men help the boys by eradicating female pollution from their bodies. This entails a series of ordeals of physical purification. One of these is nose-bleeding, in which the men thrust stems of grass into each boy's nose until the nasal membrane is pierced and blood flows out. Other such ordeals include rubbing the boy's body with something similar to stinging nettles and a series of thrashings with sticks, cassowary quill-bones, and other items. The ritual guardian ensures that the beatings are not too severe. Neighboring cultures use a variety of other techniques to purify the boys. For example, among the Wogeo, who live on a small island to the north of the eastern New Guinea mainland, a boy's tongue is scraped with a coarse leaf until it bleeds.[27] This, of course, is significant because it is through the mouth that the boy acquires tremendous pollution while breast-feeding, and it is through the mouth that he will begin to acquire jerungdu in order to become a man.

Jerungdu is found in semen: because a boy does not acquire it naturally on his own, he must acquire it in the only way he can, by "drinking" it from a man, just as a baby sucks milk from a woman to become strong. Thus, after the various rituals designed to rid him of female pollution, a boy learns the secret of the flutes, which in many New Guinea cultures are symbolic of the penis. During the ritual the boy learns how to suck on the flute, which helps instruct him in how he must suck a man's penis to obtain the "milk" inside. His ritual guardian, who is often a trusted relative, assures him of its necessity. A boy can only acquire semen from males in their teens or early twenties who have passed through various initiation rituals but have not yet fathered children. It is also forbidden for a boy to drink the semen of his ritual guardian, as that would be equivalent to incest because the guardian is actually or symbolically his maternal uncle. Pre-pubescent boys must regularly ingest semen to enable their bodies to reach puberty and masculinize. After puberty, a boy will eventually provide semen to younger boys. Thus, all Sambia men go through a period of required, yet regulated same-sex behavior. Once a man marries he is allowed to "feed" the boys only until his wife has a child. So from his late teens to mid-twenties a man regularly engages in bisexual behavior, but once his wife bears a child, he must relinquish all same-sex behavior. Thereafter he engages solely in heterosexual behavior for he has acquired his masculinity and need not repeat the ritual initiations that led to full manhood.

In Sambia culture, however, a married man still faces two serious problems. First, having sex with his wife is highly polluting, for now his body is penetrating the most polluted aspect of a woman. Thus, he regularly performs the nose-bleeding ritual to cleanse his body. The second problem is that the wife steals some of his jerungdu each time he has sex with her, making him weaker and more vulnerable to the enemy. This heightens antagonism between the sexes, and the man must also find a way to replenish his jerundgu. As he is no longer allowed to drink semen, he must acquire jerungdu from other sources, specifically from white tree sap. The sap replenishes jerungdu, but is not sufficient to turn boys into men, hence the need for the boys to ingest semen.

It is difficult to assess how common these types of ritualized behaviors are. Ian Hogbin argues that the Wogeo do not practice ritualized same-sex behavior, but from the cultural parallels between the Wogeo and the Sambia, and from Wogeo mythology it seems likely that they do.[28] Wogeo initiation begins with the scarification and bleeding of a boy's tongue to cleanse him from female pollution. After the tongue is cleansed, Hogbin indicates that a boy then learns how to play the flutes.[29] Furthermore, a Wogeo myth explains that a famous cultural hero who had been abandoned at birth kept himself alive by drinking the sticky white sap from a breadfruit tree. It also explains why all Wogeo boys must learn to blow the flutes if they desire to grow into men.[30] Certainly the key elements of ritualized same-sex behavior in the Sambia are present in the Wogeo. It is likely that Hogbin was not present when a group of boys were introduced into the initiation ceremonies, which occur approximately every three years among the Sambia, or the ritualized same-sex behavior was hidden from him by the Wogeo, who would have known that Westerners did not approve of such things due to their previous contacts with missionaries.

One might speculate that the ritualized same-sex behavior in New Guinea is simply a form of birth control but this does not appear to be the case for two reasons: first, persistent warfare helped stabilize the population by regular "weeding." This warfare was similar to feuding: an individual's death at the hand of an enemy required a retaliatory death in order to appease the dead man's spirit. Thus, rather than wiping out entire villages, this mode of war helped to maintain the population level by selectively killing a few people at a time. A second means of population control was infanticide. Gilbert Herdt notes that the Sambia had an extremely unusual male to female birth ratio, 120 males for every 100 females.[31] Combined with the Sambia preference that the first child should be a male, it appears that Sambia women frequently committed infanticide if the first child was a girl. Thus, ritualized same-sex behavior was not necessary as a means of population control, although it did provide young males with an acceptable sexual outlet that also apparently protected the group from rape and other types of sexual aggression.

Sambia relevance to causation theories. The Sambia provide us with a better understanding of what causes homosexuality. If Freud's psychoanalytical view is correct, then 100 percent of Sambia males should be homosexual because three important factors are present: distant father, domineering mother, and sexual abuse before puberty. Significantly, the boys go through puberty and adolescence with no hindrance to development of heterosexual attraction; they are completely heterosexual in behavior by their early twenties. Also relevant is the ease with which they shift from ritualized same-sex behavior during childhood and teenage years to strictly heterosexual behavior as adults, all without the aid of psychologists, electric shock therapy, reparative therapy, or other techniques used in Western society to "cure" homosexuals.[32] Herdt mentions that even though the boys' earliest sexual experiences are with males and they engage exclusively in same-sex behavior, they nonetheless have heterosexual fantasies and participate in sexual talk about females. Therefore, it is apparent that the constellation of distant father, domineering mother, and early childhood sexual abuse does not affect their inborn sexual orientation.

Herdt also briefly discusses one Sambia male who was unable to make the transition to heterosexuality. Marriages with women were arranged, but he refused to have sex with his wives and preferred to be with other males. He became a social outcast because he did not conform to the norms of Sambia society. Of interest, contrary to the peer-labeling theory, the labeling and ostracism occurred only after his preference was realized: the labeling did not cause the same-sex attraction but resulted from it.

Supporters of the psychoanalytical explanation for the cause of homosexuality may point to this one man as proof, ignoring the hundreds who were not affected. An inborn sexual orientation explains the situation much better: instead of the boys becoming homosexuals due to Western notions of bad parenting and sexual abuse, they remain heterosexuals because the majority of Sambia males have an inborn heterosexual orientation. Although they engage in homosexual behavior as youths, the transition to heterosexuality is relatively easy because that is their natural orientation.

The one exception, who was unable to make the transition, simply did not share that heterosexual orientation.

Ancient Greece

The situation just described among the New Guinea societies is also seen in "warrior based" societies such as ancient Japan and Greece. K. J. Dover indicates that the Greek expression of homosexuality developed in the Dorian military organization and spread from this region (principally Sparta and Crete) to other areas of Greece about 800 BC.[33] Gilbert Herdt explains:

> Among the ancient Dorians of Crete, the practice of boy love was created through a kind of symbolic "capture" of a desired boy by an older youth. They "eloped" in this way, and to acknowledge their sexual relationships, the family and community gave gifts and provided feasts.[34]

Thus, the festivals and ceremonies Dorian society performed for same-sex relationships were similar to those for heterosexual marriages. Such same-sex relationships were common throughout the history of ancient Greece, even into Roman times. It is also worth noting that it was also common for a heterosexual male to marry a girl in her early teens. Thus, there was little difference between homosexual and heterosexual relationships or marriages as they both involved pairings of disparate ages: an older male with a very young male or female, or even an older female with a younger one.

Africa: the Azande

The cyclical pattern of homosexual relationships among the ancient Greeks was common in other warrior societies as well. For example, the Azande of Africa represent numerous cultures on that continent that permit a male to take a younger male (generally 12 to 20 years old) as his spouse. The famous anthropologist E. E. Evans-Pritchard indicates that these marriages were socially accepted and as legitimate as heterosexual marriage: the same term applies to both heterosexual and same-sex unions. Citing an example of same-sex marriage among the Azande, Evans-Pritchard notes that the relationship was, for so long as it lasted, a legal union on the model of a normal marriage. The warrior paid bride-wealth (some five spears or more) to the parents of his boy and performed services for them as he would have done had he married their daughter. ... Also, if another man had relations with his boy he could, I was told, sue him at court for adultery.[35]

The younger male took care of the domestic chores and traveled with his husband. In fact, it was a special honor for the younger male to carry his husband's spears. These relationships and marriages, however, were not for life as it was expected that males would have children to propagate the community. When the younger male became an adult, he chose a young male to be his spouse. Evans-Pritchard also notes that a man might have both female and male spouses; also that while female homosexuality is known among the Azande, marriage between two women is not.

These societies incorporated same-sex relationships into the socialization of young males and females. This mentoring process was an important component in teaching young men to be warriors. While the marriages were seen as fully legitimate, they were not expected to be permanent because the younger male would one day have to be a mentor himself.

Anthropology and homosexuality

We have examined each of the three types of homosexual relationships described earlier by Herdt: age-structured homosexual relationships include the Sambia, ancient Greek, and Azande societies. Gender-transformed homosexual relationships are found among the Pohnpei, Butaritari, Samoa, Chukchi, and many Native American peoples. Specialized social or religious roles for homosexuals and their partners are found in Chukchi, Samoan, and various Native American societies.

It is important to recognize that many societies throughout the world traditionally recognized and accepted same-sex marriages. Among the Nandi of Kenya, three percent of all marriages are between two females.[36] The woman who wishes to initiate the marriage is expected to pay bridewealth, usually consisting of cattle, to her intended's family. This exchange initiates both a marriage and an economic union between two families, just as it does in heterosexual marriages. Other societies allowed same-sex marriages in which the ages and roles of the spouses were analogous to those in heterosexual marriages. Similarly, homosexual relationships in Western society generally parallel heterosexual relationships in that both are relatively egalitarian.

In many non-Western societies the distinction between homosexual and heterosexual has neither validity nor relevance. Cultures that distinguish biological sex from culturally prescribed gender have a flexible view of sexuality that allows them to accept same-sex marriage and adoption, with no resulting problems for the children or society. Of interest, the Bugis of Indonesia recognize five genders: man, woman, *calabai* (literally, "false-woman"), *calalai* (literally, "false-man"), and *bissu* (androgynous shaman). Marriage between people of two different genders, regardless of their sex is accepted, even if it is between a calalai and a calabai.[37] Thus, a man is able to marry a woman, a calabai, or a calalai (bissu are expected to remain celibate), while a woman is able to marry a man, a calabai or a calalai. This presents a marked contrast to the either/or situation that has prevailed in Western societies.

The supposed incompatibility of Christianity and homosexuality in the United States is not found in South Pacific cultures, nor are there any issues for homosexual couples who adopt children. Marriage is broadly defined rather than limited to unions of biological males with biological females. We see that the non-biological explanations for homosexuality do not adequately explain homosexuality in other cultures and that these explanations are actually culturally bound. This supports the view that homosexuality is at least partly biologically determined in most cases and is a natural expression of human sexuality. The latter point is demonstrated by the occurrence of homosexuality throughout the world and throughout known history.

Biological explanations for homosexual orientation are the only ones that sufficiently account for homosexuality in humans and animals. However, it is possible that some individuals engage in homosexual behavior for reasons based in the peer-labeling or psychoanalytical theories. We know that some heterosexuals, under special circumstances such as incarceration, engage in homosexual behavior.[38] We have already considered the Sambia example in which men who engaged exclusively in same-sex behavior due to cultural requirements later become strictly heterosexual. Thus, because sexuality is both an inborn characteristic and a learned or chosen behavior, it is possible for a person to have one orientation and engage in behavior associated with the other. Certainly homosexuals have had to practice heterosexual behavior throughout much of the history of Western civilization. Although such individuals altered their behavior, their orientation may not have changed at all. Naturally left-handed individuals sometimes exhibit right-handed behavior, occasionally under duress: that does not demonstrate any actual change in their inherent orientation.

"Ex-gays"

Even though Freud's psychoanalytical theory has been rejected by most psychologists, one reason for its popularity among evangelical leaders is that it permits the possibility that sexual orientation can be changed. This view has given rise to all sorts of claims by evangelical leaders. For example, Focus on the Family's The Parsonage ministry for pastors says "Homosexuality is a symptom of fallen humanity. We are not born gay (Romans 1:26-27)"; "Homosexuality is a forgivable sin as one repents of their sin and turns to God (1 Corinthians 6:9-10; Isaiah 53:6; 1 John 1:9)"; and "How should Christians respond and reach out? ... Instill hope for change (1 Corinthians 6:11)."[39] In his recent book *Outrage*, Peter Sprigg states "I must be quite blunt here. The notion that people are 'born gay' is nothing less than The Big Lie of the entire homosexual movement. Science has not proven that there is a 'gay gene' or that people are 'born gay.'"[40]

The belief that change is possible is supposedly further supported by the Bible. In modern English translations Paul appears to suggest that some Corinthians changed their homosexuality ("And such *were* some of you ..." [emphasis added], 1 Corinthians 6:11). Thus, evangelical leaders translate the biblical passage as if

Paul said that some people in Corinth were once homosexuals, implying that they have changed. For example, James Dobson's Focus on the Family ministry declares that "1 Cor. 6:11 gives clear evidence that gays can change."[41] These evangelical leaders ignore the serious problems with this translation discussed in Chapter 5: no one knows what the word translated as "homosexuals" actually means, although it is clear it does not mean homosexuals.

Gordon Robertson also relies on 1 Corinthians 6:9-11 for his belief that homosexuality can be changed:

> That is the good news, that you can be transformed by the renewing of your mind. By the renewing of the Holy Spirit, you can change to be what God intended you to be, a child of the Living God. You don't have to walk through these kinds of degradations where you are just treated like a piece of meat.[42]

Robertson's reference to meat is based on the stereotype that homosexual men are pathologically promiscuous and view one another simply as outlets for sexual energy. While there are some homosexual males who put that concept into practice, just as some heterosexuals do (otherwise prostitutes would not have much work), the implication that this is the norm denies homosexual men their humanity. Furthermore, it denies that homosexual men have the capacity and desire to have loving and fulfilling relationships.

Robert Spitzer's "ex-gay" study

Psychiatrist Robert Spitzer published a study indicating that some homosexuals can change their sexuality.[43] Spitzer's study is controversial: the American Psychological Association said the "scientific evidence does not show that conversion therapy works and that it can do more harm than good."[44] Spitzer's study is based on 45-minute interviews with 143 men and 57 women who claim to be "ex-gay." Of his informants, 21 percent were still in therapy at the time of the study, while 28 percent engaged in regular heterosexual sex before beginning therapy. Furthermore, 19 percent of the participants in the study were either involved in psychological counseling or were directors of ex-gay ministries. To qualify for the study the informants were required to have some degree of change from homosexuality to heterosexuality through what is known as reparative therapy, and the change had to have lasted a minimum of five years. Spitzer believes his study provides evidence that reparative therapy is sometimes successful.[45]

He reports that 66 percent of males and 44 percent of females achieved "good heterosexual functioning," defined in part as having sex at least once a month with someone of the opposite sex. However, only about 11 percent of the men (16 of 143) and 37 percent of the women (20 of 57) reported exclusive heterosexual desires after therapy; these figures are almost identical to the percentages of informants who did not often have same-sex attraction as teenagers.[46] In other words, 89 percent of the men and 63 percent of the women continued to have same-sex desires.

Spitzer's study was greeted warmly by evangelical organizations. Using the results as evidence, evangelical organizations proclaimed "Millions of gays and lesbians are being told by the mainstream media and the leaders of their own community that change is impossible, and that therapy will only lead to hopelessness and depression, which is simply false."[47] Focus on the Family's Bill Maier remarked "Dr. Spitzer's study clearly shows that homosexuality is not a permanent, unchangeable condition."[48] Significantly, Maier and other evangelical leaders ignored the extremely high frequency of informants who continued to have homosexual desires and all of the individuals who did not achieve the minimum amount of change required to be included in the study.

A superficial reading of Spitzer's study, combined with evangelical assumptions and arguments, creates the impression that homosexuals can change their orientation if they so desire. Closer scrutiny of the study, however, reveals major problems with this conclusion. For example, the 200 informants had to qualify by some change in their sexual behavior or desire to be *included* in the study. Thus many individuals who were unable to demonstrate change were excluded. Other studies of reparative therapy report that only about three percent of individuals who attempt the therapy achieve any degree of change.[49] A three percent success rate means that in a hypothetical group of 1,000 men and 1,000 women who desire to change their sexuality, only 30 males and 30 females would meet the minimum criteria to be included in Spitzer's study. Spitzer notes that only 66 percent of the males who met the minimum requirement for change achieved "good heterosexual functioning." Accordingly, only 20 of the original 1,000 men would reach this level. Of the 1,000 women in our hypothetical sample, only about 13 would achieve "good heterosexual functioning." Furthermore, if only 11 percent of males in Spitzer's study reported no further homosexual desires, in our hypothetical sample of 1,000 men in reparative therapy, only three (11 percent of the 30 who qualified for the study) would demonstrably change their sexuality. The results are slightly more encouraging for women: 11 of the original 1,000 females would be successful (37 percent of 30). In other words, out of 2,000 individuals only 14 (three men and 11 women), representing 0.7 percent of the individuals in the hypothetical group, would be able to change their sexuality. These results indicate that reparative therapy offers scant hope to any homosexual who wishes to become heterosexual. This is even more obvious in light of the facts that the percentage of individuals who reported complete change in their sexual desires is almost identical to the percentage of individuals who did not often have same-sex desires as teenagers. I find it highly unethical to claim that any homosexual who wants to change his or her sexuality can do so when the success rate is less than one percent. The low probability of success is mentioned by Spitzer himself:

> Obviously, this study cannot address the question of how often sexual reorientation therapy actually results in the substantial changes reported by most of the participants in this study. ... the marked change in sexual orientation reported by almost all of the study subjects *may be a rare or uncommon outcome of reparative therapy.*[50] [Emphasis added.]

Nonetheless, evangelical leaders ignore Spitzer's qualification and promote the idea that anyone who so desires can change his or her homosexuality through reparative therapy. The most that can honestly be said is that change may be possible for a very small number of individuals, particularly if they did not have same-sex attraction as teenagers.

There are, in addition, three other important points to consider in our examination of Spitzer's results: religion, marriage, and sexuality.

Religion. First, the majority of the informants shared the evangelical worldview that homosexuality is sinful and condemned by God, so there is considerable pressure for them to change their behavior. Dobson and others who state that change is possible increase this pressure. John Paulk, manager of Focus on the Family's homosexuality and gender division, and former chairman of Exodus International (which Paulk calls the largest homosexual-recovery organization in the world), was once featured in national articles and advertisements for being "ex-gay."[51] The advertisements, sponsored partly by Focus on the Family, stated that homosexuals can change their orientation and that he was living proof. Paulk also wrote an article in a Focus on the Family newsletter about his experiences "coming out" of homosexuality and being "healed" of it.[52] In the article he uses such phrases as "the same type of healing and grace that Mike and I have experienced," "homosexuality can often be treated successfully," and "individuals (like myself) who have overcome homosexuality." Only two months after writing this, Paulk was seen in gay bars. Evidently he had not overcome homosexuality, was not healed, and his homosexuality had not been treated successfully. He simply confused abstinence from same-sex behavior with healing.

To an evangelical leader, the statement that someone is "ex-gay" does not mean that the person has changed his or her sexual *orientation* but only his or her sexual *behavior.* Regina Griggs, executive director of Parents and Friends of Ex-Gays & Gays, illustrates this point: "If you have not been involved [in homosexual behavior] in over three years, which means to organizations like ours, that you have become ex-gay, you don't identify as a homosexual."[53] The situation involving former National Association of Evangelicals president Ted Haggard further demonstrates this assumption. After being outed by a male prostitute just before the 2006 national elections, Haggard entered reparative therapy. After just three weeks a spokesman declared that Haggard now realizes he is "completely heterosexual."[54] When people like Ted Haggard or John Paulk insist they truly are "ex-gay," they may have stopped living a "homosexual lifestyle," but their definitions are not explicit, and they differ from the general usage of "homosexual," so their statements can lead homosexuals to believe in the largely false hope that they can change.

Marriage. A second important consideration is that 66 percent of the men in Spitzer's study were married at the time of the study, as were 47 percent of the women (these frequencies are almost identical to the numbers who achieved "good heterosexual functioning" by having heterosexual intercourse at least once a month). This indicates there is also considerable familial pressure to change.

Sexuality. Many social scientists believe that human sexuality exists on a continuum: from heterosexuality to homosexuality, with varying degrees of bisexuality in between.[55] The continuum of sexuality raises further questions about claims of success in helping homosexuals change into heterosexuals. For example, in Spitzer's study 28 percent of participants had regular heterosexual sex before they began reparative therapy. Thus, at least one of four people included in the study were possibly bisexual, not homosexual.

It might be more accurate to state that the reported changes were simply among bisexuals who altered their *behavior* from homosexual to heterosexual. Evangelical sociologist Tony Campolo agrees, arguing those who are primarily homosexual eventually revert back to their original orientation.[56] If people who identify as homosexual come to see themselves as heterosexual, their position along the sexual orientation continuum has not shifted. A change in sexual *behavior* does not imply a change in sexual *orientation*. Most evangelical leaders, however, make no distinction between behavior and orientation. Spitzer does address this possibility in his study, although he is convinced that the reported changes were genuine.

Truly "ex-gay"?

The main criticism based on these three considerations (religion, marriage and sexuality) is that the participants may have deluded themselves into believing they had changed their sexuality, whereas it was their *behavior* that changed while their natural orientation became suppressed. While homosexuality appears to be primarily an inborn characteristic, caused partly by genetics and partly by hormones in the prenatal environment, this is not necessarily the case for *everyone*. It is entirely possible that the peer-labeling or psychoanalytical explanations of homosexuality may be true for *some* people. If so, these could be the people in Spitzer's study who appear to have changed their sexual orientation, but they would represent the exception rather than the rule.

Evangelical psychologists Stanton Jones and Don Workman also argue that some homosexuals are able to change their sexuality. Their profile of those who are able to change is sobering:

No study suggests that change comes from willingness to change or some simple set of procedures. There seems to be a consensus of opinion that change is most likely when motivation is strong, when there is a history of successful heterosexual functioning, when gender identity issues are not present, and when involvement in actual homosexual practice has been minimal.[57]

This profile does not support the predominant evangelical opinion that change is there for the asking. Jones and Workman's candidate for change appears to be either a heterosexual who has experimented with homosexual behavior, or a bisexual who has engaged primarily in heterosexual behavior. Evangelical claims that homosexuals can change if they want to simply distort the truth and ignore reality.

Results of "ex-gay" ministries

The evangelical leaders' proclamations that homosexuals can change their sexuality if they want to because it is not a permanent condition, are not only overly optimistic and deceptive, but also are potentially harmful. These proclamations ignore that the overwhelming majority of homosexuals who want to change their sexuality are not even able to make the "minimum change required" for inclusion in studies such as Spitzer's. I personally know several men, including myself, who attempted to change their sexuality through reparative therapy because we had been told it was possible. In every instance the therapy failed and most of us experienced depression, guilt, and ostracism from other evangelicals along with belief that God had abandoned or rejected us, or that God simply does not exist. Reparative therapy was a harmful experience that undermined our faith and destroyed relationships.[58] This is why the American Psychological Association issued a statement opposing reparative therapy -- it does more harm than good.[59]

Notwithstanding, many evangelicals blame the individuals who are unsuccessful at changing their sexual orientation for lack of motivation or insufficient faith in God. Blaming the individual or the parents for unusual biological traits has biblical precedent: in New Testament times, blindness was considered divine punishment for sins of the individual or parents,[60] and today people assume, for religious reasons, that a biological characteristic (homosexuality) is actually the result of personal sin or bad parenting. It seems little has changed in 2,000 years.

The use of Spitzer's study by Focus on the Family and other evangelical leaders highlights their inconsistencies on this issue. For example, in Focus on the Family's *Love Won Out* series the authors reject a scientific study that links female homosexuality to inborn biological characteristics because no other study has replicated the findings. Explaining why further studies have not been undertaken, they speculate that researchers fear the original findings would not be confirmed.[61] There are many possible reasons why the study has not been replicated, including a lack of funding, lack of necessary time to perform the analysis, or a lack of other interested researchers in this particular area of study. To suggest that it is because initial findings may not be confirmed is presumptive. Spitzer's findings also have not been replicated, yet evangelical leaders do not question the results and actually over-state them, considering the high failure rate among participants attempting to change their sexual orientation.

Exodus study

Evangelical psychologists Stanton Jones and Mark Yarhouse re-cently published the results of their study of individuals in the Exodus reparative therapy program, which funded the study. They claim that 11 individuals out of an original sample of 98 suc-cessfully changed from a homosexual orientation to heterosexual-ity, thereby replicating Spitzer's results.[62] However, one of the successful "conversions" later recanted his success, reporting his homosexual attraction was unchanged: he later left Exodus, stat-ing that faith-based therapy ministries are not "healthy or neces-sarily beneficial to participants."[63] Jones and Yarhouse nonetheless include him among their successful "conversions." Other indi-viduals considered successes report still having homosexual de-sires and attractions, even homoerotic dreams.[64] Contrary to the authors' claim, this study provides no evidence sexual orientation can be changed.

Latent heterosexuals with a homosexual problem

Don Schmierer asserts that "gender confusion," by which he means homosexuality, can be reversed to its heterosexual norm.[65] Joseph Nicolosi, former president of the National Association for Research and Therapy of Homosexuality, supports this view and believes that: "We are all heterosexual."[66] When I was in reparative therapy I once heard an evangelical leader proclaim that homosexuals are all actually "latent heterosexuals," needing only to rediscover their inborn heterosexual self. Unfortunately, a variety of harmful tech-niques were used in the 20th century to find the "latent heterosex-ual" in homosexuals.[67] Not surprisingly these efforts all failed. However, evangelical leaders argue that they have succeeded where others did not. Through what is called "reparative therapy" many evangelical leaders argue that change is indeed possible and a person can become "ex-gay." However, confusion remains as to what that change actually entails: celibacy or heterosexuality.

Robert Gagnon believes that, similar to idolatry, homosexual behavior is presented in the Bible as a willful suppression "of the obvious truth about God and God's design in the natural world."[68] However, biologist Bruce Bagemihl states that "Homosexuality is part of our evolutionary heritage as primates: anyone looking at the prevalence and elaboration of homosexual behavior among our closest relatives in the animal kingdom will be led, eventually, to this conclusion."[69] In fact, one could argue that God enjoys diversity, evidenced by the millions of species that exist and the variety of their sexual behavior and reproductive processes. Therefore, if we are to use the "obvious truth about God and God's design in the natural world" as our basis for what is appropriate behavior, then given the frequency of homosexuality throughout nature we can conclude that God created a diverse world and that homosexuality is in accord with the design. Thus, it would not be surprising that God made human sexuality a little more diverse than some would like to think.

Those who suggest that homosexuals should be discriminated against due to their sexual orientation have no support from science. If homosexuality is found throughout nature, is amoral, and is an inherited biological characteristic, does society have any legal or ethical basis for treating homosexuals differently than others? This is one of the dominant questions facing American society today and is the crux of the debate on same-sex marriage.

---

[1] Gilbert Herdt (1987, 10).

[2] Bruce Bagemihl (1999, 12). Additional articles on homosexuality in animals include Robert Epstein (February 2003), Charles E. Roselli et al. (2002) and Dinitia Smith (February 7, 2004). Smith focuses on a pair of male homosexual penguins at the Central Park Zoo that were pair-bonded for six years.

[3] Michael Alan Park (2006, 233-238).

[4] Frans de Waal (1997).

[5] Morton Kelsey and Barbara Kelsey (1999, 65). While I cannot agree that a study based on only 76 societies is "exhaustive," I do agree that homo-

sexuality is acceptable in one form or another in many or most of the world's cultures.

[6] Gilbert Herdt (1998, 63-64). Also see David F. Greenberg (1988).

[7] William H. Alkire (1965, 60).

[8] Alexandra Brewis (1996, 12).

[9] William H. Alkire (1965, 54).

[10] Paul Bahn and John Flenley (1992).

[11] Martha C. Ward (2005, 32).

[12] Alexandra Brewis (1996, 33-34).

[13] William A. Lessa (1966, 91).

[14] Edward Stein (1999).

[15] An interesting video documenting the *fa'afafine* is *Paradise Bent: Boys Will Be Girls in Samoa*, Re Angle Pictures, produced by Heather Croall (1999).

[16] Ibid (1999).

[17] Sue Farran (2004).

[18] Gilbert Herdt (1998, 106-108).

[19] The term "berdache" seen in the older literature is now considered derogatory.

[20] Walter L. Williams (1986, 2).

[21] Ibid (18).

[22] Brad Biglow, personal communication (June 16, 2005).

[23] Gilbert Herdt (1987, 1999, 2006).

[24] See Leviticus 15:19-24, 18:19 and 20:18.

[25] Gilbert Herdt (2006, 9-11)

[26] Ibid (2006, 23-24).

[27] Ian Hogbin (1970)

[28] Ibid (91).

[29] Ibid (103).

[30] Ibid (100-101).

[31] Gilbert Herdt (1987, 85).

[32] Chandler Burr (1994, 117-118). For a personal account of one man's efforts to seek a cure see Mel White (1994).

[33] K. J. Dover (1978, 185).

[34] Gilbert Herdt (1998, 67).

[35] E. E. Evans-Pritchard (1970, 1429).

[36] Marvin Harris and Orna Johnson (2003, 127-128).

[37] Sharyn Graham Davies (2007).

[38] John M. Coggeshall (1993).

[39] *The Parsonage* (1999).

[40] Peter Sprigg (2004, 37).

[41] See Bob Davies (2002, 14).

[42] Gordon Robertson (2003).

[43] Robert L. Spitzer (2003).

[44] American Psychological Association (1999, 160).

[45] Robert L. Spitzer (2003)

[46] Spitzer (2003, 407-408) suggests that 85 percent of the males and 61 percent of the females often or very often had same-sex attraction as teenagers. The tremendous similarity in the percentages that did not change with the percentages that had same-sex attraction as teenagers raises the possibility that the individuals who changed were able to do so because they were not born as homosexuals, but perhaps engaged in the behavior for reasons related to the traditional sociological or psychological theories discussed in the last chapter. Unfortunately, Spitzer does not indicate if the individuals who were able to change were among the individuals who did not have same-sex attraction as teenagers.

[47] Focus on the Family (November 6, 2003).

[48] Ibid.

[49] Ariel Shidlo and Michael Schroeder (2001) report that of 202 individuals who attempted reparative therapy only 6 achieved a "heterosexual shift," including leaders in the reparative therapy movement. E. Monsell Pattison and Myrna L. Pattison (1980) argue that only 11 out of 300 individuals who attempted reparative therapy can arguably be suggested to have been successful in changing their sexuality.

[50] Robert L. Spitzer (2003, 413).

[51] John Leland and Mark Miller (August 17, 1998).

[52] John Paulk (July 2000).

[53] Citizen Link (December 1, 2005).

[54] Neela Banerjee (February 7, 2007).

[55] Kinsey et al. (1948). Here we focus solely on gender-preference; if other aspects of sexual attraction are included, the situation becomes much more complex. Edward Stein (1999) provides an in-depth discussion on the variety of factors that affect sexual orientation. The factors extend beyond the actual sex of the person to other factors such as height, hair color, skin color, aggressiveness and so on. Stein implies that the homosexual-bisexual-heterosexual continuum is insufficient to express sexual orientation. While agreeing in principle with him, I believe that Stein is confusing a person's inborn sexual orientation (homosexual, bisexual, heterosexual, or asexual) with the specific traits to which a person is attracted. The preferred traits are quite plausibly influenced or determined by a person's social environment. Throughout his book Stein confuses these aspects of sexuality and ignores the differences between the prenatal and postnatal environments.

[56] Tony Campolo (2004, 61).

[57] Stanton L. Jones and Don E. Workman (1994, 103).

[58] See Jason Cianciotto and Sean Cahill (2006) for a more thorough discussion of ex-gay ministries.

[59] American Psychological Association (1999, 160).

[60] John 9:1-12.

[61] Focus on the Family (2001).

[62] Stanton L. Jones and Mark A. Yarhouse (2007, 285).

[63] Ibid (301).

[64] Ibid (297-298).

[65] Don Schmierer (1999).

[66] Joseph Nicolosi (2002).

[67] Chandler Burr (1994, 117-118).

[68] Robert A. J. Gagnon (2001, 286).

[69] Bruce Bagemihl (1999, 64).

8 WITH THIS RING

> *How about group marriage? Or marriage between daddies and little girls? How about marriage between a man and his donkey? Anything allegedly linked to "civil rights" will be doable.*
>
> —James Dobson[1]

Peter Sprigg correctly states that marriage "is an anthropological and sociological reality, not a legal one."[2] Marriage, however, means different things to evangelical leaders and to anthropologists. Evangelical leaders advance a supposedly traditional view that marriage is a legal bond recognized by God between one biological male and one biological female: there are no alternatives. Glenn Stanton and Bill Maier, authors of *Marriage on Trial*, explain the supposed purpose and nature of marriage:

> All societies recognize that marriage regulates sexual relationships between men and women; marriage is a durable union, lasting for life, or at least (in other societies) as long as the child is developing into young adulthood; marriage is always between men and women; marriage is always about the next generation.[3]

Therefore, allowing two people of the same sex to marry "destroys" their concept of marriage. However, anthropologists demonstrate that Stanton and Maier's analysis is incorrect.

To an anthropologist, marriage is the economic, social, and political union of two individuals and their families.[4] While this definition seems straightforward, it is actually quite vague. First, it says nothing about love as a reason for marriage, with economic, social, and political considerations taking precedence. Second, it is silent about the sexual aspect of marriage. Third, "two individuals" does not imply monogamy as opposed to polygamy. Rather, each contract involves two individuals and their families: a person can have such a contract with more than one person at a time. Fourth, the union of two individuals does not necessarily mean two adults or two people of opposite sex; it simply means two individuals. The anthropological reality of marriage is that while marriage is almost universal in human society, its forms are highly variable. The current debate about marriage calls for a detailed examination of what it means in different cultures, also helping us to understand marriage as it is described in the Bible.

Marriage is the economic, social and political union . . .

The economic and social aspects of marriage are often initiated with the exchange of either a dowry or bridewealth (also known as bride price). A dowry is essentially a woman's inheritance, given to her when she leaves her family at marriage.[5] Her husband becomes the caretaker of the dowry. If he divorces her for reasons other than her infidelity, he must give the dowry back. If she has children, the dowry will usually be divided among them upon her death. Gifts of economic value from the groom's family to the bride's are known as bridewealth, recompense for the labor lost when a daughter moves away. Frequently bridewealth is returned if the husband divorces the woman for not bearing children: infertility is regarded as the woman's fault. Both dowry and bridewealth were practiced in ancient Israel.

Modern Western society generally believes that marriage should be based on love; accordingly, marriage solely for economic or political reasons is frowned upon. However, this Western ideal only became common in the late 18th century.[6] Anthropological studies demonstrate that neither sex nor love is an inherent aspect of all marriages. The Tiwi of northern Australia are an interesting example of these points. In traditional Tiwi culture, females had to be married at all times, from birth until death.[7] The female's "father" (not necessarily the biological father), would normally arrange the marriage; if an elderly woman was widowed her son(s) would arrange the marriage upon the death of her husband. The "father" or son(s) would choose a spouse based on economic or political factors. Frequently, the "father" would give the female to a friend of his, as would the son(s). The result was that a female could be married to a male 50 years older, or 50 years younger than her. There was no requirement for a sexual relationship between the man and his wife. She was primarily an economic commodity and a potential source for additional wealth: the more wives a man had, the richer he was. Also, the more wives he had, the more daughters he would likely have as assets in future economic transactions. Although adultery was considered a serious crime in Tiwi society, it was not uncommon. Young girls became pregnant even though they never had sex with their senile husbands. Pregnancy was not seen as a sign of infidelity because the Tiwi believed that a spirit caused the pregnancy. While we might consider this a primitive view of how babies are conceived, most Christians believe that the Virgin Mary became pregnant in exactly this manner.

The Tiwi example also highlights further differences between Western notions of marriage and those expressed in many cultures around the world, including ancient Israel. The differences include the age when a person is considered eligible for marriage and the age difference between spouses. In ancient Israel, females married in their early teens, generally between 12 and 16 years old, while males normally married in their late 20s or 30s.[8] The age difference provides one explanation for why Joseph, Jesus' father, was not present during Jesus' ministry: he was probably considerably older than Mary and may have died by the time Jesus began teaching.

... of two individuals and their families

Many societies, including those in the Middle East, are oriented around the family rather than the individual. Thus, marriage involves the joining of two families, not just two individuals. Parents or relatives arrange the marriage as an economic, social, and political union of the families; it is too important a decision to be left to the bride and groom. In fact, the preferred marriage partner for an individual in ancient Israel, and in many other societies throughout the world, was a person's cousin. An arranged marriage between cousins is described in Genesis 24 where Abraham sent a servant to seek a wife for his son, Isaac. The servant went to the household of Nahor, Abraham's brother, and arranged a marriage with Rebekah, Abraham's niece. This was typical practice in biblical times and is still practiced in many places throughout the world. Arranged marriages within the extended family keep wealth within the group and strengthen kinship ties and obligations.

The aspect of marriage defined as a union of two individuals and their families does not require that the two individuals be of opposite sex. In the previous chapter we discussed some societies that allow same-sex marriages, although in many cases one individual assumes the role of the opposite gender. This is the most common arrangement in traditional cultures that recognize marriage between two members of the same biological sex. Thus, marriage is usually defined worldwide as the union of two individuals of different *gender*, not different sex. This is actually a major difference, but difficult for members of Western society to grasp because we tend not to distinguish sex from gender: sex is based on a person's genitals, while gender is the social expression of expected behaviors for both men and women. Several modern Western nations allow marriage between members of the same sex (and same gender), while others allow civil unions. There is historical evidence of same-sex marriage in Western society. In 1581 Michel de Montaigne wrote in his travel journal about a Portuguese church that performed same-sex marriages, with a Catholic Mass, employing the same ceremonies and gospel services used in heterosexual marriages.[9] The most important aspect of marriage in societies around the world is not the sex of the two individuals, but the economic, social, and political alliances they create.

Defining marriage as between two individuals does not imply that marriage is monogamous. It simply means that the economic, social, and political arrangement involves the union of two individuals, but not necessarily to the exclusion of others. This can be illustrated by considering exactly who is married in a polygamous situation. If one man has married five women, there are five marriages: the man with each of the five women. However, the women are not married to each other. Each woman is married solely to the man. Thus, in this example five separate marriage contracts have been concluded, each involving two individuals. To my knowledge, no society views all the individuals in a polygamous marriage as being married to each other. It is either one man married to each of his wives (polygyny) or, more rarely, one woman married to each of her husbands (polyandry).

In a study of 565 cultures around the world, anthropologists found polygyny in more than 74 percent of the world's cultures.[10] The second most common form of marriage was monogamy, with only 25 percent of the world's cultures being strictly monogamous. Finally, only a handful of cultures, all found in the region around Tibet and Nepal, practiced polyandry. Thus, from a cross-cultural perspective, the Western belief that marriage must be monogamous is actually a minority view.

Anthropology helps explain why polygyny is acceptable in 74 percent of world cultures, but not in industrial societies. Polygyny is usually found in societies where there are large age differences between husbands and wives. In these societies females usually marry in their early teens and, when combined with the shorter life spans of men, the age disparity creates an abundance of women of marriageable age. Therefore, polygyny helps ensure that a woman's basic needs will be met. Western societies view prohibitions against polygyny as an issue of female equality and societal fairness: monogamy eliminates potential conflicts between co-wives as well as between wealthy men who can marry many women and those who cannot. Furthermore, polygynous societies generally treat women as property to be acquired, a value completely contrary to the view in 21st century America. Thus, polygyny is considered inappropriate, even immoral, in our society.

Polygyny in the Bible

The first biblical mention of polygyny is in Genesis 4:19, which states that Lamech took two wives. Using biblical chronologies and assuming a literal Bible, Lamech was born only 874 years after creation and had his first child 1,056 years after creation, which is suggested to have occurred about 4000 BC. Thus, according to biblical tradition, polygyny was in practice by about 3000 BC. Many of the important Old Testament heroes were polygynists or had one wife and at least one concubine, female servants or slaves with whom a man could have sex without entering into a "legal" marriage. This practice is not condemned in the Old Testament, even though many evangelical leaders consider it adulterous. For example, Jacob was married to two sisters, Leah and Rachel (marrying sisters is actually condemned in Leviticus 18:18, although Jacob is never rebuked for it in the Bible), and he also had two concubines. King David had several wives and concubines, but this was nothing compared to his son Solomon, who is supposed to have had 700 wives and 300 concubines.[11] These examples demonstrate that both polygyny and concubinage were practiced in ancient Israel.

The Bible also indicates that polygyny was acceptable in Hebrew society. Old Testament laws include guidelines about who a man can and cannot marry. The Bible explicitly states that a man cannot marry two sisters,[12] but there is no prohibition against marrying two unrelated women. Polygyny is also incorporated into laws that regulate inheritance. For example, Deuteronomy 21:15-16:

> If a man has two wives, the one loved and the other unloved, and both the loved and the unloved have borne him sons, if the first-born son belongs to the unloved, then it shall be in the day he wills what he has to his sons, he cannot make the son of the loved the first-born before the son of the unloved, who is the first-born.

Not only does this passage show that polygyny was practiced, it also demonstrates that it was accepted: there is no hint of condemnation here or elsewhere in the Old Testament.

One biblical commentary cites five verses that supposedly condemn polygyny.[13] When the passages are carefully examined, however, it is clear that none of them actually condemns the practice. For example, in the original Hebrew, Deuteronomy 17:17 says that a king should not take "many wives," but does not indicate what constitutes "many." The New American Standard Bible says the king should not "multiply wives," making it appear to condemn polygyny when it actually does not.

Neither shall he multiply wives for himself, lest his heart turn away; nor shall he greatly increase silver and gold for himself.
— Deuteronomy 17:17

> But not one has done so who has a remnant of the spirit. And what did that one do while he was seeking a godly offspring? Take heed then, to your spirit, and let no one deal treacherously against the wife of your youth. "For I hate divorce," says the LORD, the God of Israel, "and him who covers his garment with wrong," says the LORD of hosts. "So take heed to your spirit, that you do not deal treacherously." – Malachi 2:15-16

> And He answered and said, "Have you not read, that He who created them from the beginning made them male and female, and said, 'For this cause a man shall leave his father and mother, and shall cleave to his wife; and the two shall become one flesh'? Consequently they are no more two, but one flesh. What therefore God has joined together, let no man separate." – Matthew 19:4-6

> An overseer, then must be above reproach, the husband of one wife, temperate, prudent, respectable, hospitable, able to teach, not addicted to wine or pugnacious, but gentle, uncontentious, free from the love of money. – 1 Timothy 3:2-3

> For this reason I left you in Crete, that you might set in order what remains, and appoint elders in every city as I directed you, namely, if any man be above reproach, the husband of one wife, having children who believe, not accused of dissipation or rebellion. – Titus 1:5-6

In context, Malachi 2:15 and Matthew 19:4 are both about divorce and do not suggest that polygyny is wrong. In fact it is difficult to understand how the Bible commentator saw any connection whatsoever to polygyny in Malachi 2:15. In Matthew 19 Jesus' statement that the man and woman become one flesh does not actually imply monogamy. A man can become one flesh with many women. She is joined to him at marriage and is entirely dependent upon him for survival. Her fortunes are tied in with his. The two people are symbolically and economically one flesh. Many evangelical leaders take Jesus' comments out of context and use them as a proof text that Jesus defines marriage as being monogamous, between one man and one woman. However, in Matthew 19 Jesus is explicitly talking about divorce; he is not defining marriage. He is stating that once two people are married they are one flesh and cannot be separated. Divorce robs a woman of the necessary means of survival because she has no economic independence, therefore divorce is prohibited.

Meanwhile, Titus 1:6 simply restates the directive in 1 Timothy 3:2 that church leaders should only have one wife. Many evangelicals take this to mean that the New Testament condemns polygyny. However, the passage only bars polygyny for church leaders, not for everyone. There is absolutely no condemnation of general polygyny in the Bible.

Another passage relevant to how the Bible "defines" marriage comes from Jesus' parable in Matthew 25:1-13. In this story Jesus talks about ten virgins who were waiting for the groom to arrive, apparently so they could marry him. Five of the virgins were not prepared and missed the ceremony so the groom married five women instead of ten. While the purpose of this parable is not to discuss the morality of polygyny, it does show that Jesus used polygyny as a legitimate example of marriage. Jesus could easily have used ten grooms to convey the same message had he believed polygyny to be wrong. In order to get around the problem of Jesus using polygyny as an example of marriage, some evangelicals I know believe that in this parable the virgins were simply attendants and not the brides preparing for the wedding. However, this view is inconsistent with Jesus' other teachings about the kingdom of heaven and with ancient Israel's culture. Thus, we see that even in the time of the New Testament, polygyny was known, practiced, and accepted. Monogamy as the *only* definition of marriage is a more recent development: it is not mandated in the Bible.

> When brothers live together and one of them dies and has no son, the wife of the deceased shall not be married outside the family to a strange man. Her husband's brother shall go in to her and take her to himself as wife and perform the duty of a husband's brother to her. And it shall be that the first-born whom she bears shall assume the name of his dead brother, that his name may not be blotted out from Israel. – Deuteronomy 25:5-6

Levirate marriage

Deuteronomy 25:5-6 highlights a further biblical command about marriage that is ignored in Western society: the levirate marriage, in which a widow marries the brother of her dead husband. The levirate marriage is mentioned in several biblical passages. For example, the Old Testament tells the story of Ruth, whose husband died without leaving her a son. Her husband had no surviving brothers for her to marry and have children with in order to continue his name. Ruth found one of her husband's relatives, Boaz, who could act as the "kinsman redeemer" and give her a child who would take on her late husband's name. The kinsman redeemer was normally the next of kin whose duty it was to vindicate a family member, redeem a family member sold into slavery, or provide a child for a deceased family member to preserve the latter's name and inheritance.[14] Ultimately, the book of Ruth suggests that the child born to Boaz and Ruth was King David's grandfather.

One is tempted to dismiss the levirate marriage command in that it obligates a man only when brothers live together, which is generally not the case in Western society. However, in ancient Israel it was the norm for brothers to live in the same household with their parents, wives, and offspring. Thus, the command is almost a universal decree that anytime a man dies without a son, his brother must marry his widow, even if the brother is already married. Furthermore, Boaz, even though he was a distant relative of Ruth's husband, recognized the importance of the spirit of this command and abided by it. This command ensures that the widow was provided for after her husband's death, an important consideration in a society where women had few rights and little potential for economic independence.

Genesis 38 tells the more sordid story of Tamar, the wife of Judah's first-born son, Er. Er died before any children were born to him. According to levirate marriage laws, which actually postdate the story if we assume a literal Bible, Tamar had to marry one of Er's brothers. Therefore, Judah instructed Onan to take Tamar and give Er a child through her. Onan refused and "wasted his seed on the ground, in order to prevent his seed becoming offspring for his brother."[15] This displeased God, who then took Onan's life. The next son was too young at the time to father children, so Tamar was forced to wait for him to come of age. After a long time had passed, the third son never fulfilled his kinsman redeemer obligation and Tamar took matters into her own hands.

She disguised herself as a prostitute, had sex with Judah, and became pregnant with her father-in-law's child. When Judah discovered that Tamar was pregnant, not knowing he was the father, he ordered that she be burned alive for her infidelity to his young son. Due to precautions she took earlier, Tamar demonstrated that Judah was the father. He then declared that she was more righteous than he, because he did not require his third son to perform the levirate marriage, and repealed the death sentence.

This story has many interesting components relevant to marriage and sexual behavior. The most important aspect for our present purposes is the biblical command about levirate marriage. Once again, while many evangelical leaders claim to uphold biblical traditions on marriage and insist that marriage is only between one man and one woman, they disregard many specific biblical commands associated with it. This is not surprising because the evangelical definition of marriage is based on modern Western culture and has little to do with the Bible. Nonetheless, it demonstrates that many evangelical leaders use the Bible selectively to support their views, and ignore the rest of what it says. This technique is also reflected in evangelical views on divorce.

Divorce, homosexuals, and marriage

About 50 years ago divorce was not common in American society. Jesus clearly states that divorce followed by remarriage is adultery, although some of the gospel accounts state that Jesus made an exception if unfaithfulness was involved.[16] Victor Furnish summarizes the biblical view of divorce as "a perversion of the created order and thus always contrary to God's will."[17] However, when one examines evangelical attitudes towards divorce and remarriage, a different picture emerges. While many evangelicals do publicly state that divorce is bad and claim to define marriage as Jesus does, some do not practice what they preach. In my experience with Bible study groups for two different evangelical churches, the majority of the married people had actually been divorced and remarried. It is highly inconsistent that many evangelical leaders denounce homosexuality by using the Bible to justify their actions, while they completely ignore Jesus' recorded words about divorce and remarriage. In fact, one Christian polling organization indicates that divorce rates are actually *higher* among evangelicals and fundamentalists than other Christians or non-Christians.[18]

In his letters to the Corinthians Paul tells Christians who are not married to remain single unless they cannot control their sexual passions.[19] Paul was under the impression that Jesus would return during his lifetime. Thus, he encouraged his followers to be like himself: to remain single and devote the rest of their lives to serving God. Paul suggests that only if sexual temptations become too great a burden should a person marry. However, while Paul allows people to marry if sexual desires are too strong for them, many evangelicals refuse to allow homosexuals the same option. They state that homosexuals must either remain celibate or marry a person of the opposite sex. However, Jesus explicitly states that not everyone is able to live a celibate life.[20] Furthermore, heterosexual marriage would do little to alleviate the natural sex drive for a homosexual.

The denial of marriage to homosexuals has additional negative repercussions.[21] Responding to conservative newspaper columnist Mona Charen, Bruce Bawer comments that the evangelical insistence on the traditional family implies a belief that it is better for homosexuals to either enter into heterosexual marriages or lead lonely, promiscuous lives:

> the *real* choice faced by society is not between traditional families and gay families, but between, on the one hand, the relative stability and monogamy of gay couples and, on the other, the relative volatility of the solitary gay or the secretly gay husband or wife.[22]

Many homosexuals, especially those who are Christian, do marry someone of the opposite sex. Many evangelical leaders encourage them to believe they can change their homosexuality and hope that in marriage heterosexual behavior will override their homosexual orientation. Nonetheless, as we saw in the last chapter, that change is unlikely to occur.

The Family Research Council (FRC) argues that "[Marriage] is about preserving the best environment for raising children and the safest, *healthiest living situation for adults*. Without strong marriages as our bedrock, our nation will suffer a devastating blow"[23] [emphasis added]. The FRC argues that a homosexual remaining in a heterosexual marriage, living a lie, and constantly denying his or her biological orientation and need for intimacy with someone of the same sex, is the healthiest living situation possible for him or her. The FRC fails to follow through with the logic of its own statements and beliefs. Traditionally, homosexuals have had to remain single or follow societal expectations and marry someone of the opposite sex. Yet evangelical leaders claim that the results of homosexuals living in this situation are high rates of depression, suicide, promiscuity and so on.[24] Based on these stereotypes, one would conclude that heterosexual marriage is *not* the "healthiest living situation" for homosexual adults. The healthiest situation is one in which society encourages homosexuals to be faithful in their relationships, adhere to the same standards that apply to heterosexuals, and enjoy the same rights and privileges. Bruce Bawer argues that "to celebrate such a person's marriage to a person of the opposite sex, is to embrace a lie about that person and to do something that is cruel to both parties in the marriage."[25] The evangelical practice of encouraging homosexuals to marry a person of the opposite sex does more to dishonor "the sanctity of marriage" than would allowing homosexuals to marry. Such marriages typically end with the heterosexual spouse feeling betrayed, the children devastated, and the homosexual internally conflicted.[26]

"The Bishop Robinson effect"

In an effort to stem the tide of growing acceptance of homosexuals, evangelical leaders support a federal constitutional amendment to define marriage as between one man and one woman. In the meantime, conservative politicians submitted several state constitutional amendments to achieve the goal of preserving "traditional marriage." Of interest, 42 states enacted anti-miscegenation laws to preserve "traditional marriage" after a proposed federal constitutional amendment banning interracial marriages failed in 1912.[27]

The FRC, an organization founded in part by James Dobson, articulates the predominant evangelical view of how same-sex marriage would destroy the institution of marriage. In response to the Massachusetts Supreme Court ruling on same-sex marriage, Peter Sprigg of the FRC said that unless we change the federal and state constitutions to "protect" marriage as only between one man and one woman, "we will lose marriage in this nation."[28] Sprigg argues that the defining characteristic of a marriage is the joining of one man and one woman. Therefore, legalizing same-sex marriage would violate this definition and destroy marriage: it would no longer be marriage because it would not solely be between one man and one woman. However, as we have seen, Sprigg's definition of marriage is not recognizable to anthropologists, sociologists, or to the vast majority of the world's cultures. Pierre Tristam issued an appropriate response to similar comments:

> Those who call themselves defenders of marriage as we have known it – as the federal 'Defense of Marriage Act' defines it, as only a union between man and woman – imply that anything different demeans marriage. But that's like saying that giving women the right to vote demeaned men's vote or that extending freedom to blacks demeaned the freedom of whites.[29]

Sprigg says that same-sex marriage will negatively affect attitudes towards marriage by encouraging heterosexuals to enter into "transient, promiscuous and unfaithful relationships."[30] Using this logic, if we are to deny marriage to groups that do not maintain permanence in marriage, then it is really the evangelicals who should be denied the right to marry, given that divorce rates are now higher among them than among other groups.[31] Once again, Sprigg's comments rely on stereotypes that are not inherent to homosexuality. Homosexuals have the same capacity as heterosexuals for engaging in monogamous, faithful, long-term marriages. This has been clearly demonstrated by the many homosexual couples who have been married, legally or otherwise, in Massachusetts, California, New York, and Oregon: some of them had been together for 52 years before they could marry. Many homosexuals desire societal support in establishing and maintaining marriages consistent with the traditional Western expectations of married behavior. This is significant when, according to theologian John Cobb, Jr., the church effectively encourages homosexuals to engage in secret and temporary liaisons, and discourages faithful, monogamous relationships.[32]

Sprigg is also concerned with what he calls "The Bishop Robinson Effect:"

> To believe that homosexual marriage would not harm heterosexual marriage, one would have to believe that no one who is in a heterosexual marriage could ever be tempted by the possibility of a homosexual relationship – and we know that that is not the case.[33]

Elsewhere, he adds that "Forty percent of the people entering 'civil unions' in Vermont were previously in heterosexual marriages – just like the new Episcopal bishop, Gene Robinson, who left his wife and children for a homosexual lover."[34] Sprigg is demonstrating his assumption that people choose to be homosexual. He fears that heterosexuals all over the country will suddenly choose to engage in homosexual behavior and abandon their heterosexual marriages for homosexual ones. Sprigg's view does not speak very highly of heterosexual marriages, or of heterosexual behavior in general. In reality he is revealing his preference that homosexuals remain in heterosexual marriages, effectively that they should live a lie that is harmful to the individual and his or her family. Jonathan Rauch argues that Sprigg's view -- homosexuals should not be allowed to marry someone of the same sex but should remain in heterosexual marriages -- highlights a double standard: no one would demand that heterosexuals only marry people they do not love or sexually desire, yet that is precisely what many evangelical leaders demand of homosexuals.[35]

Procreation and marriage

A final assertion by Sprigg is that the principal reasons for marriage are reproduction and child rearing,[36] a justification supported by former Senator Rick Santorum (R. -Pennsylvania):

> Every society in the history of man has upheld the institution of marriage as a bond between a man and a woman. Why? Be-

cause society is based on one thing: that society is based on the future of the society. And that's what? Children. Monogamous relationships. In every society, the definition of marriage has not ever to my knowledge included homosexuality. That's not to pick on homosexuality. It's not, you know, man on child, man on dog, or whatever the case may be.[37]

Senator Santorum is wrong on several points. First, he ignores that many societies around the world include same-sex unions as a legitimate form of marriage.[38] Second, monogamy is not the preferred form of marriage in the majority of cultures: three times as many prefer polygamy to monogamy.[39] Finally, not every society has the institution of marriage, evidenced by the Mosuo of southwestern China,[40] a matrilineal society in which property and familial membership are determined by the maternal lineage. Mosuo women have male lovers who visit them at night and then return to their matrilineal extended families in the morning, for a Mosuo man's responsibility is to his mother and sisters. He has no obligations to his lover or to any children he might father.

Peter Sprigg responds to the inevitable question that if marriage is solely for reproduction, then why do we allow those to marry who are infertile, do not want children, or are past childbearing age? He agrees in principle: "In fact, I would suggest that the actual, tangible public interest in childless marriages is not as great as the public interest in marriages that produce children."[41] However, he believes that this "would require an invasion of privacy or the drawing of arbitrary and inexact lines."[42] What Sprigg does not explain is why, if marriage primarily exists for procreation, it would be arbitrary to tell heterosexual couples who cannot have children that they cannot marry, but it would not be arbitrary to tell homosexual couples they cannot marry for the same reason. If the justification for marriage is procreation and the raising of children, then restricting marriage for any other reason is arbitrary. His argument also disregards the possibility of adoption as an avenue for all couples to raise children.

Jonathan Rauch disagrees with the notion that procreation is the primary purpose for Western marriage. Instead, he argues marriage is centered on two people caring for each other.[43] Rauch believes that the traditional wedding vows from the 1662 Book of Common Prayer illustrate this, given that there is no mention of children, sex, inheritance, or personal fulfillment.

Peter Sprigg recognizes that American society's view of marriage has changed over the years. Sprigg argues that the sexual revolution and the increase in divorce and "illegitimate" births have undermined marriage in the United States.[44] I am surprised that he then argues that individuals who desire to uphold faithfulness, monogamy, love and commitment to another person are actually destroying marriage. One could argue that homosexuals are defending the concept of marriage, while heterosexuals, evangelicals in particular, are destroying it through high divorce rates.

> To have and to hold from this day forward, for better for worse, for richer for poorer, in sickness and in health, to love, cherish and to obey, till death us do part.
> – Book of Common Prayer Wedding Vows

The end of civilization

James Dobson also actively opposes same-sex marriage. Early in 2004 he sent a letter to people on the Focus on the Family mailing list, setting forth his arguments against same-sex marriage.[45] He argues that due to homosexual activists, traditional marriage is in "grave danger," despite having been "celebrated by every culture on earth as the cornerstone of society."[46] Dobson defines "traditional marriage" as solely one man and one woman, ignoring that polygamy is accepted by a majority of the world's cultures and that same-sex marriages are accepted in many different societies throughout the world.

In 2003, after hearing Dobson assert during an interview that monogamy is the exclusive marital practice in most of the world's cultures, I e-mailed him for clarification.[47] Timothy Masters, one of Dobson's researchers, responded: "When the Doctor asserted that most cultures in the world have been monogamous in their approach to marriage, he was referring exclusively to contemporary civilized or industrialized societies."[48] Thus, Dobson was misleading the viewers, for he failed to mention that he was only referring to contemporary industrialized societies. Among thousands of cultures, he was referencing a very small percentage as the basis of a sweeping generalization. Ironically, Dobson dismisses all non-industrialized societies as irrelevant, but claims that his authority is based on the writings of a non-industrialized society, whose marriage practices were consistent with other non-industrialized societies, and are contrary to those of modern Western society.

Returning to Dobson's letter, with warnings that Western civilization hangs in the balance, he employs the slippery slope argument: allowing same-sex marriage will lead to polygamy, group marriage, incest, and bestiality. Dobson associates homosexuality with polygamy and incest, apparently in an attempt to convince the public that homosexuality is the moral equivalent of certain unacceptable behaviors and should therefore be opposed.

Many conservative politicians agree with Dobson's assessment. For example, commenting on the then-pending Texas sodomy law before the United States Supreme Court, Pennsylvania Senator Rick Santorum suggested that if the Supreme Court legalized homosexual acts they would be on the slippery slope to legitimizing polygamy, incest, and adultery.[49] Senator Santorum argued that if the right to privacy protects homosexual behavior, then any other consensual act must be protected as well.

Comparing homosexuals with polygamists and the incestuous, however, has no basis in clear reasoning. While associating one of the objectionable behaviors with others may strike a chord with many evangelical leaders and believers, it remains that homosexuality and, for instance, incest are different and unrelated aspects of human behavior. One does not lead to the other.

Polygamy. Andrew Sullivan highlights other flaws in the slippery slope argument, pointing out that the issue of whether government should allow only heterosexuals to marry the unrelated adult they love is completely separate from whether people should be allowed to marry more than one person at the same time.[50] Granting homosexuals an equal right to marry would not lead to polygamy, which would remain prohibited. Furthermore, that has not been the result in any of the nations where same-sex marriages or civil unions are permitted. If same-sex marriage were allowed in the United States it would simply mean that *all* Americans could enter into a monogamous marriage with an unrelated single adult they love. Under the current law, only *some* Americans can enter into a monogamous marriage with the person they love. Jonathan Rauch notes that

the hidden assumption of the argument which brackets gay marriage with polygamous or incestuous marriage is that homosexuals want the right to marry anybody they fall for. But, of course, heterosexuals are currently denied that right. They cannot marry their immediate family or all their sex partners. What homosexuals are asking for is the right to marry, not anybody they love, but *somebody* they love, which is not at all the same thing.[51] [Emphasis in original.]

Andrew Sullivan adds that when interracial marriage became legal and when women were no longer considered the legal property of their husbands there was a similar negative reaction among many evangelicals.[52] Simply put, comparisons of homosexuality with polygamy by evangelical leaders lack a reasoned foundation.

Andrew Sullivan also notes that there is no logical connection between accepting same-sex marriage and allowing polygamy: the slippery-slope argument rests on the assumption that desire to have more than one spouse is equivalent to desire to love someone of the same sex. It also confuses polygamy, an activity or behavior, with homosexuality and heterosexuality, which are states of being.[53] Jonathan Rauch argues that the "anything goes" argument put forth by evangelical leaders as a reason to prevent same-sex marriages actually exposes a significant flaw in their reasoning: it suggests "that there are no good reasons other than blind adherence to tradition to oppose plural marriage."[54]

Incest. Incest is essentially a universal taboo, although there are three well-known exceptions of institutionalized incest found among the royal families of ancient Egypt, Hawaii, and the Inca of Peru. As with polygamy, the comparison of homosexuality to sexual relations among nuclear family members is difficult to comprehend. It appears to be designed to strike a chord of repulsion among evangelicals and other people sympathetic to the evangelical leaders' message.

Incest is socially defined and takes two main forms in American society: brother-sister or parent-offspring. We consider brother-sister incest immoral because it greatly increases the possibility that any resulting children would suffer from harmful recessive genetic traits. The parent-offspring form of incest has two categories, incestuous pedophilia and incest between consenting adults. We consider incestuous pedophilia immoral for the same reason that pedophilia in general is immoral: it violates a child who is not able to resist. Parent-offspring incest, when both are consenting adults, can be considered immoral for the same reason that brother-sister incest is considered immoral: it increases the chance of genetic defects in any resulting offspring.

These reasons for the inherent immorality of incest do not apply to brother-brother incest or sister-sister incest, for those relations could not result in children. Still, these rare forms of incest are also considered immoral, perhaps because most societies view sex between members of the same family as wrong (although definitions of family membership vary). It is quite obvious why incest is generally considered immoral, but homosexuality occurs between mutually consenting non-related adults, so it has scant similarity to incest except that evangelicals do not approve of either.

The slippery slope to extinction

In his letter mentioned earlier, Dobson agrees with conservative columnist Maggie Gallagher that the central reason for marriage is for a father and mother to raise children in a "safe and loving environment." This view is blind to the role of marriage as an economic, social, and political union of two individuals and their families. From Dobson's standpoint, the traditional family "as it has been known for 5,000 years *will become extinct*" [emphasis added], resulting in "chaos such as the world has never seen before."[55] Despite his unfounded assumption that the family has been this way for 5,000 years (as we have seen, the Bible indicates polygynous families existed 5,000 years ago), Dobson presents four reasons for his belief that the family is in danger and world chaos is the only possible outcome:

Violating God's plan. First, Dobson believes that God instituted marriage as the union of one man and one woman, based on the Adam and Eve story.[56] Dobson's analysis falters on three different fronts. First, Adam and Eve had what can only be considered a family that violated "traditional family values," evidenced by Cain's murder of his brother Abel and the presumed incest that would have been necessary to continue the human race. Second, as we have already seen, in an effort to find a suitable companion for Adam, God first created the animals. However, after deciding that none of the animals would make a good companion for Adam, God created another human. The story simply explains that the appropriate partner for a human is another human. It also helps explain why a man normally marries a woman. However, the Bible does not state that this is the only possibility or the required arrangement for all humans. Third, the Genesis story gives no indication that only women can complement men "physically, spiritually and emotionally," as Dobson suggests. Even King David declared that his friend Jonathan's love surpassed that of women.

> I am distressed for you, my brother Jonathan; you have been very pleasant to me. Your love to me was more wonderful than the love of women. – 2 Samuel 1:26

Sex only in marriage. The second reason Dobson believes that same-sex marriage threatens the world is that God supposedly only allows sex in the confines of marriage.[57] Dobson ignores that the Old Testament does not condemn a man having sex with an unmarried woman, so long as her economic value is not compromised, and that the Greek word translated as "fornication" in the New Testament actually has a much narrower meaning.[58] Dobson selectively reads the Bible to make it agree with his worldview. For example, none of the quotes he mentions give specific guidelines on sexual behavior, although Genesis 1:27-28 says we should "be fruitful and multiply." That does not mean people must be married in order to multiply, or that people who are not fruitful and do not multiply are acting against the will of God. Many people are naturally infertile, which does not mean they are sinning or should be denied the right to marry.

Rejecting society's cornerstone. Dobson's third reason focuses on heterosexual marriage being the cornerstone of human society. He argues that the idea of same-sex marriage has existed "only in the last few 'milliseconds' of human history" and that every inhabited region of the world has "embraced heterosexual marriage as the norm," with no exceptions.[59] In this argument Dobson leads his readers to false conclusions. Heterosexual marriage has been *a* cornerstone of almost every civilization. However, many societies and civilizations have *also* allowed same-sex marriage and that such marriages have existed in many cultures throughout the world for as long as there have been records. Finally, Dobson's statement that every society has *always* embraced heterosexual marriage as the norm, and that there are no exceptions, is both incorrect and misleading. While Dobson is correct that in every society that has marriage, we already have seen one that does not, heterosexual marriage is the *norm*, that does not mean those societies do not *also* have same-sex marriage. It only means that same-sex marriages are *less frequent* than heterosexual ones. Dobson implies that no society has allowed same-sex marriage by suggesting first that same-sex marriage is a new phenomenon, and then that heterosexual marriage is the *norm*. Throughout the world heterosexual marriage is the norm (the most common form), but many cultures have *also* accepted same-sex marriage as an alternative.

Confusing the children. Finally, Dobson's fourth reason for why chaos will ensue if same-sex marriage is legalized focuses on children. He argues they will be condemned to temporary relationships, "involving multiple 'moms' or 'dads,'" with at least a dozen half-siblings who pass through their lives as the parents "meander from one sexual relationship to another."[60] Dobson fails to explain how this differs from the single-parent families or "blended families" that already exist due to high divorce and remarriage rates in America. It also remains to be seen how same-sex marriage might cause the decline of the traditional family because that trend already exists even though same-sex marriage was not permitted in the United States until Massachusetts legalized it in 2004. If Dobson's reasons are sufficient to ban same-sex marriage, then they are sufficient to ban heterosexual marriage, because the present state of families in America results from traditional marriage. In addition, banning same-sex marriage would not significantly affect how children are raised in this country: some children will still be raised by homosexual parents.

The only way evangelical leaders can ensure that all children are raised in families with one father and one mother is to outlaw divorce and single parent families. Contrary to the views of many evangelical leaders, studies demonstrate that children raised in homosexual families develop similarly to children in heterosexual families. Jerry Bigner and Frederick Bozett even argue that "gay fathers are found to be more sensitive and responsive to the perceived needs of children than heterosexual fathers."[61] Denying marriage to homosexuals actually ensures that any children in the family will be disadvantaged: they would not be entitled to the benefits that heterosexual families receive, such as tax exemptions and the inclusion of children in health insurance programs.

Andrew Sullivan responds to the promiscuity aspect of Dobson's statement by commenting that if marriage encourages monogamy as conservatives suggest, then promiscuous gay men are most in need of it.[62] Jonathan Rauch furthers Sullivan's argument by suggesting that even the prospect of marriage encourages sexual responsibility: one wants a good reputation and strives to be good "marriage material."[63] Rauch argues that withholding marriage from homosexuals only encourages promiscuity. At present, most homosexuals have no hope of marrying and therefore do not even think of possibilities such as abstaining until marriage. Furthermore, Morton and Barbara Kelsey suggest that cultural restrictions and practices, such as the refusal to recognize homosexual partnerships and the belief that homosexuals can change their orientation, do nothing to encourage monogamous relationships between homosexuals.[64] The double standard is apparent: many evangelical leaders accuse homosexuals of being promiscuous, but refuse to do anything to encourage monogamy: they argue that people can only have sex in marriage but then deny marriage to homosexuals.

Conservative journalist David Brooks furthers this argument:

You would think that faced with this marriage crisis, we conservatives would do everything in our power to move as many people as possible from the path of contingency to the path of fidelity. But instead, many argue that gays must be banished from matrimony because gay marriage would weaken all marriage. . . .

The conservative course is not to banish gay people from making such commitments. It is to expect that they make such commitments. We shouldn't just allow gay marriage. We should insist on gay marriage. We should regard it as scandalous that two people could claim to love each other and not want to sanctify their love with marriage and fidelity.[65]

Jonathan Rauch argues that evangelicals are actually encouraging homosexuals to just "shack up" and not expect fidelity and long-term commitment in their relationships.[66]

Send money!

Dobson's letter also appeals to his followers for money so that he can contribute $500,000 to the fight against same-sex marriage: "I have said on numerous occasions that the institution of marriage was created and ordained by God. If that is true – and I wholeheartedly believe that it is – then no wrong-headed human law can destroy it."[67] This closing remark contradicts everything Dobson has already said. For instance, he says that "the institution of marriage is in *grave danger*," that "the homosexual activist movement is poised to administer *a devastating and potentially fatal blow* to the traditional family," that "the very institution of marriage *is on the ropes*," that "Western civilization itself appears to *hang in the balance*" and with the demise of marriage "will come chaos such as the world *has never seen before*" [emphases added], presumably including Noah's flood. If he truly believes that nothing can destroy marriage, then why does he try to frighten his followers into sending money to fight same-sex marriage, threatening that if they fail in this effort marriage will be destroyed, and civilization with it?

Evidence that homosexuality destroys marriage?

To view the effects of same-sex marriage on the institution of marriage one has only to examine other countries that have legalized it, such as the Netherlands, Belgium, Spain, Canada, and South Africa. Heterosexual marriage still exists in those countries: it has not been destroyed, nor has there been a flood of heterosexuals divorcing their spouses in order to make homosexual marriages. Nonetheless, many conservatives and evangelical leaders point to Scandinavia as an example of the negative impact same-sex marriage would have on American society. For example, Stanley Kurtz of the Hoover Institution argues that marriage has been declining in Scandinavia since registered partnerships were legalized in the first half of the 1990s.[68]

Evangelical organizations follow Kurtz's lead in using Scandinavia, and in particular Sweden, as their model for what will happen to marriage in the United States if same-sex couples are given the same rights as everyone else. Evangelical pastor Ronnie Floyd says, "Visit Stockholm and you'll see not only state-sanctioned gay marriages, but every manner of sexual depravity. That culture is on the brink of collapse and its citizens seem unaware."[69] I visited Stockholm in the summer of 2007 and saw no sexual depravity, nor did the culture appear to be on the brink of collapse. Homosexual registered partnerships (contrary to Pastor Floyd's statement, same-sex marriage is actually not legal in Sweden) seem to not have had any demonstrable negative impact on the country. Still, Tony Perkins comments: "Indeed in Scandinavia where de facto gay marriage, by way of civil unions, has gained almost complete acceptance over the last decade, marriage itself has almost completely disappeared."[70]

While it is true that Sweden has the lowest marriage rate in the industrialized world (although its divorce rate is only about one-half that found in the United States[71]), the decline in marriage cannot legitimately be blamed on the acceptance of homosexual registered partnerships. Sociologists recognize that the 40 percent decline in Swedish marriages occurred in a seven- to eight-year period beginning in the 1960s,[72] long before homosexual registered partnerships were first legalized in 1995.[73] It is incomprehensible how evangelical leaders can blame homosexual registered partnerships for the precipitous decline in Swedish marriages, and marriages in other Scandinavian countries, when that decline began 30 years earlier, even before the homosexual civil rights movement started in 1969. Instead, marriages have been declining in many Western nations as a result of the growing economic independence of women and increasing numbers of couples that feel no need for church or state to sanction their relationships.[74]

Presbyterian psychologist David Myers also argues that evangelical leaders are misguided on the supposed homosexual threat to marriage and the family:

> I am reminded of C. S. Lewis's tongue-in-cheek advice from senior devil Screwtape to his apprentice devil – corrupt by diverting their attention …
>
> Could it be that those who use the anti-gay agenda to divert us from a focus on the family and from the declining well-being of America's children and youth are unwittingly heeding Screwtape's advice?[75]

Myer's argument is apt: the events or trends, such as the sexual revolution and increasing divorce, cited by evangelical leaders as evidence for the destruction of marriage, all began *before* the homosexual rights movement started in 1969. Simply put, evangelical leaders are unable to provide any valid empirical evidence that same-sex marriage will have a detrimental effect on society.

Using God's name to legitimize prejudice

Attempts by evangelical leaders to define marriage in a way that excludes same-sex marriage find no support anthropologically or sociologically. In fact, both the American Anthropological Association and the American Sociological Association have released statements opposing a constitutional amendment to prohibit same-sex marriage and other laws that discriminate against homosexuals: "The official justification for the proposed constitutional amendment is based on prejudice rather than empirical research."[76] As Derrick Jackson suggests, the motivation of evangelical leaders who fight the legalization of same-sex marriage is not based on reason: "Railing about gay marriage in a society where half of straight marriages end in divorce is gutter politics that exploits one of our deepest remaining strains of bigotry."[77] Pierre Tristam elaborates:

Where, exactly, is the damage being done now that homosexuals can marry in the eyes of the law? How is the institution of marriage being 'violated' when rights to marry between consenting adults are being extended rather than restricted? I don't see how my marriage is going to be affected by the fact that, say, my gay neighbors can now go to Boston and marry. It's their affair, their luck, their freedom. . . . Some folks reason that way still. Their self-importance depends on the second-class status of others. Superiority by race, sex or creed is no longer openly acceptable, but you can still send gays to the back of the bus and call yourself respectable, especially when you invoke tradition.[78]

A similar argument was adopted by the Massachusetts Supreme Court: banning same-sex marriage "works a deep and scarring hardship on a very real segment of the community for no rational reason." The *New York Times* commented

The court's logic is persuasive. It notes that marriage is both a social institution and a privileged legal status for things like child custody and survivor benefits. Denying gays the benefits of marriage deprives them of equal protection. The court rejected the state's arguments, including its chief one, that "marriage's primary purpose is procreation." Heterosexuals can marry, the court noted, even if they are unable to have children. The ban is simply about prejudice, the court concluded . . The Constitution has never been amended to take away minority rights, and now would be a poor time to start.[79]

Anthropological and sociological evidence shows that homosexuals are no threat to American society, though they may be a threat to the evangelical perception of God. As John McNeill observes, "Only a sadistic God would create hundreds of thousands of humans to be inherently homosexual and then deny them the right to sexual intimacy."[80] Many evangelical leaders are caught in a difficult situation because they believe that the literal Bible is "God's word" and that God condemns homosexuality and homosexuals. The choice for many evangelical leaders is that either homosexuality is a chosen or learned behavior, or that God allowed people to be homosexual from birth. Because they will not believe that God would make people homosexual and then condemn them to hell for it, it must be a learned behavior. And if it is a learned behavior, it represents a willful rejection of God's natural law: for this reason, no rights or privileges should be extended to homosexuals.

In order to believe homosexuality is a learned or chosen behavior, evangelical leaders must deny scientific findings on the subject. They then fight the "gay agenda" for equal rights, using their idea of God to shield them from accusations of prejudice: they believe it is appropriate to discriminate against homosexuals because God does as well. In reality, their position has no reasonable foundation. The Bible is not without error, it does not clearly condemn homosexuals, and homosexuality is not a learned behavior: science demonstrates that it is biologically determined and found throughout nature. The assertion of many evangelical leaders that an entire group of people should be discriminated against because of biological characteristics is not defensible and denies Jesus' teachings on loving one's neighbor as oneself.

Preserving civilization by preserving marriage

In this chapter we have examined how evangelical leaders and anthropologists define marriage. Representing the evangelical view, Ronnie Floyd explains that in his view same-sex marriage is an oxymoron because God supposedly only recognizes marriage between a man and a woman: "Remember, it was Adam and Eve, not Adam and Steve."[81] However, biblical examples show that in ancient Israel marriage was polygynous, between cousins, arranged by the parents or other family members and entailed significant age differences between the spouses, with females getting married in their early teens. There is obviously a disconnect between what many evangelicals believe their authority is (the Bible), and what it actually is (modern Western culture).

The reality of marriage is that same-sex marriage has existed in many cultures throughout the world, is considered equivalent to heterosexual marriage, and has not destroyed marriage in those cultures. The resistance of many evangelical leaders to same-sex marriage appears to stem more from prejudice rooted in tradition than anything else. This is evident when one considers that many evangelical leaders ignore biblical passages that condemn divorce, remarriage, tattoos, charging interest, and overeating, and they ignore many other biblical commands, such as a virgin who is raped must marry her rapist with no opportunity for divorce and that if a man has sex with a woman during her menstrual period, they are both to be exiled.

Some politicians also employ a selective interpretation of the Bible. For example, in October 2003 Republican representative Zach Wamp of Tennessee referred to homosexuality as a sickness, an aberration, and a sin that needs to be controlled. His view of what policy should be "is based on the biblical values from the Old Testament forward."[82] Those who claim that the literal Bible is "God's word," and that policy should be based on it, might consider the statement of William Sloane Coffin, former senior minister of the Riverside Church in New York City:

> Let's be done with the hypocrisy of claiming 'I am a biblical literalist' when everyone is a *selective* literalist, especially those who swear by the anti-homosexual laws in the Book of Leviticus and then feast on barbecued ribs and delight in Monday-night football, for it is *toevah*, an abomination, not only to eat pork but merely to touch the skin of a dead pig.[83] [Emphasis in original.]

Nonetheless, evangelical leaders attempt to ensure the state's definition of marriage is based on one religious tradition's perspective, even though other Christian denominations, such as the Quakers and the United Church of Christ, allow and bless same-sex marriages. However, religious freedom precludes one religious tradition from forcing its views on society. Certainly Jesus never forced others to adhere to his views: the action is completely contrary to his ideals as expressed in the gospels. In fact, he argued that we should render unto the government that which is in the government's domain.[84] In other words, given that it is the government that defines who can and cannot marry and determines the benefits and privileges extended to those it allows to marry, we should not allow one religious tradition's definition of marriage to override other traditions.

Although scientific research demonstrates that evangelical arguments on homosexuality and same-sex marriage are incorrect, some evangelical leaders nonetheless maintain that homosexuals should not be afforded equal rights in American society. They view homosexual attempts to gain equal marital rights as part of a larger agenda, which they see as a significant and dangerous threat to American society.

---

[1] James Dobson (2004, 49-50).

[2] Peter Sprigg (November 19, 2003).

[3] Glenn T. Stanton and Bill Maier (2004, 121).

[4] See Stephanie Coontz (2005) for a thorough discussion on marriage.

[5] Daniel G. Bates and Elliot M. Fratkin (2003, 292).

[6] Stephanie Coontz (2005, 7).

[7] See C. W. M. Hart et al. (1988) for more on the Tiwi.

[8] Philip J. King and Lawrence E. Stager (2001, 37).

[9] Michel de Montaigne (1997, 22).

[10] Irwin Altman and Joseph Ginat (1996), George P. Murdock (1967) and Daniel G. Bates and Elliot M. Fratkin (2003, 293-298).

[11] 1 Kings 11:3.

[12] Leviticus 18:18.

[13] *Thompson Chain-Reference Bible* (1983, 1377).

[14] Philip J. King and Lawrence E. Stager (2001, 38-39).

[15] Genesis 38:9. This verse was once used as a condemnation of masturbation.

[16] See Matthew 5:32, 19:9; Mark 10:11-12; and Luke 16:18.

[17] Victor Paul Furnish (1994, 23).

[18] This information derives from the Barna Research Group, in Southeast Christian Church (Winter 2004, 3).

[19] 1 Corinthians 7.

[20] Matthew 19:10-12.

[21] See Gilbert Herdt and Robert Kertzner (2006) for a more thorough discussion.

[22] Bruce Bawer (1993, 112).

[23] Family Research Council (November 19, 2003).

[24] See Chapter 9 and Don Schmierer (1999) and Peter Sprigg (November 18, 2003) for a more thorough discussion of the stereotypes.

[25] Bruce Bawer (1997, 255).

[26] Andrew Sullivan (1995, 104).

[27] Stephanie Coontz (2005, 213).

[28] Peter Sprigg (November 18, 2003).

[29] Pierre Tristam (November 26, 2003).

[30] Peter Sprigg (October 28, 2003).

[31] Barna Research Group, in Southeast Christian Church (Winter 2004, 3).

[32] John B. Cobb, Jr. (1999, 93).

[33] Peter Sprigg (2004, 90).

[34] Peter Sprigg (October 28, 2003).

[35] Jonathan Rauch (2004, 97).

[36] Peter Sprigg (March 2, 2004).

[37] Quoted in Associated Press (April 22, 2003).

[38] This subject is addressed more fully in Chapters 7 and 8.

[39] Irwin Altman and Joseph Ginat (1996), George P. Murdock (1967) and Daniel G. Bates and Elliot M. Fratkin (2003, 293-298).

[40] Lu Yuan and Sam Mitchell (November 2000).

[41] Peter Sprigg (March 2, 2004).

[42] Ibid.

[43] Jonathan Rauch (2004, 24).

[44] Peter Sprigg (November 19, 2003).

[45] His arguments are also found in James Dobson (April 2004).

[46] James Dobson (January 20, 2004).

[47] *Larry King Live*, September 5, 2003, CNN.

[48] Timothy Masters, personal communication (September 24, 2003).

[49] Associated Press (April 22, 2003).

[50] Andrew Sullivan (1997, 279).

[51] Jonathan Rauch (1997, 286).

[52] Andrew Sullivan (1997, 280).

[53] Ibid (279).

[54] Jonathan Rauch (2004, 128).

[55] James Dobson (January 20, 2004).

[56] Ibid.

[57] Ibid.

[58] James B. Nelson (1994, 81) and Walter Wink (1999, 39). James Strong's (1991) influential dictionary of the Greek New Testament indicates that *porneia*, translated as "fornication," refers specifically to "harlotry," including adultery and incest.

[59] James Dobson (January 20, 2004).

[60] Ibid.

[61] Jerry J. Bigner and Frederick W. Bozett (1997, 261-263).

[62] Andrew Sullivan (1997, 281).

[63] Jonathan Rauch (2004, 21).

[64] Morton Kelsey and Barbara Kelsey (1999, 64).

[65] David Brooks (November 22, 2003).

[66] Jonathan Rauch (2004, 93).

[67] James Dobson (January 20, 2004).

[68] Stanley Kurtz (March 10, 2004).

[69] Ronnie W. Floyd (2004, 127).

[70] Tony R. Perkins (May 1, 2004).

[71] J. Ross Eshleman (2003, 490).

[72] Ibid (324).

[73] Denmark was the first nation to recognize homosexual civil unions in 1989. Other European nations followed Denmark's lead, including Norway in 1993, Sweden in 1995 and many other western European nations thereafter, including France and the United Kingdom. New Zealand approved legislation legalizing civil unions in December 2004. The Netherlands became the first nation to grant full marriage rights to homosexuals in 2001, followed by Belgium in 2003, Canada and Spain in 2005, and South Africa in 2006. Vermont became the first American state to grant homosexual civil unions, followed recently by Connecticut and New Jersey, while Massachusetts was the first to legalize same-sex marriage in May 2004.

[74] See Stephanie Coontz (2005) for a more thorough discussion.

[75] David G. Myers (1999, 69-70). The book he references is C. S. Lewis (1961).

[76] American Sociological Association (April 2004) and American Anthropological Association (January 2005). The quote is from the ASA statement.

[77] Derrick Jackson (November 19, 2003).

[78] Pierre Tristam (November 26, 2003).

[79] *New York Times* (November 20, 2003).

[80] John J. McNeill (1994, 53).

[81] Ronnie W. Floyd (2004, 151).

[82] Human Rights Campaign (October 22, 2003).

[83] William Sloane Coffin (1999, 108).

[84] Matthew 22:21.

9 THE CROSS VERSUS THE RAINBOW

For nearly sixty years, the homosexual activist movement and related entities have been working to implement a master plan that has had as its centerpiece the utter destruction of the family.

— James Dobson[1]

The homosexual rights movement is an effort by homosexuals and others to gain the same rights and privileges that most Americans have. In evangelical circles it is referred to as the "gay agenda," seen by many evangelical leaders as a stealthy attempt by homosexuals to abolish Christian morality and undermine American society. It causes great concern among evangelicals because they believe it will help bring about the end of American civilization. Therefore, many evangelical leaders encourage their followers to oppose homosexuals' attempts to gain equality. Consequently, Christians who are homosexual frequently find themselves caught in the crossfire.

The proponents of the "gay agenda" have done an exceptionally poor job of informing the homosexual community about their agenda and how they plan to carry it out. Most homosexuals I know are unaware that such an agenda even exists. In an effort to find out what the "gay agenda" really is, and why so many evangelical leaders are concerned about it, I examined the mission statements of four important homosexual advocacy groups:

The Human Rights Campaign. "HRC is a bipartisan organization that works to advance equality based on sexual orientation and gender expression and identity, to ensure that gay, lesbian, bisexual and transgender Americans can be open, honest and safe at home, at work and in the community."[2]

The Gay & Lesbian Alliance Against Defamation (GLAAD) "is dedicated to promoting and ensuring fair, accurate and inclusive representation of people and events in the media as a means of eliminating homophobia and discrimination based on gender identity and sexual orientation."[3]

Parents, Families and Friends of Lesbians and Gays. "PFLAG promotes the health and well-being of gay, lesbian, bisexual and transgendered persons, their families and friends through: support, to cope with an adverse society; education, to enlighten an ill-informed public; and advocacy, to end discrimination and to secure equal civil rights. Parents, Families and Friends of Lesbians and Gays provides opportunity for dialogue about sexual orientation and gender identity, and acts to create a society that is healthy and respectful of human diversity."[4]

National Gay and Lesbian Task Force Foundation (NGLTFF). "Founded in 1973, the National Gay and Lesbian Task Force Foundation (The Task Force) is the oldest national organization working to eliminate prejudice, violence and injustice against lesbian, gay, bisexual and transgender people."[5]

From these mission statements we can see that the purposes of these groups are to:

1. Secure equality for homosexuals.
2. Ensure that homosexuals do not suffer from discrimination.
3. Promote a society that is respectful of human diversity, and thereby ensure that homosexuals and other minorities are not the victims of physical violence.
4. Ensure that homosexuals are fairly represented in the media.

As a Christian I know that violence and discrimination are inconsistent with Jesus' teachings, while honesty and a society that respects all humans regardless of their beliefs or characteristics are consistent with his teachings. As the goals of the homosexual advocacy groups are consistent with what Jesus taught, it remains unclear exactly why many evangelical leaders feel threatened by their aims. In order to understand why evangelicals actively oppose homosexual efforts toward equality, we will examine their perceptions of and responses to the "gay agenda."

The gay agenda according to evangelicals

There is no shortage of evangelical writings on the "gay agenda," including Alan Sears and Craig Osten's *The Homosexual Agenda: Exposing the Principal Threat to Religious Freedom Today.*[6] They refer to Kirk and Madsen's 1989 book *After the Ball: How America Will Conquer Its Fear and Hatred of Gays in the '90s*[7] for an explanation of the "gay agenda." Sears and Osten point out that *After the Ball* highlights a number of stealth techniques homosexuals should use in winning over American sentiment. However, Kirk and Madsen's book appears to be more influential among evangelicals than among homosexuals. Didi Herman wrote: "*After the Ball* was widely criticized and uninfluential within lesbian and gay communities, but it was taken up by the [Christian Right] as representative of the movement as a whole in its advocacy of 'stealth techniques.'"[8]

After the Ball actually elaborates on six points raised in an earlier article by Marshall Kirk and Erastes Pill that provided guidelines for how homosexuals could gain acceptance in American society:[9]

1. Talk about gays and gayness as loudly and as often as possible.
2. Give homosexual protectors a just cause.
3. Make gays look good.
4. Make the victimizers look bad.
5. Get funds from corporate America.
6. Portray gays as victims, not as aggressive challengers.

In order to demonstrate how evangelical leaders construct and perceive the "gay agenda," I will examine each of these points separately along with representative evangelical responses.

Talk about gays and gayness as loudly and as often as possible

Kirk and Pill's recommendation to talk about gays and gayness as loudly and as often as possible is in part intended to increase the familiarity and normalcy of homosexuality. The more something is discussed, the more familiar and less foreign it becomes. This tactic encouraged homosexuals to "come out of the closet." Many evangelical leaders, however, oppose homosexuals being open about their lifestyles; they would rather not see public proclamations of relationships most of them consider sinful.

Sears and Osten argue that homosexual activists intentionally hide the "unseemly side" of homosexual behavior, including its supposed link to pedophilia, in order to gain wider acceptance.[10] However, homosexuality and pedophilia *are* different. Homosexual behavior is between consenting adults: pedophilia is not. The assumed association between homosexuality and pedophilia denigrates homosexuals by association with criminal behavior. One could more easily associate pedophilia with heterosexuality: the most common form of pedophilia is between an adult male and a young girl.[11]

Although it may seem to evangelical leaders that homosexuals are constantly talking about their sexuality, many people fail to recognize that homosexuals talk about it considerably less than heterosexuals. Any time a heterosexual mentions a spouse, children, or a date, wears a wedding ring, has a picture of a family member on a desk at work or school, he or she is proclaiming his or her sexuality. Heterosexuals are so accustomed to hearing people talk about their intimate and familial relationships that they do not realize how frequent it happens, mainly because it is the societal norm. Talk of homosexuality is not an ingrained part of society, so it appears more common than it is: consider how often heterosexuals kiss or hold hands in public and compare that to how often homosexuals are seen doing the same. Heterosexuals simply talk about or demonstrate their sexuality much more often than homosexuals. Thus, the intent of Kirk and Pill's encouragement for homosexuals to talk about gays and gayness as loudly and as often as possible may be to bring familiarity with and awareness of homosexuality to the same level as heterosexuality.

Give homosexual protectors a just cause

Kirk and Pill encourage homosexuals to behave responsibly to ensure that the unacceptable behavior of some does not lead to denial of social justice to all. If it is demonstrated that homosexuals are treated unequally for their inborn biological difference, Kirk and Pill expect that Americans will eventually recognize that inherent injustice and begin treating homosexuals with acceptance and fairness. Many evangelical leaders believe this would be a bad thing.

As Sears and Osten observe,

> this strategy ties naturally into the almost natural inclination of people on the left side of the political spectrum to embrace any group that they become convinced has been "wronged" in the past. While there have been groups with legitimate grievances (e.g., African-Americans), radical homosexual activists have tried to piggyback on these legitimate efforts to right past wrongs to move the ball forward for their agenda.[12]

This argument ignores history: homosexuals have been wronged in the past. They have been killed, jailed, castrated, and subjected to other abuses, such as forced frontal lobotomies and hysterectomies for no other reason than that they were homosexual.[13] Add to this physical, verbal, and emotional harassment, ostracism from their families, and persecution by religious authorities and it becomes clear that homosexuals do have legitimate grievances, Sears and Osten notwithstanding. The American Psychological Association affirms that

> homosexuals are frequently the targets of discrimination and violence. This threat of violence and discrimination is an obstacle to lesbian and gay people's development. In a 1989 national survey, 5% of the gay men and 10% of the lesbians reported physical abuse or assault related to being lesbian or gay in the last year; 47% reported some form of discrimination over their lifetime. Other research has shown similarly high rates of discrimination or violence.[14]

Robert Gagnon dismisses the significant levels of violence against homosexuals as "relative[ly] rare incidents" and actually accuses homosexuals of exploiting the situation to stifle freedom of speech (particularly of evangelical Christians) and manipulating society into endorsing homosexuality.[15]

Gagnon argues that there are six negative effects that the acceptance of homosexuality can have on society:[16]

1. It will lead to more people engaging in same-sex behavior, thereby increasing the frequencies of health-related problems and decreasing life expectancy.
2. It will lead to more pedophilia and pederasty.

3. It will lead to increased acceptance of promiscuity.
4. It will cause "the total annihilation of societal gender norms."
5. It will marginalize those who believe homosexuality is sinful behavior.
6. It will harm homosexuals because God deems it to be sinful.

It is worth noting that Gagnon relies heavily on Paul Cameron to argue his first two points, even though Cameron is known to have fabricated his data.[17] Meanwhile, Gagnon's third and fourth points are not supported by sociological or anthropological research and are based in evangelical stereotypes of homosexuals. I believe Gagnon's fifth point is legitimate. For example, gluttony has traditionally been considered one of the seven deadly sins and is condemned throughout the Bible. Overeating is a primary cause of many significant health problems which cause decreased life expectancy and significant financial burdens for American taxpayers; both these points are specifically mentioned by Gagnon in his arguments against accepting homosexuality. If Christians spoke out against those who habitually overeat in the same way that they speak against homosexuals, Christians would be marginalized. Their marginalization would not result solely from the declaration that gluttony is a sin: if Christians approached the subject as many do homosexuality, they would be marginalized by the outright distortions, fabrications, and callousness with which they treat "sinners." It is one thing to believe in good faith that a behavior is wrong; it is altogether another thing for Christians to treat others in ways they would not want to be treated themselves.

Through such examples, we see that many evangelicals attempt to portray homosexuals in the most negative ways. Evangelical leaders believe the "homosexual lifestyle" is inherently hopeless, hedonistic, filled with despair, disease, substance abuse, high rates of mental illness, suicide, and social ostracism; that it includes frequent acts of pedophilia, and that homosexual relationships are inherently short-lived, promiscuous, and filled with domestic violence.[18] Evangelical leaders also argue that the "homosexual lifestyle" leads to a decreased life expectancy for homosexuals, not because of rampant homophobia but because of the characteristics associated with the "homosexual lifestyle."[19]

Certain aspects of these perceptions are accurate. Some members of the homosexual community are highly promiscuous and abuse drugs and alcohol, as do some members of the heterosexual community. Domestic violence and sexually transmitted diseases are not exclusive to the homosexual community: the majority of AIDS victims worldwide are women and children.[20] Accusations of child sexual abuse are simply evangelical leaders' attempts to equate homosexuals with pedophiles. I also question the reliability of data that suggest homosexuals have a shortened life expectancy. It is nearly impossible to get accurate reports on such issues because many homosexuals are not out of the closet and are not included in these studies.

Finally, mental illness is certainly an issue faced by some homosexuals: attempting to live a lie by hiding or denying one's sexuality, or facing threats of violence when one is honest about it, is enough to cause anyone some mental or emotional problems. These factors contribute directly to higher suicide rates among homosexuals, especially for teens who are two to three times more likely to commit suicide than their heterosexual counterparts.[21]

Evangelical leaders do not view the higher suicide rates among homosexual teens as the result of society's prejudice, but as the result of the natural consequences of a person straying, consciously or otherwise, from God's intended use of his or her body.[22] Such beliefs are inconsistent with scientific research. Due to lack of evidence that homosexuality is a pathological disorder, the American Psychiatric Association removed homosexuality from its official manual listing emotional and mental disorders in 1973. The American Psychological Association explicitly states that "Psychologists, psychiatrists and other mental health professionals agree that homosexuality is not an illness, mental disorder or emotional problem."[23] Nonetheless, one southern judge recently stated that "gays and lesbians should be put in some type of mental institution."[24]

Bruce Bawer believes that the propaganda of Focus on the Family leads to the higher suicide rate among gay teens, and notes that James Dobson is "more willing to sacrifice the lives of gay youth – who, devastated by hatred, commit suicide at an alarming rate – than to change the societal attitudes that cause them to take their own lives."[25]

Evangelical leaders ignore or deny the testimonies of homosexuals who lead well-adjusted and happy lives. Instead, they place greater emphasis on the testimonies of "ex-gays" who say they were unhappy as homosexuals. There is no evidence that their unhappiness was an inherent result of being homosexual. On the contrary, it appears to be the result of their being outcasts of their faith community, consigned to hell because of their sexuality. Tony Campolo relates this rejection to the higher suicide rates of homosexual teens:

> Believing that God created them for rejection, many homosexual people reject the God whom they believe has rejected them. The despair that such a theology can create has driven some gays to suicide. I wonder how much such teachings about God are responsible for the large number of teenage suicides each year, making suicide the second major cause of death in the United States. Believing God hates them, some homosexual young people come to hate themselves, and in self-loathing they end their lives.[26]

Evangelical psychologists Stanton Jones and Mark Yarhouse admit that "social hostility toward homosexuals is bound to be an influencing factor in any measure of emotional stability."[27] The importance of the social environment for a person's mental health cannot be overemphasized. It permeates the home, work, and social areas of everyone's daily life. Facing constant hostility and pressure to hide an important and deeply personal aspect of one's life is simply not healthy.

Contrary to the views of Peter Sprigg, James Dobson and others, Tony Campolo correctly realizes that there is no single "homosexual lifestyle," just as there is no single heterosexual lifestyle.[28] Some homosexuals are monogamous, some are promiscuous, and some are celibate. Homosexuals, like heterosexuals, have lifestyles that are far too varied for such sweeping generalizations.

Kirk and Pill's admonition that homosexuals should behave responsibly to avoid such negative stereotyping is something evangelical leaders might be expected to encourage rather than resist, given their criticisms of those who lead hedonistic lives.

Make gays look good

In an interview with Pete Winn of Focus on the Family, Craig Osten indicates there is a deliberate attempt by homosexuals to "make gays look good" through media campaigns and various television programs such as *Will & Grace* and *Queer Eye for the Straight Guy*.[29] He states that these shows portray homosexuals as the "most normal, stable people in America." This is an obvious exaggeration as neither of the main homosexual characters on *Will & Grace* are portrayed as the most normal or stable people in America. Will and Jack are portrayed as average people who are trying to find fulfilling relationships while balancing their jobs and social lives. Perhaps Osten finds that they are portrayed unrealistically because he carries a stereotype about homosexuals.

Robert Knight of the Culture and Family Institute provides an example of the evangelical stereotype that homosexuals actively recruit children into their lifestyle by suggesting that the Harvey Milk High School in New York City, a school set up for homosexual students to avoid persecution and harassment, is "where they isolate kids and *encourage* them to be homosexual"[30] [emphasis added]. In reality, the students are there specifically because they *already* identify as homosexual. The students do not need to be encouraged by anyone to be, or become, homosexual.

A further misconception about homosexuals is provided by Scott Ross of the Christian Broadcasting Network: "Homosexuals are no longer confined primarily to the arts as they were once thought to be. They now include doctors, lawyers, teachers, politicians, architects, businessmen, and ministers."[31] Ross may be surprised to learn that homosexuals were never confined primarily to the arts, it was just safer to be open about one's sexuality in that community. Homosexuals have always been doctors, lawyers, teachers, politicians, police, athletes, journalists, soldiers and ministers who simply could not feel safe if they let others know about that aspect of their lives. This is demonstrated in the film *Brokeback Mountain*: fear of discovery dominated Ennis' life, and his lover, Jack, was apparently murdered for being homosexual. Societal oppression of homosexuals increased their internal conflict, even as they struggled to meet society's expectations. Their own lives as well as their wives' and children's were tragically affected. It is true that if homosexuals were not allowed to work, the arts and entertainment communities would suffer greatly, as would society in general. Nonetheless, homosexuals have always been the neighbors who appear normal in every way, mainly because they are normal in every way, although they have a sexual orientation that occurs in a minority of people. When evangelical leaders see homosexuals portrayed in a way that does not fit their stereotypes, they regard it as part of an agenda to make homosexuals look normal. What many evangelical leaders do not recognize is that most homosexuals do not fit their stereotypes and *are* just like other normal, stable Americans.

Personally, I identify with Will from *Will & Grace*. I am an educated, middle-aged, single male who is not promiscuous, acts normally, dresses like other men, has a stable job, and does not "encourage" children to be homosexual; I am not a pedophile, nor do I support anyone who is. When the show debuted, I was pleased finally to see a television character that I could relate to. It was a very long wait. While evangelical leaders may see the show as a subversive aspect of the "gay agenda," I see it as an honest portrayal of some homosexual men, and an inclusive look at American society. It represents one of the objectives in Kirk and Pill's outline and of GLAAD: to fight for fairness in the media concerning the representation of homosexuals.

Because many evangelical leaders have internalized a negative stereotype of homosexuals, they perceive any positive portrayal of them as a dishonest manipulation of public perception. It is the evangelical leaders, however, who are manipulating the public by constantly associating homosexuals with pedophiles and labeling homosexual men as pathologically promiscuous. As Bruce Bawer comments: "It's a grotesque paradox: certain people who happen to have been born gay want to be foursquare pillars of our society – Scouts, soldiers, clergymen. But they can't, unless they lie about their homosexuality."[32] Yet, conservative Christian leaders, the supposed societal pillars, spread anti-gay propaganda that depicts homosexuals as drag queens or leather fetishists. Homosexual advocacy groups, such as GLAAD, are working to help Americans look beyond the stereotypes to see who homosexuals truly are: their next door neighbor, best friend, son or daughter, uncle or aunt, or anyone else a person would never expect to be unusual because they are normal in every way.

Make the victimizers look bad

Kirk and Pill's advice to "make the victimizers look bad" might be restated as "make the evangelical leaders look bad," for they are the most active group opposed to equal rights for homosexuals. Theologian John Cobb, Jr. affirms this: the Christian church usually gives some support to the oppressed, but for homosexuals it has traditionally been the leading oppressor.[33] Evangelical leaders attempt to justify their opposition by arguing that homosexuality is not an inborn biological characteristic. They also ignore that American citizens are protected from discrimination based on their religious affiliation, even though that is clearly not an inborn biological characteristic and can certainly be changed.[34]

As with Robert Knight's argument that "true compassion means opposing homosexuality in all its forms,"[35] it appears that the evangelical leaders employ an Orwellian doublespeak. James Dobson responded to a letter from a homosexual man by stating "I hope you can see that our opposition to the gay and lesbian tidal wave is not an expression of hate but one of *social justice and common sense*"[36] [emphasis added]. To Dobson, social justice is to withhold equal rights from homosexuals, and to require them to deny their sexuality and remain in the closet. Dobson even appeals to the homosexual correspondent's sense of fairness by asking how he would feel if Christians lobbied for protected legal status or "should be given a job and shielded from termination just because we are Christians?"[37] Christians, however, already have such protection. It *is* illegal to fire an employee because of his or her religious beliefs; Christians are already included in hate-crime legislation because of their lifestyle choice. I do not know of a single homosexual who argues that he or she *should be given* a job simply for being homosexual. Rather, the argument is that they *should not be denied* a job because of their sexuality, just as Christians cannot be denied a job because of their chosen religion. Bruce Bawer summarizes the homosexual position: they are not seeking preferential treatment; they simply wish not to be treated differently than anyone else in their personal lives, careers, or relationships simply for being gay.[38]

Dobson's prediction that homosexuals would fight the inclusion of Christians under hate-crime and other non-discriminatory legislation "tooth and nail"[39] is unfounded: these laws were passed without opposition. I cannot remember a single complaint from the homosexual community about religion being included in hate-crime legislation. Thus, many evangelical leaders oppose homosexuals having the same rights and protections that Christians already have based on their own lifestyle choice. I find it hard to understand that people who claim to follow Jesus' command to treat others the way they *want* to be treated would actively oppose the protection of a group of people under hate-crime legislation who frequently are victims of hate-crimes.[40] By doing so they imply that to kill a Christian because he or she is Christian is motivated by hate but to kill a homosexual because of his or her homosexuality is not. If such a crime is not motivated by hate, exactly what do evangelical leaders identify as the motivation?

Dobson's response to the gay correspondent continues by suggesting one must understand Christians feel victimized because of their religious views. Dobson appears to be saying that because many evangelicals *feel* victimized, they are allowed to victimize homosexuals. This attitude is contrary to Jesus' teachings.[41]

Dobson suggests that granting homosexuals the right to marry someone of the same sex would be a *special* right. Jan LaRue of the Concerned Women for America agrees with this assessment: "Homosexuals are seeking a special right. They already have the same right to marry the rest of us have – the right to marry a person of the opposite sex."[42] Glenn Stanton, co-author of *Marriage on Trial* and senior analyst for marriage and sexuality at Focus on the Family, agrees:

> Current marriage law treats everybody equally. We do not ban people from marrying based on sexual orientation. But we do have some criteria. You can't marry someone in your close family. You have to marry an adult. You can't marry someone who's already married. And you have to marry somebody of the opposite sex. . . . Marriage treats homosexuals the same. We don't care what their orientation is. We only care whether they meet the basic criteria.[43]

With the exception of same-sex marriage, the banned aspects listed by Stanton were integral aspects of "biblical marriage" as described in the Old Testament. We have already seen how the evangelical view of marriage differs from the customs of ancient Israel and those mentioned in the Bible.

Peter Sprigg explains the marriage rights of all Americans in greater detail, associating homosexuals with pedophiles, polygamists and the incestuous:

> "Gay citizens" already have the same right to marry as anyone else – subject to the same restrictions. No one may marry a close blood relative, a child, a person who is already married, or a person of the same sex. However much those restrictions may disappoint the incestuous, pedophiles, polygamists, and homosexuals, the issue is not discrimination. It is the nature of marriage itself.[44]

Jonathan Rauch responds that there are no people who are only able to experience emotional and erotic love with a member of their nuclear family. Thus, comparisons with incest are invalid. He adds:

> If therefore, the rule is that the law should give everyone a realistic hope of marrying *somebody* he loves – not zero people, not two people, not three people, but one person – there is no other group in the country whose situation is comparable to homo-

sexuals', because only homosexuals are barred, by law, from marrying *anyone* they love.[45] [Emphasis in original.]

When one examines the cross-cultural diversity in marriage, it becomes clear that Sprigg's statement regarding "the nature of marriage" has little meaning (Chapter 8). What evangelical leaders ignore is that if homosexuals are given the "special" right to marry someone of the same sex, heterosexuals would also have that same right, thereby making it *equal*, not special. It would also give homosexuals the *equal* privilege to marry someone they love.

Many evangelical leaders feel they should oppose homosexual equality because they believe homosexuality is a sin. However, they do not support the notion that gluttons should be denied housing or barred from all-you-can-eat buffets even though they believe gluttony is sinful, or that men who lust after women should be fired solely because of their sinful ways. Many evangelicals hold to a double standard that winks at the "sins" of some, usually ones they commit, but condemns the "sins" of others. This is in direct contrast to Jesus' admonition that before we even raise the issue of someone else's sin we must eliminate our own;

> Do not judge lest you be judged yourselves. For in the way you judge, you will be judged; and by your standard of measure, it shall be measured to you. And why do you look at the speck in your brother's eye, but do not notice the log that is in your own eye? Or how can you say to your brother, 'Let me take the speck out of your eye,' and behold, the log is in your own eye? You hypocrite, first take the log out of your own eye, and then you will see clearly enough to take the speck out of your brother's eye. – Matthew 7:1-5

nor should we judge others, for God will judge us as well. Nonetheless, evangelical leaders regularly cast homosexuals in a negative light based on their preconceived stereotypes. Kirk and Pill suggest homosexuals should make the "anti-gay victimizers" look bad: all homosexuals need to do to achieve this is to present the evangelical leaders' comments in context.

Get funds from corporate America

Evangelical leaders also oppose Kirk and Pill's strategy aimed at

securing corporate funding, which includes convincing corporations to be fair in their benefit programs. If corporations include
unmarried heterosexual partners in their benefits programs, they
should also include homosexual partners. Many evangelical leaders certainly do not approve of including unmarried heterosexual
partners, although they tend not to raise much of a fuss. That is
certainly not the case when companies include homosexual partners.[46]

Evangelicals frequently state that no sin is worse than any
other, but they encourage protests and boycotts of companies that
advertise during television shows with homosexual themes. They
do not object to television programs with story lines of adultery,
pre-marital sex, lust, gluttony, lying, stealing, murder and so
forth. Most evangelicals view these behaviors as sinful, but homosexuality seems to be the only one singled out for boycotts and
protests. The Southern Baptist denomination maintained a long
boycott of Disney because of its gay-friendly policy. If evangelical
leaders were consistent in their behavior and protested or boy-
cotted every sponsor of every show that features unacceptable behavior, there would not be many shows left for them to watch,
and they would certainly be very limited in the merchandise they
could purchase. Despite evangelical opposition, homosexual activists hope to gain a measure of equality by encouraging corporations to be fair in how they treat homosexual employees.

Portray gays as victims, not as aggressive challengers

Kirk and Pill mention that homosexuals should make known how
they are treated by highlighting that homosexuals are victims of
crimes for no other reason than their sexual orientation. In comparison, many evangelical leaders believe that the "gay agenda" is
aggressively and ruthlessly pursued by homosexuals who undermine the traditional family and traditional American society.
Craig Osten comments that homosexuals have "exploited things
like the tragic murder of Matthew Shepard" and demonize Christian leaders who have love and compassion for homosexuals.[47]

While "love and compassion" for homosexuals sounds noble, evangelical leaders use these terms differently than most people.

As Sears and Osten explain,

> we are called to love our neighbors. For the sincere Christian, this means many things (see Matt. 25:31-46) but especially introducing them to the love and saving grace of Jesus Christ (Matt. 28:18). And what is the greatest obstacle to faith and life in Jesus Christ? It is a person's sinful nature. If a person cannot see or be told or be allowed to hear or read that their ignorance, their behavior, their sin is blocking them from God's full plan for them, they may miss the abundant life, the eternal life that Christ died to provide for all kinds of persons, including those trapped in sexually disordered behavior . . . We must love homosexual men and women, and because of this love for them we must want to see them redeemed from a lifestyle of certain, ultimate despair.[48]

Because many evangelicals believe homosexuality is a sin that will condemn its practitioners to hell, love and compassion means doing whatever they can to oppose homosexuals. "Love" is about saving souls, not about treating others with compassion, respect, and dignity: to do so is regarded as enabling sinful behavior.

Exploiting Matthew Shepard

For those who are not familiar with the tragic death of Matthew Shepard, he was a student at the University of Wyoming (my *alma mater*) who was tied to a fence post, pistol-whipped and left to die outside of Laramie by two young men on October 6, 1998. Their apparent motive was hatred of homosexuals: at one point they claimed Matthew made a pass at them, which supposedly "justified" their brutal act of murder.[49] About a month after Matthew Shepard's death, a New York theatrical company visited Laramie and interviewed about 200 members of the community. The result was a very moving play, *The Laramie Project*. Gene Edward Veith, the cultural editor of *World* magazine, describes the play as not

> just about the Shepard killing but about the ordinary folks of Laramie, Wyo. – and thus, America – and the extent to which their 'hate' contributed to the mindset that led to his murder. . . .

Any human being – and certainly a Christian – will feel empathy and compassion for Matthew Shepard, both as he is portrayed in the play and as the real-life victim of a cruel murder. … This evocation of compassion is completely appropriate for such a horrific crime. Nonetheless, it can short-circuit moral reflection on lifestyle choices. For example, one would think that the AIDS epidemic would be powerful evidence that homosexual behavior is not a good idea. And yet, making the public feel sorry for those plagued by this disease (as Shepard was) has made people more sympathetic to the homosexual cause.[50]

Veith's comments are interesting on several fronts. First, he explains how homosexuals "exploit" the murder of Matthew Shepard by drawing attention to hate-crimes against themselves. He perceives telling a fact-based story of how and why a brutal murder occurred is exploitation. He is correct that the population of Laramie is not unusual: they are ordinary, good-natured, and kind people. That is why I found the murder of Matthew Shepard so deeply disturbing. I lived in Laramie for almost seven-years and was shocked to hear that such a brutal crime happened there. The people of Laramie, and Wyoming in general, have a live-and-let-live attitude. *The Laramie Project* accurately portrays this spirit; watching the play brought back many positive memories of the town and its citizens. The play also drives home the fact that such crimes and prejudice against homosexuals do exist, even in the most unassuming of places.

A second observation from Veith's comment on *The Laramie Project* is that he believes homosexuals are trying to deceive the general public by not portraying what he considers the realities of homosexual life. I can personally assure Veith that the reality of being homosexual in Laramie is portrayed accurately in the play. Veith's view of homosexual life is based on evangelical stereotypes, not on actual experience.

Third, the vast majority of people in the world with AIDS are heterosexual, not homosexual.[51] In addition, a majority of the victims are women and children, not men. If we were to use Veith's own words and logic we would conclude that "the AIDS epidemic would be powerful evidence that *heterosexual* behavior is not a good idea." Obviously this statement is ridiculous, just as Veith's statement is in regards to homosexuality. It is not sexual orientation that increases AIDS infections, but certain aspects of sexual behavior, drug use, and poverty. What is truly distressing is that many evangelical leaders regularly use the AIDS epidemic to further their own crusade against homosexuals. For example, Pat Robertson, referencing the apostle Paul's lifetime, states: "They didn't have AIDS in those days, but I am sure they had plenty of these other diseases and they were getting their share of them. These people are prone to all kinds of diseases because the thing is unnatural."[52] Robertson overlooks that heterosexuals get the same diseases as homosexuals. That does not automatically imply that heterosexuality is unnatural, just as it has no implication on homosexuality being natural or unnatural. What is unfortunate is that evangelical leaders continue to think of AIDS as a "gay disease," even though the majority of people in the world who have it are heterosexual. I wonder how AIDS can be effectively fought with such stereotypical attitudes still common in the United States?

In his critique of *The Laramie Project*, Veith adds the play "demonizes the other side, not just the murderers but those who 'hate' – and, by association, those who oppose homosexual behavior."[53] Many evangelical leaders refuse to accept any responsibility for the violent treatment of homosexuals, even though their comments, teachings and sermons sometimes fuel the fires of hatred. In addition to portraying homosexuals as AIDS-plagued individuals, evangelical leaders regularly accuse homosexuals of preying on children and sometimes portray all homosexual men as cross-dressers. In addition, many evangelical leaders regularly misuse scripture to make it sound as if there are a large number of verses that condemn homosexuality when only one possibly mentions aspects of both male and female homosexuality. Some evangelical leaders also frequently quote Leviticus 20:13, which appears to state that homosexual men should be put to death. Meanwhile, they ignore many other things the Bible declares to be worthy of death or exile, such as disobeying parents, working on the Sabbath, and having sex with a woman during her menstrual period.[54] These attitudes foster an environment that creates hostility toward homosexuals, with the logical result being violence against them.

Hate-crimes. The FBI reports that 7,163 hate-crime incidents occurred in 2005 (Table 6).[55] The manner in which Focus on the Family's Steve Jordahl presented the data, in an article entitled "FBI's Hate Crime Report Debunks Gay 'Victim' Myth," reveals the organization's bias.[56] The article's title contradicts the FBI statistics, which indicate sexual orientation accounts for one out of every seven reported hate-crimes.

Jordahl's article begins: "Racial crimes top the list, followed by religion. Near the bottom ... crimes committed because of sexual orientation." Sexual orientation is third out of the five categories included, exactly in the middle of the list, not "near the bottom." Jordahl omits the percentage for sexual orientation bias: "Fifty-five percent of hate crimes were committed because

Table 6: 2005 Hate Crime Statistics

Category	Percent
Racial bias	54.7
Religion	17.1
Sexual orientation	14.2
Ethnicity/national origin	13.2
Mental/physical disability	0.7

of racial bias, 17-percent based on religion and once again, sexual orientation came in a distant third." His statement is accurate if one interprets it to say that sexual orientation bias is a distant third to racial bias. However, his phrasing incorrectly implies that sexual orientation bias is a distant third to religious bias. The percentage of crimes due to sexual orientation bias is only slightly lower than those directed at religious groups, usually Jewish or Muslim.

Finally, Jordahl quotes Focus on the Family's gender issues analyst, Caleb H. Price: "The problem is that, when gay activists come to the table to play their victim card – they are bluffing. The card isn't even in their hand." However, the FBI statistics clearly demonstrate that gay activists have a legitimate grievance. They are not "bluffing."

Sears and Osten argue that it is harder every day to share the gospel with homosexuals because of "limits on religious freedom or hardened hearts."[57] I believe they find it more difficult not because of the two items Sears and Osten mention, but rather because many evangelical leaders are not honest in their discussion of homosexuality. They treat homosexuals as enemy combatants, attacking their character and actively opposing laws that would recognize their dignity and humanity, yet expect them to be receptive to messages of love, forgiveness, and reconciliation.

The perfect moral law of God

As their focus on the "gay agenda" indicates, evangelical leaders live in a reality quite different from the rest of American society. Their reality emphasizes the "persecution" Christians supposedly suffer at the hands of the judicial system. For example, Tom McClusky maintains "As Massachusetts is showing us and as Vermont already showed us, it's this judicial tyranny that's . . . trying to force these things [same-sex marriage] on the public."[58] After Roy Moore was removed as the Alabama Chief Justice for refusing to remove the Ten Commandments monument he had personally placed in an Alabama courthouse, James Dobson remarked:

> The Court of the Judiciary has confirmed Judge Thompson's ruling – and the opinion of all judicial tyrants – that elected officials can neither publicly acknowledge God, nor proclaim the truth that the laws of this country are based on the perfect moral law of God. Who would have thought we would arrive at a day in this country when a man could be stripped of his livelihood simply for acknowledging his Creator?[59]

The laws of the United States are not based on the "perfect moral law of God." Of the actions forbidden by the Ten Commandments, only murder and theft are illegal in this country. There are many other laws in the Old Testament that are not part of the American legal code. For example, the Bible forbids a man having sex with a woman during her menstrual period, not paying people their wages on the same day they work for you, breeding together two different kinds of cattle, sowing two different crops in the same field, wearing clothing made of mixed fabric, shaving or grooming sideburns, having a tattoo, and going to a fortune teller.[60] While these prohibitions may not have much to do with morality here and now, they did in ancient Israel. All of these "perfect moral laws of God" are found in the same passage as the Leviticus prohibitions that supposedly relate to male homosexuality. This raises the issue of why many evangelical leaders accept the possible prohibitions on male homosexuality but ignore the other prohibitions found in the same code of laws.

Other laws found in Leviticus dictate the "eye for an eye" system of retribution: "And if a man injures his neighbor, just as he has done, so it shall be done to him: fracture for fracture, eye for eye, tooth for tooth; just as he has injured a man, so it shall be inflicted on him."[61] However, Jesus contradicted this "perfect law of God" when he taught that it is wrong to take such retribution, that we should instead turn the other cheek.[62] The Bible indicates that when considering crimes that deserve the death penalty, Jesus stated that only the person who is sinless should execute the judgment, a teaching ignored by many evangelicals who support the death penalty.[63] Additional biblical laws indicate that a woman who is not a virgin on her wedding day and anyone who works on the Sabbath must be put to death, that rabbit and pork are not to be eaten, and that a person is not allowed to touch the skin of a dead pig.[64] One can only imagine what God must think of college football where people touch the skin of a dead pig and work on the Sabbath!

The Bible also declares immoral an important aspect of our economic system: "You shall not charge interest to your countryman: interest on money, food, or anything that may be loaned at interest."[65] Furthermore, the Bible says "Cursed is he who distorts the justice due an alien."[66] This passage is relevant to the situation at Guantanamo Bay in Cuba where foreign prisoners are denied legal counsel, a fair and speedy trial, and many other rights held by American citizens.

In addition to other biblical laws that are not encoded in the American legal system, evangelical leaders also ignore Old Testament commands about church attendance. In Deuteronomy 23:2 we find "No one of illegitimate birth shall enter the assembly of the LORD; none of their descendants, even to the tenth generation, shall enter the assembly of the LORD." The evangelical explanation for not observing this command is based on Peter's vision in Acts 10 where God instructs Peter to eat the forbidden foods: they are no longer unclean because Jesus' death caused all things unclean to become clean. According to Acts 10, Peter understood this to include people who were previously considered unclean under Old Testament laws. There is reason to believe that this declaration would also include homosexuals because it includes all people who did not conform to the physical norm, such as the illegitimate, blind, lame, deformed, disfigured, hunchbacks, and dwarves.[67]

If we changed American society to comply with biblical laws, we would have a society that would not be very different from that of Afghanistan under the Taliban. Adulterers, rebellious children, women who had pre-marital sex, and anyone working on the Sabbath would receive the death penalty. Girls who were raped would be forced to marry their rapists. Divorce would only be an option for men, not for women. No one would be allowed to make images of any living being, human or animal, or of anything in heaven or under the earth. In addition to many other prohibitions, a husband would not be allowed to have sex with his wife during her menstrual period, under penalty of exile. Women would be required to wear modest clothing and have their heads covered, could not braid their hair, or wear pearls or gold (including wedding rings). They could not have authority over a man or talk in church: women would have to be entirely submissive to their husbands.[68] These biblical injunctions represent the basic teachings on matters relating to society. They illustrate that our laws are not founded on "the perfect moral law of God," as Dobson argues. Nonetheless, many evangelical leaders attempt to force their morality and beliefs on all Americans by actively pursuing an agenda of their own.

The evangelical agenda

The notion of an evangelical agenda is not simply a product of paranoia. Joe Dallas from Focus on the Family states that evangelicals do have a collective agenda.[69] Evangelical leaders seemingly desire to create a society, based on their interpretation of the Bible, in which their views are forced upon all others in American society. As we have seen, many homosexual advocacy groups have an agenda centered on achieving equal rights for homosexuals. The main difference between the "gay agenda" and the evangelical agenda is that the latter is designed to *deny* rights and privileges to others, while the former attempts to *gain* equal rights with others.

Evangelical leaders have an image of how American society, and in particular the American family, should look. This family is one modeled after *Leave it to Beaver*, *I Love Lucy* and other television programs of the 1950s and early 1960s. The mother stays at home and raises the well-mannered children. The father provides financially and is the unquestioned leader. Nicely manicured lawns and a white picket fence reflect the wholesomeness of the family. The only change evangelical leaders would seemingly make is to have the hypothetical Cleavers and Ricardos attend church every Sunday.[70]

Historian Stephanie Coontz highlights that the image of the wholesome 1950s is a distortion of reality.[71] She notes that magazine covers during that decade focused on the out-of-control teenagers. Coontz comments that considerable violence committed by teenagers also "went unreported because it was directed at what then were considered 'legitimate targets,' such as African Americans."[72] In addition, teenage birth rates in the late 1950s were nearly twice what they were during the 1990s.

Homosexuals do not fit into the 1950s television shows or familial images cherished by evangelical leaders. Many evangelical leaders believe that if homosexuals are accepted in society, God will eventually destroy America for its acceptance of sin, just as God destroyed Sodom and Gomorrah. Thus, for many evangelical leaders, the stakes are very high: either return to the nostalgic 1950s television family and society (a society that treated homosexuals as criminals and mentally ill, and treated blacks and other minorities as less than full citizens), or be wiped off the face of the earth by God. However, many evangelical leaders deceive themselves about the "family values" presented in the Bible. As theologian and author Chris Glaser observes, the traditional family values movement is more concerned with the *status quo* than with biblical norms: "The 'traditional family' of the Old Testament would have been polygamous and treated women and children as possessions."[73]

The evangelical agenda has a number of important aspects that affect all Americans. For example, many evangelical leaders are trying to have evolution removed from the classroom and replaced by creation science or intelligent design, to make abortion illegal, to reinstate God in public life, to establish conservative courts that judge according to the majority, and to ensure that homosexuals do not attain equal rights.

David Limbaugh believes evangelicals should "refuse to go to the back of the bus" and fight for their "right" to assert the evangelical worldview over all Americans.

We have an obligation as Christians to struggle for our religious liberties. . . . if we don't fight in the political world we can expect our freedoms to erode even more rapidly. *We have to have political freedom in order to evangelize.* It's that simple.[74] [Emphasis added.]

The evangelical leaders' goal in reestablishing school prayer and Bible reading, displaying Ten Commandments monuments, promoting abstinence-based sex education, refusing to allow evolution to be taught in science classes, and opposing homosexuality is evangelizing. This is precisely why the writers of the Constitution placed safeguards to prevent the establishment of religion: state and federal governments are not to be used to promote one religious belief at the expense of others. Religious freedom is a guarantee for all, not just for the religious majority. Evangelical leaders have every right to promote their faith and try to win converts but they have no right to use the government to achieve these goals. The American ideal of freedom of belief does not permit one group to force its religious beliefs on others.

A recent controversy in Shepherdsville, Kentucky highlights one evangelical leader's attempt to promote his beliefs at the expense of other faiths. Ninie O'Hara, the executive editor of *The Southeast Outlook*, a newspaper associated with the Southeast Christian Church in Louisville, explains the controversy:

> Last year, a Bullitt County elementary school teacher disseminated information from the Koran, the Islamic holy book, during a religious studies section of curriculum. . . . Little Flock Senior Pastor Ronald Shaver came to the superintendent and wanted the teacher fired. [Superintendent] Eberbaugh met with Shaver to resolve the issue. The teacher was not fired, but the religious studies course was.[75]

Thus, although Pastor Shaver wanted the teacher fired for discussing what the Koran says in a religious studies course, an entirely appropriate setting for discussing religion and religious teachings, a compromise was reached and the class is no longer taught. Pastor Shaver apparently believes that no one should be allowed to teach what other religions say, even in a religious studies class. As with the controversy on evolution, many evangelical leaders only want the aspects of science or religion that are consistent with their interpretation of the Bible to be taught in schools. They attempt to censor anything that is inconsistent with their beliefs. It is unfortunate that Pastor Shaver and others do not respect other beliefs or recognize that working to suppress other religious teachings is not in their best interest. If they believe it is legitimate to suppress other beliefs, what is to stop others from suppressing evangelical beliefs?

In fact, David Limbaugh believes that Christians are the ones being discriminated against and are actually the victims of persecution in the United States:

> I'm talking about discrimination against Christians – where Christians are singled out and treated with disrespect, they're impugned and not accorded the same amount of tolerance everyone else is, and that the people who tout tolerance as the highest virtue do not give that same respect to Christians, ironically.[76]

Limbaugh states that the reason Christians are discriminated against is because they believe in absolute truth:

I know certain other religions say they do, too, but we represent the dominant force in society – the dominant force that advocates traditional values, the Judeo-Christian ethic, and some secularists don't think they can countenance the coexistence of Christian values with their own values. They require – in many cases – that we accept the homosexual agenda and that we not only tolerate homosexual activists and treat them civilly and with respect, but that we treat their ideas as equally valid.[77] [Emphasis added.]

It is interesting to compare the two statements by Limbaugh. In the first one he complains that Christians are treated with disrespect, that they have their character attacked (impugned) and are not accorded the same amount of tolerance as others. However, in the second quote Limbaugh complains that evangelicals are *expected* to treat homosexual activists "civilly and with respect." I cannot help but think that if evangelical leaders desire respect, tolerance, and equality, then they should extend the same to other groups, whether or not they agree with them. Jesus taught that we are to treat others the way we *want* to be treated, not the way we perceive that we are treated.[78]

A disturbing aspect of the unquestioned authority that many evangelicals give to a literal Bible is that it can then be used to oppress groups that were not accepted as equal in ancient Mediterranean societies. Massachusetts Supreme Judicial Court Chief Justice Margaret Marshall wrote in the decision to allow same-sex marriage that the state's Constitution "forbids the creation of second-class citizens."[79] That is precisely, however, what many evangelical leaders are trying to do. They do not want homosexuals to have the same rights and privileges as heterosexuals. This attitude stems from evangelical beliefs, which they attempt to impose on the rest of society. Let us remember that if it were not for liberal judges who went against the will of the people, segregation of blacks from whites might still be a reality in American society and interracial marriage could still be illegal in many states. This would especially be true in the southern "Bible-belt" states where discrimination against blacks was most pronounced.

Despite frequent complaints of "activist judges" and "judicial tyranny" by evangelical leaders, the courts serve as a check to discriminatory laws that are determined by the will of the people through the legislature. The founders of this country recognized the potential for the tyranny of the majority when they instituted the means of checks and balances between the executive, legislative and judicial branches of government. The courts have agreed that rights should not be determined by a popular vote but by criteria based on social justice, that "all men are created equal." Obviously the founding fathers did not apply the criteria to *all* humans at that time. However, as the decades passed more and more Americans have been given the same rights, privileges and freedoms that heterosexual land-holding white males received when the United States became a nation. Evangelical leaders cannot legitimately extol the virtues of the American system of democracy, with its system of checks and balances, and then denounce the courts for executing their responsibility to check the legislative and executive branches.

Two agendas

We have discussed several stereotypes that evangelical leaders have of homosexuals. These stereotypes reflect assumptions and beliefs that significantly impact how many evangelicals view and treat homosexuals: the views are deep-seated and underlie evangelical actions in fighting against the "gay agenda." The stereotypes ease evangelical consciences by helping to justify the unjust treatment of homosexuals. Because homosexuals supposedly prey on children, many evangelical leaders believe that homosexuals should not be given equal rights. Because homosexuals are inherently promiscuous and unfaithful, many evangelicals believe that homosexuals should not be allowed to marry. These stereotypes comfort evangelicals as they disobey Jesus' command to treat others the way evangelicals want to be treated.[80]

Evangelical leaders believe that attempts by homosexuals to attain equal rights should be opposed at all costs. Many evangelical leaders believe that God will stop blessing the United States and possibly destroy it should homosexuals succeed in their efforts to gain equality. Unfortunately, a small minority of homosexuals is more than happy to help the evangelical cause through obscene behavior at Gay Pride events, which are then used by evangelical leaders as a depiction of the "typical" homosexual. However, just as homosexuals have aspects of their community that are rather unsightly, so too does the heterosexual community. The main difference is that evangelical leaders separate heterosexuals from the uglier aspects of the heterosexual community but directly associate the undesirable aspects of the homosexual community with all homosexuals.

Many evangelical leaders ignore the significant amount of hate-crimes against homosexuals that are reported every year to authorities. Instead of examining the motivations for the murder of Matthew Shepard and working out of love and compassion to ensure that such a crime would never happen again, many evangelical leaders simply express their condolences and move on. They ignore evidence that violates their stereotypes of homosexuals and protest anything that portrays homosexuals in a more realistic and representative manner. Evangelical leaders then encourage their followers to fight the "gay agenda," to resist the homosexual activists who are supposedly trying to destroy America, to oppose all legislation that would protect homosexuals from discrimination in the work place and in housing, and to fight the inclusion of homosexuals in any type of hate-crime legislation.[81] After all these efforts, evangelical leaders then express surprise and anger when the homosexual community accuses them of fostering and promoting an environment that encourages hostility and violence. Instead, evangelical leaders argue that they are simply "loving" homosexuals and showing them their "compassion" by opposing them at every turn.

The restriction or denial of homosexual rights through legislative efforts does not bring about a more just society but creates a divided and discriminatory one. Bruce Bawer summarizes what the homosexual rights movement seeks to achieve: abolish the inequities homosexuals live with and allow them to live in a safe environment. He explains that no one can prevent a person from being gay, regardless of what laws are imposed. However, it is possible to prevent homosexuals from being honest about themselves, which is in no one's interest. Bawer explains: "Dishonesty about homosexuality only breeds ignorance – and as a result of that ignorance, hate is sown in places where there might be love, distrust where there might be understanding, antagonism and violence where there might be harmony and peace."[82]

However, the battle against homosexuality is only one aspect of the evangelical agenda to reshape American society. Other aspects include reintroducing God into schools, courtrooms, and in government, preventing evolution from being taught, abolishing abortion, and opposing what they call "judicial tyranny." Many evangelical leaders believe it is necessary to put America back on its "Christian foundation" in order to retain God's blessing and protection of this country. Putting homosexuals back in the closet is not enough. The clock must be rolled back to the 1950s when this country was, in the evangelical view, wholesome, just, and moral. Of course, to believe that the 1950s were a moral time in American society is to ignore segregation and injustice against blacks. This is no oversight: "Bible-believing" Christians, especially in the South, were at the forefront of the efforts to retain segregation and, in the previous century, defend slavery. Until very recently Bob Jones University in South Carolina prevented interracial dating among its students, using the Bible as its justification. In addition, many southern private Christian schools were established to preserve segregation through legal channels.[83] Bruce Bawer summarizes these actions: "The Religious Right didn't grow out of a love for God and one's neighbor – it grew out of racism, pure and simple."[84]

I fully believe that evangelical leaders do not realize the implications of what they demand. For example, placing restrictions on science education would have far reaching consequences, for the same scientific knowledge and principles that explain the origins of humans have also provided our medical knowledge and ability to fly to the moon. Many evangelical leaders look at the past through rose-colored glasses and do not see the injustice and in-humanity that has been a part of American society. They do not recognize that by working to oppress one group within American society, they are negatively impacting all of American society. One cannot have a healthy society if a significant minority of the population suffers discrimination. It is equivalent to trying to have a happy family when one of the children is constantly being abused. It would be impossible for that family to be healthy.

Bruce Bawer discusses the reasoning behind the actions of many evangelicals and the potential threat underlying them. He suggests that evangelicals

> are taught to view their fellow Americans not as having been 'created equal,' … but as being saved or unsaved, children of God or creatures of Satan; they are taught not to respect those most different from themselves but to regard them as the en-emy, to resist their influence, and to seek to restrict their rights. This is not only morally offensive, it's socially dangerous – and it represents for obvious reasons, a very real menace to democ-ratic civil society.[85]

If evangelical leaders wish to live their lives in accordance with certain biblical teachings, while ignoring others, that is their pre-rogative. When they act to compel other Americans to do the same, however, I must object: biblical law and order would create a repressive society with freedom and societal rights accorded only to heterosexual males. The Bible can be a valuable guide for life, but only when understood in its historical, cultural, and liter-ary contexts.

---

[1] James Dobson (2004, 19).
[2] Human Rights Campaign (no date).
[3] Gay & Lesbian Alliance Against Defamation (no date).
[4] Parents, Families and Friends of Lesbians and Gays (no date).
[5] National Gay and Lesbian Task Force Foundation (no date).
[6] Alan Sears and Craig Osten (2003).
[7] Marshall Kirk and Hunter Madsen (1989).

[8] Didi Herman (1997, 86).

[9] Marshall K. Kirk and Erastes Pill (November 1987).

[10] Alan Sears and Craig Osten (2003, 20).

[11] Steven E. Barkan (2001, 293).

[12] Alan Sears and Craig Osten (2003, 22).

[13] Chandler Burr (1994, 117-118).

[14] American Psychological Association (July 1998).

[15] Robert A. J. Gagnon (2001, 29).

[16] Ibid. (471-485).

[17] Gary Sanders (1999, 199).

[18] Don Schmierer (1999), Peter Sprigg (November 18, 2003) and Andrew Sullivan (1995, 106).

[19] Don Schmierer (1999).

[20] Susan L. McCammon *et al.* (2004, 412-413). Also, see www.unaids.org, which reports that HIV is found in 39 percent of the adult population in two southern African nations.

[21] Shelly Reese (1999, 140).

[22] See Focus on the Family (2002a, 14) for more information on the evangelical response to higher suicide rates among homosexual teens.

[23] American Psychological Association (1999, 157).

[24] ABC News (April 12, 2003). George County (Mississippi) Justice Court Judge Connie Wilkinson also referenced Romans 1 to suggest that those who break God's law, specifically referring to homosexuals, and those who engage in homosexuality are "worthy of death."

[25] Bruce Bawer (1997, 255).

[26] Tony Campolo (2004, 62-63).

[27] Stanton L. Jones and Mark A. Yarhouse (2000, 106-107).

[28] Tony Campolo (2004, 57).

[29] Craig Osten, in Pete Winn (July 25, 2003).

[30] Robert Knight, in Pete Winn (August 21, 2003).

[31] Scott Ross (2003).

[32] Bruce Bawer (1993, 101).

[33] John B. Cobb Jr. (1999, 90).

[34] Edward Stein (1999, 303).

[35] Robert Knight, in Pete Winn (August 21, 2003).

[36] James Dobson (1997, 523).

[37] Ibid. (522-523).

[38] Bruce Bawer (1993, 87).

[39] James Dobson (1997, 523).

[40] Stuart Shepard (November 14, 2003).

[41] See Matthew 19:19, 22:39; Mark 12:31; and Luke 10:27-28 for four examples.

[42] Jan LaRue (September 16, 2003).

[43] Glenn Stanton, in Pete Winn (August 21, 2003).

[44] Peter Sprigg (October 28, 2003).

[45] Jonathan Rauch (2004, 126-127).

[46] In 2006 conservative evangelical organizations supported legislation designed to remove employment benefits from homosexual couples in Alaska and Michigan. See Wendy Cloyd (July 3, 2006) and Jessica Stollings (July 10, 2006).

[47] Craig Osten, in Pete Winn (July 25, 2003).

[48] Alan Sears and Craig Osten (2003, 206).

[49] This sentiment was echoed by evangelical pastor Jimmy Swaggart who publicly declared in September 2004 that he would kill any homosexual man who expressed a romantic interest in him (see Matt Nagle, September 24, 2004).

[50] Gene Edward Veith (October 2003).

[51] See Susan L. McCammon *et al.* (2004, 412-413, 437) and www.unaids.org.

[52] Pat Robertson (August 11, 2003).

[53] Gene Edward Veith (October 2003).

[54] See Deuteronomy 21:18-21, Numbers 15:32-36 and Leviticus 20:18.

[55] Federal Bureau of Investigation (October 2006).

[56] Steve Jordahl (October 18, 2006).

[57] Alan Sears and Craig Osten (2003, 207).

[58] Tom McClusky, in Keith Peters (December 1, 2003).

[59] Focus on the Family (November 13, 2003).

[60] Leviticus 18:19; 19:13, 19, 27, 28 and 31.

[61] Leviticus 24:19-20.

[62] Matthew 5:39.

[63] John 8:1-11, although this passage is not found in the earliest manuscripts of John's gospel.

[64] Deuteronomy 22:20-21; Numbers 15:32-36; Leviticus 11:7; and Deuteronomy 14:8, respectively.

[65] See Deuteronomy 23:19 for one example.

[66] Deuteronomy 27:19.

[67] For example, Leviticus 21:17-20 prohibits many of these people from being priests because they were not pure.

[68] See 1 Corinthians 11 and 1 Timothy 2.

[69] Joe Dallas (1999, 10).

[70] Stephanie Coontz (1997).

[71] Ibid.

[72] Ibid (28).

[73] Chris Glaser (1994, 154).

[74] David Limbaugh, in Pete Winn (November 20, 2003).

[75] Ninie O'Hara (February 12, 2004).

[76] David Limbaugh, in Pete Winn (November 20, 2003).

[77] Ibid.

[78] For example, Luke 10:25-29.

[79] Quoted in Derrick Jackson (November 19, 2003).

[80] "And just as you want men to treat you, treat them in the same way" (Luke 6:31).

[81] For example, consider the following quote from Keith Peters (November 14, 2003): "It is important to contact your senators and representative and ask them to oppose any hate-crimes bill that would include protection for the vague and subjective – as well as self-declared – concept of 'sexual orientation.'"

[82] Bruce Bawer (1993, 25).

[83] Bruce Bawer (1997, 143-144).

[84] Ibid (144).

[85] Ibid (10).

10 THE RAINBOW CROSS

> *Is Jesus about enforcing rules that deny equality, freedom, and personal integrity to a considerable proportion of the creatures God made in his image? Or is he about love?*

> — Bruce Bawer[1]

This book has examined how homosexual Christians are taught to perceive themselves by evangelical leaders, how many evangelicals view reality, how they view homosexuality and how they try to use God's name to legitimize prejudice against homosexuals. Many evangelical leaders are somewhat abusive towards homosexuals in word and action. There are also many evangelicals and other Christians who, as Bruce Bawer notes, strive as Jesus did to see those who are different "not as threatening foreigners but as fellow children of God."[2]

I have argued that the basic assumptions evangelical leaders have about the world are very different from those held by other Christians and non-Christians. Evangelical leaders believe the Bible is God's literal and inerrant word. Biblical errors and contradictions are explained away or ignored, as are many passages that condemn behavior that is widely practiced among evangelicals and other members of Western societies. As Richard Hays notes, evangelical leaders turn a blind eye to inconvenient biblical teachings, even those of Jesus: "Some of the most urgent champions of 'biblical morality' on sexual matters become strangely equivocal when the discussion turns to the New Testament's teachings about possessions."[3] According to James Nelson, the number of biblical passages on homosexuality is paltry compared to hundreds on economic matters.[4] Many biblical passages explicitly condemn the wealthy. For instance, Luke 18:24-25 quotes Jesus: "How hard it is for those who are wealthy to enter the kingdom of God! For it is easier for a camel to go through the eye of a needle, than for a rich man to enter the kingdom of God." This is not an isolated statement. Nonetheless, evangelical leaders rarely attempt to dictate social policy based on these words of Jesus, but condemn homosexuals on the basis of a single biblical passage that may relate to general homosexuality. Although Jesus clearly condemned divorce and remarriage, recent studies of divorce rates among fundamentalist and evangelical Christians found them higher than in most other segments of society; in addition, remarriage is common in evangelical churches.[5]

Pierre Tristam observes that some evangelical leaders uphold a tradition that is actually rooted in prejudice: "Superiority by race, sex or creed is no longer openly acceptable, but you can still send gays to the back of the bus and call yourself respectable, especially when you invoke tradition."[6] Certainly not every evangelical is prejudiced against homosexuals; many otherwise kind, sincere, and genuine evangelicals simply follow the example and teachings of their leaders. Most are not aware of the cultural and historical contexts of biblical passages interpreted to condemn homosexuality. They have simply accepted, without question, the basic assumptions of the evangelical worldview.

Today many Americans recognize that homosexuals are not accurately represented by the usual stereotypes. Our younger generations are much more accepting of homosexuals, for they see that discrimination against homosexuals is equivalent to discrimination against left-handed people, the disabled, and racial minorities. As more homosexuals come into the open, Americans realize that the people they have been discriminating against are their relatives, neighbors, friends, teachers, leaders, heroes, and many otherwise typical Americans with whom they interact on a daily basis. For their part, evangelical leaders find the tide of public opinion turning against them: polls from the Pew Research Center indicate that opposition to gays serving in the military, adopting children, and marrying have all declined substantially in the last few years; opposition to same-sex marriage decreased from 65 percent in June, 1996, to 51 percent in March, 2006 and disapproval of gays adopting children declined from 57 to 48 percent between 1999 and March, 2006.[7] In response to these trends, evangelical leaders urgently press for a constitutional definition of marriage as solely between one man and one woman, for they know how important marriage is to homosexuals. As Andrew Sullivan observes,

> Marriage is not simply a private contract; it is a social and public recognition of a private commitment. As such, it is the highest public recognition of personal integrity. Denying it to homosexuals is the most public affront possible to their public equality.[8]

James Dobson not only supports a constitutional amendment to define marriage but also decries the Supreme Court's anti-sodomy law decision: "The Justices have ruled that homosexuals have the constitutional right to practice sodomy. . . . Morality is no longer the basis for our interpretation of the law."[9] It is questionable, however, whether biblical morality was ever the basis for American law or its interpretation. Was the law based on morality when slavery was legal or when segregation was practiced under Jim Crow regulations? Was it moral that women were denied the right to vote? Was it ethical when child labor was common and the working day was up to 16 hours long, or when the age of consent for females was ten years? Was it based on morality when Japanese Americans were interned for no other reason than their ancestry? Dobson is harking back to the "good old days," ignoring the lessons of history as well as Ecclesiastes 7:10: "Do not say, 'Why is it that the former days were better than these?' For it is not from wisdom that you ask about this."

Many evangelicals sincerely subscribe to the idea that they are to "hate the sin but love the sinner." By speaking out against homosexuality and opposing equal rights for homosexuals, evangelicals believe they are being loving toward homosexuals by making them aware that God does not approve of their sexual behavior.[10] However, popular evangelical author Philip Yancey, discussing his conversations with homosexuals who are Christian, realized that each one had "tales of rejection, hatred, and persecution," while half had been disowned by their families. He recognized that while many Christians say they should love homosexuals but give them a message of judgment, only the latter is actually done.[11]

Homosexuals who are evangelical constantly face such judgments, which confront them with the dilemma of choosing between loving another person or practicing their Christian faith. If they are unable to overcome their homosexual desires, they are condemned for lack of faith. If they choose their faith, they are effectively condemned to celibacy, a lifestyle that is rarely forced upon people: even many people who are incarcerated have conjugal visitation rights.

Many evangelicals cannot accept that homosexuality is biologically determined because that would undermine their views of the Bible and of God: it would be a cruel God who "makes" people homosexual and then condemns them to hell for it. James Dobson explicitly cites this as one reason he rejects a biological basis for homosexuality.[12] Thus, the only possible conclusion is that a person chooses or learns to be homosexual; if homosexuality is chosen or learned, it can also be changed.

Many evangelicals are unaware that their basic assumptions about the Bible are mistaken, especially as it relates to homosexuality. Some, hiding behind the cloak of ignorance, fail to notice the disconnect between their leaders' attitude toward homosexuals and the example of love, adherence to the Golden Rule, and inclusion set by the man they acknowledge as God. In Matthew 7, Jesus explicitly denounces judging and focusing on the sins of others without first removing one's own sins. Although Jesus repeatedly taught the Golden Rule, when we examine the attitudes of many evangelical leaders toward homosexuals and homosexuality, we see it is not the standard they follow. While evangelical leaders have the right to express their opinions and beliefs, they do not have the right to impose them upon the rest of society.

The apostle Paul declares that all the primary distinctions that separated people in ancient Israel -- male and female, Greek and Jew, slave and free -- are abolished for Christians.[13] Those who focus on the spirit of Paul's statement believe he meant all boundaries between all people, not just the three divisions explicitly mentioned. If Paul were writing today, he might include "black and white" and "straight and gay" in his list. Thus, the struggle of evangelicals against homosexuals does not comport with Paul's vision of seeing all people as equal in the eyes of Jesus.

The response of mainline Christians

The predominant evangelical response to homosexuality does not represent all of Christianity. Christian communities such as the Quakers and the United Church of Christ are more welcoming of homosexuals; among them, homosexual Christians can practice their faith with integrity and honesty. The treatment of homosexuals in many denominations has been influenced partly by the scholarly investigations of theologians and historians. Still, mainline Christians are routinely castigated by evangelicals for their support of homosexuals and for considering the cultural and historical contexts of the Bible in their interpretation. Alan Sears and Craig Osten argue that many mainline churches are supportive of homosexuals because they are no longer concerned about the gospel and that their *raison d'etre* is the promotion of homosexuality.[14]

Biblical scholars and theologians like James Nelson recognize the dangers of a superficial and literal reading of the Bible. He observes that homosexual behavior is condemned when it violates the purity code, involves prostitution, is in the context of idolatry, or is pedophilic in nature: however, the same can be said about those behaviors in a heterosexual context. Simply, Nelson argues "the major questions that concern us in the present debate simply are not directly addressed in Scripture."[15] Nelson's analysis represents a primary difference between the evangelical view of the Bible and the mainline Protestant denominations. Many evangelical leaders look only at the "letter of the law" and generally do not bother with contextual intricacies; the mainline churches place more emphasis on the "spirit of the law" and on the cultural, historical, and scriptural contexts.

A second difference between evangelicals and mainline Christians is their respective attitudes toward science. Many evangelical leaders are suspicious of science, primarily due to scientific findings about the origins of humans. Evangelicals are taught that the Bible is the literal and inerrant "word of God," so they believe anything that contradicts it is wrong. Because scientific findings contradict the book of Genesis, evangelical leaders conclude that science is wrong. Then, because they believe science is wrong about human origins, they decide it is also wrong about the causes of homosexuality. In contrast, many mainline Protestant denominations do not accept the evangelical doctrine of a literal and inerrant Bible, which is not included in any of the early Christian church's creedal statements: it apparently became official doctrine among fundamentalist churches only in 1895.[16] As such, mainline churches comfortably incorporate scientific knowledge in their worldview.

Recognizing that humans are not different from animals in their basic anatomy and physiology, many mainline Christians accept that homosexuality is a natural phenomenon. Realizing that homosexuality is an inborn characteristic, is natural, and is morally neutral, some denominations now apply the "spirit of the biblical tradition" to include homosexuals, and even allow them to serve in positions of authority. These denominations accept homosexuals as church members and some even bless same-sex unions. The Episcopal Church received worldwide news coverage in 2003 when it ordained its first openly homosexual bishop.

Mainline Protestant churches can be inclusive because they have a different view of scripture than most evangelicals. C. S. Lewis, one of the most respected Christian authors of the 20th century and a former Cambridge professor, summarizes their approach to the Bible by recognizing the Holy Spirit's influence on the authors, redactors, and editors, and those who preserved and canonized particular texts:

On all of these I suppose a Divine pressure; of which not by any means all need have been conscious.

The human qualities of the raw materials show through. Naïvety, error, contradiction, even (as in the cursing Psalms) wickedness are not removed. The total result is not "the Word of God" in the sense that every passage, in itself, gives impeccable science or history. It carries the Word of God; and we (under grace, with attention to tradition and to interpreters wiser than ourselves, and with the use of such intelligence and learning as we may have) receive that word from it not by using it as an encyclopedia or an encyclical but by steeping ourselves in its tone or temper and so learning its overall message.[17]

This approach to the Bible does not require a literal interpretation. In addition, science does not have to manipulate its findings to fit the Bible, but is respected as a separate means of inquiry. Lewis highlights that by integrating the scientific approach with religious understanding, we can better understand humanity and our place within the universe. Rather than dismissing evolutionary theory because it does not agree with the Bible, mainline Christians consider it possible that God used evolution to advance humanity. The importance of creation stories is not in *how* God created the universe but that *God* created the universe. C. S. Lewis supports this interpretation by suggesting the creation story in Genesis 2 simply illustrates the ancient belief that God could only make one thing out of something else. He writes:

For on any view man is in one sense clearly made "out of" something else. He is an animal; but an animal called to be, or raised to be, or (if you like) doomed to be, something more than an animal. On the ordinary biological view … one of the primates is changed so that he becomes man; but he remains still a primate and an animal. He is taken up into a new life without relinquishing the old.[18]

Here Lewis treats the Genesis stories not as divinely revealed facts of how God created us, but as myth that carries meanings easily understood by the people. The Genesis account differs from many other Mediterranean creation myths: rather than being begotten by the gods, humans were created as distinct entities with no divine blood running through them. In Egypt, pharaohs claimed to have divine blood; and the Greeks have stories of semi-divine individuals; but the Hebrews were mere mortals who had the God-given abilities to reason and be creative. They also had the knowledge of good and evil, but were not God themselves. Therefore, they believed that humans are accountable to a higher power for their actions.

Many evangelical leaders take a simplified but literal approach to these stories, in spite of all scientific evidence, and then use the stories in questionable ways. As we have seen, many evangelical leaders refer to Adam and Eve as evidence that God meant marriage as the union of one male and one female, but, of course, they ignore all the biblical passages that discuss polygamy without condemnation and the possibility that Jesus himself considered polygamy a legitimate form of marriage.[19] A scholarly, mainline Christian interpretation of the same story, by way of contrast, is offered by Victor Furnish. He argues that the passage explains why a man marries a woman: the passage is descriptive, not prescriptive, explaining what is typical behavior for humans.[20]

Is the Bible relevant to the debate on homosexuality?

The literal approach to scripture employed by many evangelical leaders is not universal among Christians, nor is it required of Christian believers. Furthermore, the literal interpretation is not consistent with the beliefs of the early Christian church which generally regarded the Old Testament as allegory.[21] For contemporary Christians, Robert Gagnon lists five criteria to determine whether biblical comments on homosexuality are still valid:[22]

1. Is the context for the biblical situation similar to the modern situation?
2. Are the biblical arguments still convincing?
3. Do modern scientific insights contradict the biblical arguments?
4. Is there a consistent Christian understanding and practice over the centuries?
5. Is the Holy Spirit leading the church to change its position?

As we have seen throughout this book, biblical comments on homosexuality do not hold up very well to Gagnon's examination.

First, the biblical situation is not comparable to the contemporary situation: biblical condemnations of homosexual behavior were related to ritual purity, including temple prostitution. In the ancient Mediterranean basin, temple prostitution was common, but in modern Western culture homosexual relationships are usually based on love and devotion. Second, the scientific approach to homosexuality demonstrates that it is an inborn characteristic, that it is not a psychological pathology, and that it does not result primarily from social factors such as poor parenting, sexual abuse, or peer pressure. Third, while the Christian church has generally condemned homosexuality, John Boswell provides evidence that the church also had periods of tolerance: certainly the modern church does not speak with a unified voice on the matter. Finally, it is difficult to assess whether the work of the Holy Spirit justifies changing the biblical position: there are no unquestioned criteria for such a judgment, nor are different Christian denominations in agreement about homosexuality, although the trend among them favors accepting it. Applying Gagnon's criteria leads to the view that biblical comments on same-sex behavior are no longer valid, even if we accept a literal interpretation of the Bible.

Homosexual Christians

One question frequently arises among evangelicals who have homosexual friends: Can a person be homosexual and Christian? I have argued that these two identities are not mutually exclusive.[23] Many Christian denominations accept homosexual people into fellowship and positions of leadership. If we define "Christian" as someone who follows the teachings of Jesus, of course a lesbian or gay man can be Christian. Jesus most often gave his followers positive commands, such as to obey the Golden Rule. There is certainly no record of Jesus condemning homosexuals or homosexuality. James Nelson notes that

> even on such a major issue as sexual intercourse between unmarried consenting adults there is no explicit prohibition in either Hebrew Scripture or the New Testament ... Indeed, the Song of Solomon celebrates one such relationship."[24]

Based on Jesus' teachings, the debate should not be whether a homosexual can be a Christian but whether a rich person can be a Christian.

I have also argued that even evangelical homosexuals can practice a faith in God that is rooted in integrity and honesty. They can draw from C. S. Lewis' understanding of biblical inspiration, which requires attention to its underlying themes and tones: that God commands us to live by the Golden Rule, to embrace the outcast, to help the poor and needy, and to live a life of humility. In addition, biblical interpretation should incorporate our increased knowledge and understanding of the world, recognizing that ancient Mediterranean societies did not have a scientific view of nature and held many incorrect beliefs about their world. For example, we can still accept a sinful condition in humanity and the biblical solution -- harmony and reconciliation between God and humans through the death of Jesus -- without having to believe the stories are literally true.

I agree with the Bible that it is not good for people to be alone, and that celibacy is a lifestyle to which few are called. While evangelical Christianity presents homosexuals with a choice between faith or the lifestyle to which they are naturally inclined, mainline Christian churches are not hampered by biblical literalism. C. S. Lewis advised that sex, in accord with love and good faith, and promoting the well-being of all involved, can be holy and glorify God.[25] Homosexuals can be Christians and pursue their right to happiness within bonded relationships. Lewis offers no license for sexual promiscuity, for he rejects selfish sexual gratification and always requires an honest consideration of what is best for the people involved.

Evangelical stereotypes notwithstanding, being homosexual does not require promiscuity and licentiousness. Many homosexuals conduct themselves with integrity, faith, justice, and compassion. They practice Christian values according to the biblical statement of what God wants from us: "He has told you, O man, what is good: and what does the Lord require of you but to do justice, to love kindness, and to walk humbly with your God?"[26] The word translated as "kindness" means to take care of other people as if they were family. This is the message that flows through the Bible and is the trademark of Jesus' followers: that we love one another, treat others as we would be treated, refrain from judging others, and that we live humbly.

All humans are equal; some are more equal than others

We have examined ways in which evangelical reality differs from that of other Americans and Christians. The disparities create confusion in public debates on issues of national concern. Evangelicals assume that human biology is inherently different from other animals', that evolution did not happen, that the Bible is literally true in all its detail, that homosexuality is a learned behavior originating in humanity's rebellion against God, that homosexuality is defined by behavior rather than orientation, and that this country's laws are based on the Ten Commandments. These assumptions, which underlie evangelical opposition to homosexuality, are not supported by scientific evidence nor Christian values. We have also examined how homosexual Christians are taught to perceive themselves as inherently unhappy, immoral, and promiscuous deviants by evangelical leaders. The unfortunate consequences of these teachings abound. Gilbert Herdt and Robert Kertzner demonstrate that the well-being of homosexuals and their children is seriously impacted by the denial of marriage rights.[27] The denial reinforces stigma associated with homosexual orientation and creates conflicting messages to teens: they are told to wait until marriage to have sex, and then are denied the possibility of marriage.

If we are to create a truly just and fair society it is extremely important to understand the motivations and actions of evangelical leaders, many of whom believe God will eventually destroy American civilization if homosexuals are given rights, even though God refused to "blink an eye" during slavery and segregation. Evangelicals rewrite history to convince followers that the American past was a glorious time of moral behavior, while ignoring institutionalized injustice that persisted through much of it. Many evangelical leaders misrepresent basic scientific findings and distort biological principles to convince their followers and the public that homosexuality is a learned behavior that can be changed. The fact is that an extremely small percentage of homosexuals who attempt to change achieve a *behavioral* change that brings them sexual or emotional fulfillment. Evangelicals also

misrepresent what the Bible says about homosexuality by ignoring its cultural, historical, and scriptural contexts, which render irrelevant all the passages used in the debate. Finally, they manipulate people's fears to gain their federal and state constitutional
amendments that would deny certain Americans the same basic
rights and privileges all citizens are supposed to have: life, liberty,
and the pursuit of happiness.

Contrary to the views of evangelical leaders, the reshaping of
American laws and morality according to those of ancient Israel
would not be in our best interests. In fact, this would be a difficult
feat to accomplish because there is no consistency within the Bible: it was written over time and reflects changing cultural values
held in several eastern Mediterranean societies. Furthermore,
many of the values expressed in the Bible are antithetical to those
held by most Americans, evangelicals included. James Nelson addresses this in his discussion of biblical sexual morality, indicating
we no longer view women as the property of men, menstrual
blood and semen as unclean; we do not proscribe sex when females are menstruating or accept polygamy, concubinage, and
prostitution; nor do we enforce the levirate marriage regulations.[28]

Many evangelical leaders argue that homosexuals should be
denied equal rights and should also remain celibate. They believe
that abstaining from sexual intercourse is much more important
than seeking fulfillment through an intimate relationship. They
essentially argue that God (if we take Genesis 2:18 literally) was
wrong in proclaiming "it is not good for man to be alone" by insisting that homosexuals should not enter into relationships with
people who might fulfill their social, emotional, physical, and sexual needs. Using God's name to legitimize their prejudice, evangelical leaders issue a new commandment for homosexuals:
"Thou shalt not love!"

Western civilization has a long history of overcoming prejudice
and discrimination. Since the Renaissance, Western societies have
recognized the humanity of left-handed individuals, the landless,
women, people of non-European descent, and people of different
religious beliefs. Now sexual minorities are proclaiming their humanity, but tradition and those who cling to it once again oppose

development of a truly just society in which all people are fully equal because *all people* are made in the image of God. By following in the spirit of Jesus' teachings with perseverance and reason, that vision can be achieved; until then, we will continue to demonstrate the Orwellian proclamation that all humans are equal, but some are more equal than others.

---

[1] Bruce Bawer (1997, 314).

[2] Ibid (183).

[3] Richard B. Hays (1994, 5).

[4] James B. Nelson (1994, 79).

[5] This information derives from the Barna Research Group referenced in *Discover* magazine from the Southeast Christian Church in Louisville, Kentucky (Winter 2004:3). Also see S. Kenneth Chi and Sharon K. Housenecht (1985), Norval D. Glenn and Michael Supanic (1984) and Stephanie Coontz (2005, 287).

[6] Pierre Tristam (November 26, 2003).

[7] The Pew Research Center for the People and the Press (March 22, 2006).

[8] Andrew Sullivan (1995, 179).

[9] James Dobson (August 28, 2003).

[10] Alan Sears and Craig Osten (2003, 206).

[11] Philip Yancey (1997, 166).

[12] James Dobson (1997, 513-514).

[13] 1 Corinthians 12:13.

[14] Alan Sears and Craig Osten (2003, 20).

[15] James B. Nelson (1994, 80).

[16] See Bruce Bawer (1997, 88-90).

[17] C. S. Lewis (1958, 111-112).

[18] Ibid (115-116).

[19] Matthew 25:1-13.

[20] Victor Paul Furnish (1994, 22-23).

[21] See John Boswell (1980, 137-143) and David F. Wright (1990, 103-106).

[22] Robert A. J. Gagnon (2001, 342).

[23] The large membership of www.gaychristian.net indicates that there are many homosexual Christians around the world.

[24] James B. Nelson (1994, 81).

[25] C. S. Lewis (1964, 115-116).

[26] Micah 6:8.

[27] Gilbert Herdt and Robert Kertzner (2006).

[28] James B. Nelson (1994, 81).

REFERENCES

ABC News. November 2000. "2000 The Vote: Exit Polls."
abcnews.go.com/sections/politics/2000vote/general/
exitpoll_hub.html
— April 12, 2003. "Judge: Put Gays in Mental Institutions."
www.abcnews.com,
www.agrnews.org/issues/170/nationalnews.html
Alkire, W. H. 1965. *Lamotrek Atoll: Inter-island Socioeconomic Ties*. Prospect
Heights, Illinois: Waveland Press.
Altman, I., and J. Ginat. 1996. *Polygamous Families in Contemporary Society*.
Cambridge: Cambridge University Press.
American Anthropological Association. December 2004. "Creationism
Lite." *Anthropology News* 45 (9):23.
— January 2005. "2004 President's Report: Working Together." *Anthropology News* 46(1): 21.
American Psychological Association. July 1998. "Answers to Your Questions about Sexual Orientation and Homosexuality."
www.apa.org/topics/orientation.html
— 1999. "Therapists Should Not Try to Change Anyone's Sexual Orientation," in *Homosexuality: Opposing Viewpoints*, ed. M. E. Williams, pp.
156-160. San Diego: Greenhaven Press.
American Sociological Association Member Resolution, April 2004.
www2.asanet.org/public/marriage_res.html
Ankerberg, J., and J. Weldon. 1994. *The Facts on Homosexuality. Scientific
Research and Biblical Authority: Can Homosexuals Really Change?*
Eugene: Harvest House.
Anonymous. 2000. *Big Daddy?* Ontario: Chick Publications.
Anonymous. March 11, 2002. "No Easy Victory." *Christianity Today*
46(3):50.
Aristotle. 1976. *Ethics*, translated by J. A. K. Thomson. London: Penguin.
Associated Press. April 22, 2003. "Sen. Rick Santorum's Comments on
Homosexuality in an AP Interview." sfgate.com/article.cgi?file=/
news/archive/2003/04/22/national1737EDT0668.DTL
— May 6, 2004. "Report: U.S. Losing Ground in Science Education."
Bagemihl, B. 1999. Biological Exuberance: *Animal Homosexuality and
Natural Diversity*. New York: St Martin's Press.
Bahn, P., and J. Flenley. 1992. *Easter Island, Earth Island*. London: Thames
and Hudson.

Bailey, J. M. and D. S. Benishay. 1993. "Familial Aggregation of Female Sexual Orientation." *American Journal of Psychiatry* 150:272-277.

Bailey, J. M., M. P. Dunne and N. G. Martin. 2000. "Genetic and Environmental Influences on Sexual Orientation and Its Correlates in an Australian Twin Sample." *Journal of Personality and Social Psychology* 78:33.

Bailey, J. M. and R. C. Pillard. 1991. "A Genetic Study of Male Sexual Orientation." *Archives of General Psychiatry* 48:1089-1096.

Bailey, J. M., R. C. Pillard, M. C. Neale and Y. Agyei. 1993. "Heritable Factors Influence Sexual Orientation in Women." *Archives of General Psychiatry* 50:217-223.

Banerjee, N. February 7, 2007. "Ousted Pastor 'Completely Healed,'" *The New York Times*.

Barkan S. E. 2001. *Criminology: A Sociological Understanding.* 2nd ed. Upper Saddle River: Prentice Hall.

Bates D. G., and E. M. Fratkin. 2003. *Cultural Anthropology.* 3rd ed. Boston: Allyn and Bacon.

Bawer, B. 1993. *A Place at the Table: The Gay Individual in American Society.* New York: Touchstone.

– 1997. *Stealing Jesus: How Fundamentalism Betrays Christianity.* New York: Three Rivers Press.

Behe, M. J. 1996. *Darwin's Black Box: The Biochemical Challenge to Evolution.* New York: Touchstone.

– February 7, 2005. "Design for Living," *The New York Times*.

– October 2005. "Kitzmiller v. Dover Area School District." www.talkorigins.org/faqs/dover/ day11pm.html#day11pm132

Bell, A. P., M. S. Weinberg, and S. K. Hammersmmith. 1981. *Sexual Preference: Statistical Appendix.* Bloomington: Indiana University Press.

Bellis, A. O. 1999. "Christians Should Accept Homosexuality," in *Homosexuality: Opposing Viewpoints*, ed. M. E. Williams, pp. 126-132. San Diego: Greenhaven Press.

Berglund, H., P. Lindström and I. Savic. 2006. "Brain Response to Putative Pheromones in Lesbian Women." *Proceedings of the National Academy of Sciences of the United States of America* 103:8269-8274.

Bigner J. J. and F. W. Bozett. 1997. "Parenting by Gay Fathers," in *Same-Sex Marriage: Pro and Con*, ed. Andrew Sullivan, pp. 261-263. New York: Vintage.

Biran, A., and H. Shanks. 1994. "'David' Found at Dan." *Biblical Archaeology Review* 20 (2):26-39.

Black D., G. Gates, S. Sanders and L. Taylor. 2000. "Demographics of the Gay and Lesbian Population in the United States: Evidence from Available Systematic Data Sources." *Demography* 37:139-154.

Bogaert, A. F. 2006. "Biological versus Nonbiological Older Brothers and Men's Sexual Orientation." *Proceedings of the National Academy of Sciences of the United States of America* 103:10771-10774.

Boswell, J. 1980. *Christianity, Social Tolerance, and Homosexuality. Gay People in Western Europe from the Beginning of the Christian Era to the Fourteenth Century.* Chicago: University of Chicago Press.

Bottéro, J. and M.-J. Stève. 1993. *Il Était une Fois la Mesopotamie.* Paris: Gallimard.

Boyarin, D. 1995. "Are There Any Jews in 'The History of Sexuality'?" *Journal of the History of Sexuality* 5:333-355.

Brand, T., J. Kroonen, J. Mos and A. K. Slob. 1991. "Adult Partner Preference and Sexual Behavior of Male Rats Affected by Perinatal Endocrine Manipulations." *Hormones and Behavior* 25:323-341.

Brewis, A. 1996. *Lives on the Line: Women and Ecology on a Pacific Atoll.* Fort Worth: Harcourt Brace.

Brooks, D. November 22, 2003. "The Power of Marriage," *The New York Times.*

Burr, C. 1994. "Homosexuality and Biology," in *Homosexuality in the Church: Both Sides of the Debate,* ed. J. S. Siker, pp. 116-134. Louisville: Westminster John Knox Press.

Byne, W., S. Tobet, L. Mattiace, M. S. Lasco, E. Kemether, M. A. Edgar, S. Morgello, M. S. Buchsbaum and B. L. Jones (2001). "The Interstitial Nuclei of the Human Anterior Hypothalamus: An Investigation of Variation within Sex, Sexual Orientation and HIV Status." *Hormones & Behavior* 40:86-92.

Cahill, L. S. 1994. "Homosexuality: A Case Study in Moral Argument," in *Homosexuality in the Church: Both Sides of the Debate,* ed. J. S. Siker, pp. 61-75. Louisville: Westminster John Knox Press.

Calimach, A. 2002. *Lovers' Legends: The Gay Greek Myths.* New Rochelle: Haiduk.

Campbell, A. F., and M. A. O'Brien. 1993. *Sources of the Pentateuch: Texts, Introductions, Annotations.* Minneapolis: Fortress Press.

Campolo, T. 2004. *Speaking My Mind: The Radical Evangelical Prophet Tackles the Tough Issues Christians are Afraid to Face.* Nashville: W Publishing.

Carman. 2000. "America Again." From *Heart of a Champion* (Sparrow/EMD records).

Chadwick, D. H. November 2001. "Evolution of Whales." *National Geographic 200* (5):75-77.

Chi S. K., and S. K. Housenecht. 1985. "Protestant Fundamentalism and Marital Success: A Comparative Approach." *Sociology and Social Research* 69:351-375.

Cianciotto, J., and S. Cahill. 2006. *Youth in the Crosshairs: The Third Wave of Ex-gay Activism.* New York: National Gay and Lesbian Task Force Policy Institute.

Citizen Link. December 1, 2005. "Vatican Ruling Allows Ex-Gays in Priesthood." www.family.org/cforum/news/a0038781.cfm

Cloyd, W. July 3, 2006. "Alaska Family Council Gets Under Way." www.family.org/cforum/news/a0041124.cfm

CNN News. November 2004. Election Results. us.cnn.com/ELECTION/2004/pages/results/states/US/P/00/epolls.0.html

Cobb, J. B., Jr. 1999. "Being Christian about Homosexuality," in *Homosexuality and Christian Faith: Questions of Conscience for the Churches,* ed. W. Wink, pp. 89-93. Minneapolis: Fortress Press.

Coffin, W. S. 1999. "Liberty to the Captives and Good Tidings to the Afflicted," in *Homosexuality and Christian Faith,* ed. W. Wink, pp. 105-110. Minneapolis: Fortress Press.

Coggeshall, J. M. (1993). "Ladies Behind Bars: A Liminal Gender As Cultural Mirror," reprinted in *Talking About People: Readings in Cultural Anthropology,* eds. W. Haviland and R. Gordon, 3rd ed., pp. 116-120. New York: McGraw-Hill.

Cohen, K. M. 2002. "Relationships among Childhood Sex-atypical Behavior, Spatial Ability, Handedness, and Sexual Orientation in Men." *Archives of Sexual Behavior* 31(1):129-143.

Comfort, R. No date. *Evolution, The Evidence: For and Against.* Bellflower: Living Water Publications.

Concerned Women for America. No date. "Action Alert: The Boy Scouts Need Your Help!" congress.cwfa.org/cwfa/issues/alert/?alertid=3057761

Coontz, S. 1997. *The Way We Really Are: Coming to Terms with America's Changing Families.* New York: Basic Books.

— 2005. *Marriage, a History: How Love Conquered Marriage.* New York: Penguin.

Corey, L., and K. K. Holmes. 1980. "Sexual Transmission of Hepatitis A in Homosexual Men." *New England Journal of Medicine* 302:435-438.

Corp, N., and R. W. Byrne. 2004. "Sex Differences in Chimpanzee Handedness." *American Journal of Physical Anthropology* 123:62-68.

Countryman, L. W. 1988. *Dirt, Greed and Sex: Sexual Ethics in the New Testament and their Implications for Today*. Philadelphia: Fortress Press.

Crary, D., March 7, 2004, "Gay-rights Foes See Opportunity in Furor." Associated Press.

Crompton, L. 2003. *Homosexuality & Civilization*. Cambridge: The Belknap Press.

Crouse, J. S. January 21, 2004. "Domestic Agenda Gets Hefty Boost in State of the Union." www.beverlylahayeinstitute.org/articledisplay.asp?id=5129&department=BLI&categoryid=dotcommentary

Dailey, T. J. 2004. *The Bible, the Church & Homosexuality: Exposing the 'Gay' Theology*. Washington: Family Research Council.

Dallas, J. 1999. *How Should We Respond?: An Exhortation to the Church on Loving the Homosexual*. Love Won Out series, Focus on the Family.

Darwin, C. 2004. *The Origin of Species*. New York: Barnes & Noble Classics.

Davies, B. 2002. *When a Loved One Says "I'm Gay."* Love Won Out series, Focus on the Family.

Davies, P. 1999. *The 5th Miracle: The Search for the Origin and Meaning of Life*. New York: Touchstone.

Davies, S. G. 2007. *Challenging Gender Norms: Five Genders among the Bugis in Indonesia*. Belmont: Thomson Wadsworth.

de Montaigne, M. 1997. "A Strange Brotherhood," in *Same-Sex Marriage: Pro and Con*, ed. A. Sullivan, p. 22. New York: Vintage Books.

de Waal, F. 1997. *Bonobo: The Forgotten Ape*. Berkeley: University of California Press.

Denton, M. J. 1998. *Nature's Destiny: How the Laws of Biology Reveal Purpose in the Universe*. New York: The Free Press.

Dobson, J. C. 1997. *Solid Answers: America's Foremost Family Counselor Responds to Tough Questions Facing Today's Families*. Wheaton, Illinois: Tyndale House.

—August 28, 2003. "Restoring the Foundations: Repealing Judicial Tyranny." family.org/fmedia/misc/a0027564.cfm

— January 20, 2004. Letter to Focus on the Family supporters from James C. Dobson.

— April 2004. Family News From Dr. James Dobson.

— 2004. *Marriage Under Fire: Why We Must Win This Battle*. Sisters, Oregon: Multnomah Press.

Douglas, J. D. (ed.). 1982. *The New Bible Dictionary*. 2nd ed. Wheaton, Illinois: Tyndale House.

Dover, K. J. 1978. *Greek Homosexuality*. Cambridge: Harvard University Press.

Eckert, E., T. J. Bouchard, J. Bohlen and L. L. Heston. 1986. "Homosexuality in Monozygotic Twins Reared Apart." *British Journal of Psychiatry* 160:407-409.

Egertson, P. W. 1999. "One Family's Story," in *Homosexuality and Christian Faith: Questions of Conscience for the Churches*, ed. W. Wink, pp. 23-30. Minneapolis: Fortress Press.

Epstein, R. February 2003. "Am I Anti-Gay?" *Psychology Today* 36 (1):7.

Eshleman, J. R. 2003. *The Family*. 10th ed. Boston: Allyn and Bacon.

Evans-Pritchard, E. E. 1970. "Sexual Inversion among the Azande." *American Anthropologist*, 72:1428-1434.

Fagan, B. M. 2001. *In the Beginning: An Introduction to Archaeology*. 10th ed. Upper Saddle River, New Jersey: Prentice Hall.

Falwell, J. No date. "Why did I do it?" www.falwell.com/ press%20statements/prsarchives/prswhy.htm

Family Research Council. November 19, 2003. "Mass. Supreme Court Rules in Favor of 'Gay Marriage.'" www.frc.org/index.cfm?i=PR03K06&f=PG03I03

Family Research Council. December 12, 2003. "A Pro-Family Win: Abercrombie Cancels Catalog For Good." press.arrivenet.com/notforprofit/article.php/113128.html

Farran, S. 2004. "Transsexuals, Fa'afafine, Fakaleiti and Marriage Law in the Pacific: Considerations for the Future." *Journal of the Polynesian Society* 113 (2):119-142.

Federal Bureau of Investigation. October 2006. "Uniform Crime Reporting Program: Hate Crime Statistics 2005." www.fbi.gov/ucr/hc2005/index.html

Fernea, E. W., and R. A. Fernea. 2003. "Symbolizing Roles: Behind the Veil," in *Conformity and Conflict: Readings in Cultural Anthropology*, ed. J. Spradley and D. W. McCurdy, 11th ed., pp. 253-260. Boston: Allyn and Bacon.

Floyd, R. W. 2004. *The Gay Agenda: It's Dividing the Family, the Church, and a Nation*. Green Forest, Arkansas: New Leaf Press.

Focus on the Family. 2001. *The Heart of the Matter: The Roots and Causes of Female Homosexuality*. Love Won Out series, Focus on the Family.

— 2002a. *Teaching Captivity? How the Pro-Gay Agenda Is Affecting Our Schools ... And How You Can Make a Difference.* Love Won Out series, Focus on the Family.

— 2002b. *The Truth Comes Out: The Roots and Causes of Male Homosexuality.* Love Won Out series, Focus on the Family.

— April 24, 2003. "Dobson Defends Senator Santorum against Gay Activists." www.family.org/welcome/press/a0025665.cfm

— July 1, 2003. "Santorum's Wisdom." Focus on the Family's Citizen Link, www.family.org/cforum/feature/a0026715.cfm

— November 6, 2003. "Homosexual Activists Withholding Truth on Reparative Therapy." www.family.org/welcome/press/a0028749.cfm

— November 13, 2003. "Dobson Decries Chief Justice Moore's Removal from Office." www.family.org/welcome/press/a0028833.cfm

— No date (a). www.family.org/cforum/fosi/origins/

— No date (b). "About Dr. Dobson." www.family.org/docstudy/aboutdrdobson.cfm

— No date (c). www.family.org/welcome/aboutfof/a0005554.cfm

Foster, D. No date. "Articles of Faith and Freedom." Witness Ministries, www.witnessfortheworld.org/aof.html

Furnish, V. P., 1994. "The Bible and Homosexuality: Reading the Texts in Context," in *Homosexuality in the Church: Both Sides of the Debate*, ed. J. S. Siker, pp. 18-35. Louisville: Westminster John Knox Press.

Gagnon, R. A. J. 2001. *The Bible and Homosexual Practice: Texts and Hermeneutics.* Nashville: Abingdon Press.

Gay & Lesbian Alliance Against Defamation. No date. www.glaad.org/about/index.php

Glaser, C. 1994. "The Love that Dare Not Pray Its Name: The Gay and Lesbian Movement in America's Churches," in *Homosexuality in the Church: Both Sides of the Debate*, ed. J. S. Siker, pp. 150-157. Louisville: Westminster John Knox Press.

Glenn, N. D. and M. Supancic. 1984. "The Social and Demographic Correlates of Divorce and Separation in the United States: An Update and Reconsideration." *Journal of Marriage and the Family* 46:563-575.

Gore, R. April 2003. "The Rise of Mammals." National Geographic 203 (4):5-37.

Greenberg, D. F. 1988. *The Construction of Homosexuality.* Chicago: The University of Chicago Press.

Haley, M. 2001. *Straight Answers: Exposing the Myths and Facts About Homosexuality.* Love Won Out series, Focus on the Family.

Hall, J. A. Y., and D. Kimura. 1994. "Dermatoglyphic Asymmetry and Sexual Orientation in Men." *Behavioral Neuroscience* 108:1203-1206.

Hamer, D., and P. Copeland. 1994. *The Science of Desire: The Search for the Gay Gene and the Biology of Behavior*. New York: Simon and Schuster.

Hanson, K. C., and D. E. Oakman. 1998. *Palestine in the Time of Jesus: Social Structures and Social Conflicts*. Minneapolis: Fortress Press.

Harris, M. and O. Johnson. 2003. *Cultural Anthropology*, 6th ed. Boston: Allyn and Bacon.

Harry, J. 1990. "A Probability Sample of Gay Males." *Journal of Homosexuality* 19:89-104.

Hart, C. W. M., A. R. Pilling and J. C. Goodale. 1988. *The Tiwi of North Australia*. 3rd ed. New York: Holt, Rinehart and Winston.

Hays, R. B. 1994. "Awaiting the Redemption of our Bodies: The Witness of Scripture Concerning Homosexuality," in *Homosexuality in the Church: Both Sides of the Debate*, ed. J. S. Siker, pp. 3-17. Louisville: Westminster John Knox Press.

Heider, K. G. 2001. *Seeing Anthropology: Cultural Anthropology through Film*. 2nd ed. Boston: Allyn and Bacon.

Helminiak, D. A. 1999. "Scripture, Sexual Ethics, and the Nature of Christianity." *Pastoral Psychology* 47 (4):261-271.

— 2000. *What the Bible Really Says about Homosexuality: Millenium Edition*. San Francisco: Alamo Square Press.

Herdt, G. 1987. *The Sambia: Ritual and Gender in New Guinea*. Fort Worth: Harcourt Brace Jovanovich College Publishers.

— 1998. *Same Sex, Different Cultures: Exploring Gay and Lesbian Lives*. New York: Westview Press.

— 1999. *Sambia Sexual Culture: Essays from the Field*. Chicago: The University of Chicago Press.

— 2006. *The Sambia: Ritual, Sexuality, and Change in Papua New Guinea*. 2nd edition. Belmont, California: Wadsworth.

Herdt, G., and R. Kertzner. 2006. "I Do, but I Can't: The Impact of Marriage Denial on the Mental Health and Sexual Citizenship of Lesbians and Gay Men in the United States." *Sexuality Research and Social Policy Journal of NSRC* 3:33-49.

Herman, D. 1997. *The Antigay Agenda: Orthodox Vision and the Christian Right*. Chicago: The University of Chicago Press.

Hershberger, S. L. 1997. "A Twin Registry Study of Male and Female Sexual Orientation." *Journal of Sex Research* 34:212-222.

Hogbin, I. 1970. *The Island of Menstruating Men: Religion in Wogeo, New Guinea.* Prospect Heights, Illinois: Waveland Press.

Hopkin, M. December 7, 2004. "Left-handers Flourish in Violent Society." *Nature* published online soi:10.1038/news041206-6.

Human Rights Campaign. October 22, 2003. "HRC Condemns Anti-Gay Remarks of U.S. Rep. Zach Wamp." www.hrc.org/newsreleases/2003/031022wamp.asp

Human Rights Campaign. No date. www.hrc.org/Template.cfm?Section=About_HRC

Hurtado, L. W. 1990. "How the New Testament Has Come Down to Us," in *The History of Christianity*, eds. T. Dowley, J. H. Y. Briggs, R. D. Linder and D. F. Wright, pp. 130-136. Oxford: Lion Publishing.

Jackson, D. November 19, 2003. "Mass. Court Cuts Through the Homophobia." *Boston Globe.*

Jacobs, A. January 30, 2004. "Georgia Takes on Evolution." *The New York Times.*

Jerry Falwell Ministries. No date. www.falwell.com/?a=qa#Anchor-32075

Johanson, D., and M. Edey. 1990. *Lucy: The Beginnings of Humankind.* New York: Simon Schuster.

Jones, S. L. 1994. *The Gay Debate.* Downers Grove, Illinois: Inter Varsity Press.

Jones, S. L. and D. E. Workman. 1994. "Homosexuality: The Behavioral Sciences and the Church," in *Homosexuality in the Church: Both Sides of the Debate*, ed. J. S. Siker, pp. 93-115. Louisville: Westminster John Knox Press.

Jones, S. L. and M. A. Yarhouse. 2000. *Homosexuality: The Use of Scientific Research in the Church's Moral Debate.* Downers Grove, Illinois: Inter Varsity Press.

Jones, S. 1997. *In the Blood: God, Genes and Destiny.* London: Flamingo.

Jordahl, S. October 18, 2006. "FBI's Hate Crime Report Debunks Gay 'Victim' Myth." www.family.org/cforum/fnif/news/a0042340.cfm

Kallestrup, P., R. Zinyama, E. Gomo, E. Dickmeiss, P. Platz, J. Gerstoft, and H. Ullum. 2003. "Low Prevalence of Hepatitis C Virus Antibodies in HIV-Enemic Area of Zimbabwe Support Sexual Transmission As the Major Route of HIV Transmission in Africa." *AIDS* 17:1400-1402.

Kangas, S. 1999. "Homosexuality is Biologically Determined," in *Homosexuality: Opposing Viewpoints*, ed. M. E. Williams, pp. 17-21. San Diego: Greenhaven Press.

Kelsey, M. and B. Kelsey. 1999. "Homosexualities," in *Homosexuality and Christian Faith: Questions of Conscience for the Churches*, ed. W. Wink, pp. 63-66. Minneapolis: Fortress Press.

King, P. J. and L. E. Stager. 2001. *Life in Biblical Israel*. Louisville: Westminster John Knox Press.

Kinsey, A. C., W. B. Pomeroy and C. E. Martin. 1948. *Sexual Behavior in the Human Male*. Philadelphia: Saunders.

Kinsey, A. C., W. B. Pomeroy, C. E. Martin and P. H. Gebhard. 1953. *Sexual Behavior in the Human Female*. Philadelphia: Saunders.

Kirk, M. K., and H. Madsen. 1989. *After the Ball: How America Will Conquer Its Fear and Hatred of Gays in the '90s*. New York: Doubleday.

Kirk, M. K., and E. Pill. November, 1987. "The Overhauling of Straight America," *Guide Magazine*.

Kitamoto, T. 1997. "Conditional Disruption of Synaptic Transmission Induces Male-Male Courtship Behavior in Drosophila." *Proceedings of the National Academy of Sciences USA* 99(20):13232-13237.

Kurtz, S. March 10, 2004. "Death of Marriage in Scandinavia." *Boston Globe*.

Lanning, K. V. 1992. *Child Molesters: A Behavioral Analysis*. 3rd ed. Quantico, Virginia: Behavioral Science Unit, Federal Bureau of Investigation.

LaRue, J. September 16, 2003. "Talking Points: Why Homosexual Marriage is Wrong." www.cwfa.org/printerfriendly.asp?id=4589&department=legal&categoryid=family

Leland, J., and M. Miller. August 17, 1998. "Can Gays 'Convert'?" *Newsweek* pp. 46-52.

Lemaire, A. 1994. "'House of David' Restored in Moabite Inscription." *Biblical Archaeology Review* 20 (3):30-37.

Lessa, W. A. 1966. *Ulithi: A Micronesian Design for Living*. Prospect Heights, Illinois: Waveland Press.

LeVay, S. 1993. *The Sexual Brain*. Cambridge: MIT Press.

Lewis, C. S. 1943. *Mere Christianity*. New York: Touchstone.

— 1955. *Surprised by Joy: The Shape of My Early Life*. New York: Barnes & Noble.

— 1958. *Reflections on the Psalms*. New York: Harcourt.

— 1961. *The Screwtape Letters*. New York: Touchstone.

— 1964. *Letters to Malcolm: Chiefly on Prayer*. New York: Harcourt.

Macionis, J. J. 2001. *Sociology*. 8th ed. Upper Saddle River, New Jersey: Prentice Hall.

Malina, B. J. 2001. *The New Testament World: Insights from Cultural Anthropology*. Louisville: Westminster John Knox Press.

Markoe, G. E. 2000. *Peoples of the Past: Phoenicians*. London: The British Museum Press.

Martin, D. B. 1996. "Arsenokoites and Malakos: Meanings and Consequences," in *Biblical Ethics and Homosexuality: Listening to Scripture*, ed. R. L. Brawley, pp.117-136. Louisville: Westminster John Knox Press.

McCammon, S. L., D. Knox and C. Schacht. 2004. *Choices in Sexuality*. 2nd ed. Cincinnati: Atomic Dog Publishing.

McConville, G. 1996. *The Old Testament*. London: Teach Yourself Books.

McDowell, J. 1999. *The New Evidence That Demands a Verdict*. Nashville: Thomas Nelson.

McGreevey, J. M. 2006. *The Confession*. Los Angeles: Regan.

McNeill, J. J. 1994. "Homosexuality: Challenging the Church to Grow," in *Homosexuality in the Church: Both Sides of the Debate*, ed. J. S. Siker, pp. 49-58. Louisville: Westminster John Knox Press.

Meyer-Bahlburg, H.F.L, T. M. Exner, G. Lorenz, R. S. Gruen, J. M. Gorman and A. A. Ehrhardt. 1991. "Sexual Risk Behavior, Sexual Functioning, and HIV-Disease Progression in Gay Men." *Journal of Sex Research*, 28(1):3-27.

Mosher, W. D., A. Chandra and J. Jones. 2005. "Sexual Behavior and Selected Health Measures: Men and Women 15-44 Years of Age, United States, 2002." Advance Data from Vital and Health Statistics, 362. Hyattsville, Maryland: National Center for Health Statistics, 2005.

Murdock, G. P. 1967. *Ethnographic Atlas*. Pittsburgh: University of Pittsburgh Press.

Murray, O. 2001. "Life and Society in Classical Greece," in *The Oxford Illustrated History of Greece and the Hellenistic World*, eds. J. Boardman, J. Griffin and O. Murray, pp. 198-227.

Mustanski, B. S., J. M. Bailey, and S. Kaspar. 2002. "Dermatoglyphics, Handedness, Sex, and Sexual Orientations." *Archives of Sexual Behavior* 31:113-122.

Mustanksi, B. S., M. L. Chivers, and J. M. Bailey. 2002. "A Critical Review of Recent Biological Research on Human Sexual Orientation." *Annual Review of Sex Research* 12:89-140.

Mustanski, B. S., M. G. DuPree, C. M. Nievergelt, S. Bocklandt, N. J. Schork, and D. H. Hamer. 2005. "A Genomewide Scan of Male Sexual Orientation." *Human Genetics* 116:272-278.

Myers, D. G. 1999. "Accepting What Cannot Be Changed," in *Homosexuality and Christian Faith: Questions of Conscience for the Churches*, ed. W. Wink, pp. 67-70. Minneapolis: Fortress Press.

Nagle, M. September 24, 2004. "Jimmy Swaggart Threatens to Kill Any Gay Man Who 'Looks at Me Like That.'" *Seattle Gay News* 32 (39):5.

National Gay and Lesbian Task Force Foundation. No date. www.thetaskforce.org/aboutus/index.cfm

National Geographic. August 2004. "They Might Not Be Giants: Reading the Bones of a Mythic Race."

Nelson, J. B. 1994. "Sources for Body Theology: Homosexuality as a Test Case," in *Homosexuality in the Church: Both Sides of the Debate*, ed. J. S. Siker, pp. 76-90. Louisville: Westminster John Knox Press.

New American Standard Bible: Reference Edition. 1975. Iowa Falls: World Bible Publishers.

New Revised Standard Bible. 2001. 3rd ed. Oxford: Oxford University Press.

New York Times. November 20, 2003. "A Victory for Gay Marriage."

Nicolosi, J. 2002. "The Condition of Male Homosexuality," speech presented at the *Love Won Out* conference, Dallas, TX, May 6, 2000.

O'Hara, N. February 12, 2004. "Church Protests Superintendent's Decision to Ban Lunchtime Visits." *The Southeast Outlook.* Louisville: Southeast Christian Church.

Olyan, S. M. 1994. " 'And with a Male You Shall Not Lie the Lying Down of a Woman': On the Meaning and Significance of Leviticus 18:22 and 20:13." *Journal of the History of Sexuality* 5:179-206.

Ovid. 2005. *The Metamorphoses.* New York: Barnes & Noble Classics.

Parents, Families and Friends of Lesbians and Gays. No date. www.pflag.org/index.php?id=188

Park, M. A. 2003. *Introducing Anthropology: An Integrated Approach.* 2nd ed. New York: McGraw Hill.

— 2006. *Biological Anthropology.* 5th ed. Boston: Mayfield.

The Parsonage. 1999. "Homosexuality: How Should the Church Respond?" Focus on the Family, www.family.org/pastor/resources/sos/a0006413.html

Pattison, E. M. and M. L. Pattison. 1980. "Ex-gays: Religiously Mediated Change in Homosexuals." *American Journal of Psychiatry* 137:1553-1562.

Paulk, J. July 2000. *Family News from Dr. James Dobson.* Colorado Springs: Focus on the Family.

Peleg, Y. 2005. "Love at First Sight? David, Jonathan, and the Biblical Politics of Gender." *Journal for the Study of the Old Testament* 30:171-189.

Peoples, J., and G. Bailey. 2000. *Humanity: An Introduction to Cultural Anthropology.* 5th ed. Belmont, California: Wadsworth.

Perkins, T. R. May 1, 2004. "Take a Stand for Marriage." Speech presented at May Day for Marriage, Seattle, Washington. www.frc.org/get.cfm?i=PD04E01

Peters, K. November 14, 2003. "Hatch Capitulates on Hate-Crimes Bill." *Family News in Focus.* www.family.org/cforum/fnif/news/a0028855.cfm

— December 1, 2003. "FMA Introduced in Senate." Family News in Focus. www.family.org/cforum/fnif/news/a0029019.cfm

Pew Research Center for the People and the Press. March 22, 2006. people-press.org/reports/display.php3?ReportID=273

Porac, C., and S. Coren. 1981. *Lateral Preferences and Human Behavior.* New York: Springer-Verlag.

Quammen, D. November 2004. "Darwin's Big Idea: Was Darwin Wrong?" *National Geographic* 206 (5):2-35.

Ratzinger, J. Cardinal. 1994. "Letters to the Bishops of the Catholic Church on the Pastoral Care of Homosexual Persons," in *Homosexuality in the Church: Both Sides of the Debate,* ed. J. S. Siker, pp. 39-48. Louisville: Westminster John Knox Press.

Rauch, J. 1997. "Marrying Somebody," in *Same-Sex Marriage: Pro and Con,* ed. A. Sullivan, pp. 285-288. New York: Vintage.

— 2004. *Gay Marriage: Why It Is Good for Gays, Good for Straights, and Good for America.* New York: Times Books.

Reese, S. 1999. "Schools Should Stress Acceptance of Homosexuality," in *Homosexuality: Opposing Viewpoints,* ed. M. E. Williams, pp. 138-143. San Diego: Greenhaven Press.

Rennie, J. July 2002. "Answers to Creationist Nonsense," *Scientific American,* pp. 78-85.

Robertson, G. 2003 Homosexuality: Roots and Ramifications. www.cbn.com/spirituallife/biblestudyandtheology/discipleship/gordonteaches_corinth0307.aspx

Robertson, P. 2001. Answers to 200 of Life's Most Probing Questions. www.cbnindia.org/200Questions/article.php?topic=14

—September 2001a. "Robertson's Statement Regarding Terrorist Attack on America." www.patrobertson.com/PressReleases/TerroristAttack.asp

— September 2001b. "Pat Robertson Addresses Comments Made By Jerry Falwell." www.patroberstson.com/PressReleases/falwell.asp

— August 11, 2003. Pat Robertson Responds to the Episcopal Church Homosexual Controversy. www.cbn.com/spirituallife/perspectives/EpiscopalControversy 81103.asp

— 2004. *The Ten Offenses: Reclaim the Blessings of the Ten Commandments.* Nashville: Integrity.

Roetzel, C. J. 1998. *The Letters of Paul: Conversations in Context.* 4th ed. Louisville: Westminster John Knox Press.

Roselli, C. E. November, 2002. Paper presented at *Annual Society for Neuroscience meeting*, Orlando, Florida.

Roselli, C. E., J. A. Resko and F. Stormshak. 2002. "Hormonal Influences on Sexual Partner Preference in Rams." *Archives of Sexual Behavior* 31(1):43-49.

Ross, S. 2003. "The Not So Gay Way: A Look at Homosexuality." www.cbn.com/700club/scottross/commentary/Not_So_Gay_Way.aspx

Ruse, M. 2005. *The Evolution-Creation Struggle.* Cambridge: Harvard University Press.

Sanders, G. 1999. "Homosexual Parenting is Not Harmful to Children," in *Homosexuality: Opposing Viewpoints*, ed. M. E. Williams, pp. 193-200. San Diego: Greenhaven Press.

Savic, I., H. Berglund, and P. Lindström. 2005. "Brain Response to Putative Pheromones in Homosexual Men." *Proceedings of the National Academy of Sciences of the United States of America* 102(20):7356-7361.

Schmierer, D. 1999. "An Ounce of Prevention." *Focus on the Family Magazine.* www.family.org/fofmag/pp/a0024031.cfm

Schwartz, P., and V. Rutter. 1998. *The Gender of Sexuality.* Thousand Oaks: Pine Forge Press.

Scroggs, R. 1983. *The New Testament and Homosexuality.* Minneapolis: Augsburg Fortress.

Sears, A., and C. Osten. 2003. *The Homosexual Agenda: Exposing the Principal Threat to Religious Freedom Today.* Nashville: Broadman & Holman.

Seton-Williams, M. V. 1993. *Greek Legends and Stories*. New York: Barnes & Noble Books.

Shackelford, D. June, 1999. "Was Adam a UFO (unidentified figurative object)?" *Creation* 21(3):42-43.

Shaw, I. (ed.). 2000a. *The Oxford History of Ancient Egypt*. Oxford: Oxford University Press.

Shaw, I. 2000b. "Egypt and the Outside World," in *The Oxford History of Ancient Egypt*, ed. I. Shaw, pp. 314-329. Oxford: Oxford University Press.

Shepard, S. November 14, 2003. "Hate Crimes Down, FBI Says." Family News in Focus. www.family.org/cforum/fnif/news/a0028853.cfm

Shidlo, A., and M. Schroeder. 2001. Paper presented at the annual meeting of the American Psychiatric Association, New Orleans.

Siker, J. 1994. "Homosexual Christians, the Bible, and Gentile Inclusion: Confessions of a Repenting Heterosexist," in *Homosexuality in the Church: Both Sides of the Debate*, ed. J. S. Siker, pp. 178-194. Louisville: Westminster John Knox Press.

Sillitoe, P. 1998. *An Introduction to the Anthropology of Melanesia: Culture and Tradition*. Cambridge (UK): Cambridge University Press.

Sloan, C. P. November 2006. "Origin of Childhood." *National Geographic* 210 (5):148-159.

Smith, D. February 7, 2004. "Love that dare not squeak its name." *The New York Times*.

South Carolina Republican Party. 2004. We the People: The Platform of the South Carolina Republican Party. www.scgop.com/documents/platform.asp.

Southeast Christian Church. Winter 2004. *Discover Magazine*. Louisville: Southeast Christian Church.

Spitzer, R. L. 2003. "Can Some Gay Men and Lesbians Change Their Sexual Orientation? 200 Participants Reporting a Change from Homosexual to Heterosexual Orientation." *Archives of Sexual Behavior* 32:403-417.

Spong, J. S. 1991. *Rescuing the Bible from Fundamentalism*. San Francisco: Harper.

Sprigg, P. October 28, 2003. "Questions on Same-Sex Unions Answered: Responding to Andrew Sullivan." www.frc.org/get.cfm?i=PV03J01

— November 18, 2003. "Gay Marriage: Massachusetts Ruling." Transcript of online discussion, www.washingtonpost.com/wp-dyn/articles/A56938-2003Nov18.html

— November 19, 2003. "Questions and Answers: What's Wrong with Letting Same-Sex Couples Legally Marry?" www.frc.org/get.cfm?i=IF03H01

— March 2, 2004. "What Is the Public Purpose of Marriage." www.frc.org/get.cfm?i =PD04B01

— 2004. *Outrage: How Gay Activists and Liberal Judges are Trashing Democracy to Redefine Marriage.* Washington: Regnery.

Sprigg, P., and T. Dailey. 2004. *Getting It Straight: What the Research Shows about Homosexuality.* Washington: Family Research Council.

Stanton, G. T., and B. Maier. 2004. *Marriage on Trial: The Case against Same-Sex Marriage and Parenting.* Downers Grove, Illinois: Inter Varsity Press.

Stein, E. 1999. *The Mismeasure of Desire: The Science, Theory, and Ethics of Sexual Orientation.* Oxford: Oxford University Press.

Stein, L. D. October 21, 2004. "Human Genome: End of the Beginning." *Nature* 431:915-916.

Stollings, J. July 10, 2006. "Conservative Group Sues University over Gay-Partner Benefits." www.family.org/cforum/fnif/news/a0041174.cfm

Strong, J. 1991. "A Concise Dictionary of the Words in The Greek Testament; with Their Renderings in the Authorized English Version," in *The Complete Word Study: New Testament*, ed. S. Zodhiates, pp. 5-79. Chattanooga: AMG.

Sullivan, A. 1995. *Virtually Normal: An Argument about Homosexuality.* New York: Vintage.

— 1997. "Three's a Crowd," in *Same-Sex Marriage: Pro and Con*, ed. A. Sullivan, pp. 278-282. New York: Vintage.

Thompson Chain-Reference Bible, New International Version. 1983. Indianapolis: B.B. Kirkbride Bible Co. and Grand Rapids: Zondervan Bible Publishers.

Time. November 24, 2003. Volume 162 (21).

Tristam, P. November 26, 2003. "Piety's Ruse: Invoking Sanctity to Label Different as Second Class." *Daytona (Florida) Beach News-Journal.*

Tuaolo, E. 2006. *Alone in the Trenches: My Life As a Gay Man in the NFL.* Naperville, Il: Sourcebooks.

United Nations. 2001. Demographic Yearbook, 1999. Issue 51: 550-552.

Veith, G. E. October, 2003. "The Progaganda Project." Focus on the Family's *Citizen Magazine.* www.family.org/cforum/ citizenmag/features/a0028130.cfm

Walker, T. December 2001-February 2002. "Shifting Sands: How Do We Handle Conflicts between Geology and the Bible?" *Creation* 24(1):36-37.

Ward, M. C. 2005. *Nest in the Wind: Adventures in Anthropology on a Tropical Island.* 2nd ed. Prospect Heights, Il: Waveland Press.

White, M. 1994. *Stranger at the Gate: To Be Gay and Christian in America.* New York: Plume.

Wilkinson, L. 1999. "Does Methodological Naturalism Lead to Metaphysical Naturalism?" in *Darwinism Defeated? The Johnson-Lamoureux Debate on Biological Origins,* eds. P. E. Johnson and D. O. Lamoureux, pp. 167-174. Vancouver (Canada): Regent College.

Williams, W. L. 1986. *The Spirit and the Flesh: Sexual Diversity in American Indian Culture.* Boston: Beacon Press.

Wilson, G. and Q. Rahman. 2005. *Born Gay: The Psychobiology of Sex Orientation.* London: Peter Owen.

Wink, W. 1999. "Homosexuality and the Bible," in *Homosexuality and Christian Faith,* ed. W. Wink, pp. 33-49. Minneapolis: Fortress Press.

Winn, P. July 25, 2003. "Q & A: The Homosexual Agenda." Focus on the Family's *Citizen Link.* www.family.org/cforum/feature/a0027070.cfm

— August 21, 2003. "The 'Overgaying' of America." Focus on the Family's *Citizen Link.* www.family.org/cforum/feature/a0027430.cfm

— November 20, 2003. "They Want to Sweep Us Away." Focus on the Family's *Citizen Link.* www.family.org/cforum/feature/a0028909.cfm

Wright, D. F. 1990. "What the First Christians Believed," in *The History of Christianity,* ed. T. Dowley, J. H. Y. Briggs, R. D. Linder and D. F. Wright, pp. 101-122. Oxford: Lion Publishing.

Xiridou, M., R. Geskus, J. de Wit, R. Coutinho, and M. Kretzschmar. 2003. "The Contribution of Steady and Casual Partnerships to the Incidence of HIV Infection among Homosexual Men in Amsterdam." *AIDS* 17:1029-1038.

Yancey, P. 1997. *What's So Amazing about Grace?* Grand Rapids: Zondervan.

Youth on the Rock. No date. youthontherock.com/viewtopic.php?t=1319&postdays=0&postorder=asc&start=15

Yuan, L., and S. Mitchell. November 2000. "Land of the Walking Marriage." *Natural History.* New York: *American Museum of Natural History.*

Zimmer, C. November 2006. "From Fins to Wings." *National Geographic* 210 (5):110-135.

Zodhiates, S. 1994. *The Complete Word Study: Old Testament.* Chattanooga: AMG.

INDEX OF GENERAL SUBJECTS

INDEX OF GENERAL NAMES

INDEX OF BIBLICAL CITATIONS, SUBJECTS AND NAMES

STUDY GUIDE

Chapter 1: The Rainbow and the Cross

1. The author grew up in the late 1960s and 1970s. Would his experiences be different if he was a teenager today?
2. The author mentions repressing all sexual desires as he grew up. How might that affect a person's health and overall well-being?
3. Why might a person want to change his or her sexual orientation? Are some of those reasons more compelling than others? Why?
4. How important are emotional, relational, physical, and sexual intimacy for humans and other primates?
5. Not all Christians or Christian denominations are opposed to homosexuality. Why does it seem that only one "Christian" view is portrayed in the media? Does it represent all Christians?

Chapter 2: Evangelical Reality

1. In the foreword Daniel Helminiak argues that one cannot reason with the irrational. Why does he describe evangelical arguments as irrational? Is it possible to reason with evangelical leaders?
2. Why do some evangelicals believe that homosexuals are "doing the devil's work"?
3. Why do liberal Christians not voice their views on homosexuality as loudly as evangelicals? Or do they?
4. If God is just, all-knowing, and loving, how can many evangelicals believe that God could condemn homosexuals for their sexual orientation? Is that a fair assessment of evangelical views? Why or why not?
5. Why do evangelicals focus on supposed anti-gay biblical passages rather than the command to love one's neighbor? Does their argument that by focusing on the former they are doing the latter stand up to close scrutiny?

Chapter 3: Faith versus Science

1. How does the "debate" about evolution relate to the "debate" about homosexuality?
2. Why do evangelicals want to remove evolution from school curricula?
3. What effects might result if evolution were not taught in public schools?
4. How could reinterpreting scientific findings to conform to a literal interpretation of the Bible impact society?

5. Are churches that accept the possibility of evolution, such as the Roman Catholic Church or Episcopal Church, more tolerant of homosexuality? What other factors influence their views?

Chapter 4: The Bible: Culture and History

1. Many Christians used to interpret the Bible as supporting slavery. Today most Christians find the practice abhorrent and contrary to God's will, but the biblical texts have not changed. How does culture influence our interpretation of the Bible?
2. Why do conservative Christians still condemn homosexuality and use Leviticus 18:22 and 20:13 as justification, when they also consider many Old Testament laws outdated, or simply ignore them?
3. What relevance does a text written thousands of years ago have in contemporary society? Explain.
4. If the Narcissus story is about homosexuality, then what is implied by Narcissus' death? What about similar themes in modern stories, such as *Brokeback Mountain*?
5. Can a majority of Christian leaders throughout history be wrong about what the Bible says about homosexuality? Why or why not?

Chapter 5: Fade to Gray: The Bible and Homosexuality

1. Academics argue that "homosexuality" and "heterosexuality" are modern Western concepts. Does the lack of Old Testament passages on homosexuality support or refute this idea? Why?
2. The Old Testament is more restrictive about female sexuality than male sexuality, but it mentions male-male sexual behavior and is silent on female-female sexual behavior. How might this apparent discrepancy be explained?
3. Most scholars now recognize that Sodom's crime was lack of hospitality. Why do so many people still believe it was homosexuality?
4. It seems that every attempt to find support for condemning homosexuality in the Bible falls short, yet many evangelical leaders persist in citing biblical authority for their opposition to it. What motivates this behavior?
5. Does understanding the Bible's cultural and historical contexts discredit what was written? How can one decide what should be accepted as truth? What does it mean today for a biblical passage to be "true"?

Chapter 6: Gender Confusion?

1. What causes sexual orientation and why does it matter?

2. What impact do scientific findings about homosexuality have on evangelical beliefs? Discuss the view of an inerrant Bible and Paul's comment in Romans 1 that homosexuality is unnatural.
3. The scientific investigation for what causes homosexuality focuses primarily on males rather than females. What are some reasons for this inequality?
4. Many evangelical leaders argue that Bailey and Pillard's twin study demonstrates that homosexuality is not genetic. Based on that argument, it would also demonstrate that heterosexuality is not genetic because some twin pairs exhibit both orientations. How would evangelicals respond to that point?
5. Is the presence of homosexuality in nature relevant to the societal "debate" on homosexuality? Explain.

Chapter 7: Diverse Sexualities: An Anthropologist's Perspective

1. Based on the anthropological evidence, is it more appropriate to use the terms "homosexual" and "heterosexual," or "homogender" and "heterogender?" Would the use of the latter terms impact evangelical opposition to same-sex relationships? Why or why not?
2. In Micronesia if two girls want to be in a relationship, one of them changes her gender identity to male. Is this "male" more aptly described as a lesbian conforming to societal rules or as a female-to-male transgender individual? Do you think he actually feels that he was meant to be a man? How do the limits of English terminology affect our understanding of other cultures?
3. Why does American culture appear to be so "homophobic" as compared to other cultures? Is that a fair assessment? Explain.
4. If more evangelicals understood how other cultures view homosexual behavior, do you think it would make them more accepting? Are we culturally preconditioned to view anyone who is different as being bad?
5. Most psychologists consider reparative (ex-gay) therapy   unethical. Discuss the arguments for and against this view.

Chapter 8: With This Ring

1. Compare and contrast what anthropologists see as the purpose of marriage and what American society seems to believe it is. Discuss whether same-sex marriages can be incorporated into either view.
2. List some of the important components of marriage in American society. Have they changed over the years? How and why?
3. Why are many evangelical leaders opposed to same-sex marriage even though it would not directly impact their lives? Or would it?

Explain.

4. Why do you think some Americans are more willing to allow civil unions than marriage for homosexuals? Discuss the arguments for and against that position.

5. Many evangelical leaders often use strong language about the impact of same-sex marriage on American society. Is this is a scare tactic or do you agree it could end civilization? Explain.

Chapter 9: The Cross versus the Rainbow

1. Why do you think *After the Ball* was not widely accepted by homosexual leaders? The authors seem to make reasonable points that are consistent with the marketing plans of many companies.

2. Bruce Bawer suggests that the religious right developed from racism rather than from love for one's neighbor. Is that is a fair assessment? Why or why not?

3. What are some concrete steps that could be taken to reduce the number of hate-crimes against sexual minorities?

4. How do the media reinforce society's stereotypes of homosexuals?

5. David Limbaugh states that Christians are discriminated against because they believe in absolute truth. Is this a fair assessment? Explain.

Chapter 10: The Rainbow Cross

1. Do you believe society will ever eradicate homosexuality? Would this be a good thing? Explain.

2. Many evangelicals say they are to "hate the sin and love the sinner." Why do you think many homosexuals find this approach degrading and patronizing?

3. Explain why some homosexuals ostracize gay Christians.

4. Many homosexual Christians find themselves ostracized from both Christian and gay communities. Why do they choose to embrace two conflicting identities?

5. How have your views about, or understanding of, homosexuality and evangelical uses of the Bible, been changed by this book?

About Haiduk Press

The haiduks were quasi-legendary folk heroes who to this day are regarded as romantic, Robin Hood figures, and are an integral part of the folklore of the villages and towns of Hungary and Romania. Inspired by their example, Haiduk Press was formed to publish non-fiction works that gently challenge the cultural status quo and conventional wisdom.

www.haidukpress.com
haidukpress@gmail.com

Cover and text design by Gyuri Negulescu-Marconi,
ilustrator2005@gmail.com; www.marconimedia.ro;
Text edited for Haiduk Press by Bea Ferrigno, wrdwyz@gmail.com.